Welcome

THE
EVERYTHING
PARENT'S GUIDES®

AS A PARENT, you're swamped with conflicting advice and parenting techniques that tell you what is best for your child. THE EVERYTHING® PARENT'S GUIDES get right to the point about specific issues. They give you the most recent, up-to-date information on parenting trends, behavior issues, and health concerns—providing you with a detailed resource to help you ease your parenting anxieties.

THE EVERYTHING® PARENT'S GUIDES are an extension of the bestselling *Everything*® series in the parenting category. These family-friendly books are designed to be a one-stop guide for parents. If you want authoritative information on specific topics not fully covered in other books, THE EVERYTHING® PARENT'S GUIDES are the perfect resource to ensure that you raise a healthy, confident child.

Visit the entire Everything® series at www.everything.com

THE
EVERYTHING.
PARENT'S GUIDE TO
Children with Dyslexia

Dear Reader,

I have a son who could not read until age eleven. That was ten years ago; now my son is an avid reader who did well in high school and won admission to a number of selective colleges, and is now living on his own, embarking on an exciting and rewarding career. There was a time that I feared a diagnosis of dyslexia, thinking it would mean that something was terribly wrong with my son's brain. Instead, I learned that dyslexia is merely one facet of something wonderfully right with my son's brain—it is the flip side of his extraordinary creativity, his wonderful sense of humor, his quick grasp of mathematical concepts, and his knack for solving problems.

In 1995, I became the Webmaster for the "Dyslexia, the Gift" Web site at *www.dyslexia.com*. Almost as soon as the site went up, I was deluged with e-mail from people all over the world, mostly from parents like you desperately seeking help for their kids. In the years since, I have been privy to hundreds of success stories like my son's—but I also have met many parents who are simply overwhelmed by contradictory information and choices that they face. I cannot give you a crystal ball to predict your child's future, but I hope that I can help guide you through the maze.

I feel tremendously privileged to be able to write this book, to share much of what I have learned over the years—and to learn new things myself in the course of my research. I hope you will find this book to be a valuable reference and starting point, and I hope that it will also help you find some of the answers you are looking for. Your journey will be different than mine, but if you have faith in your child, I think you will find that you are just as richly rewarded at the end.

Abigail Marshall

THE
EVERYTHING®
PARENT'S GUIDE TO
CHILDREN
WITH
DYSLEXIA

All you need to ensure
your child's success

Abigail Marshall

Adams Media
Avon, Massachusetts

This book is dedicated in loving memory to
Elizabeth "Misty" Davis.

Publishing Director: Gary M. Krebs
Managing Editor: Kate McBride
Copy Chief: Laura MacLaughlin
Acquisitions Editor: Kate Burgo
Development Editor: Karen Johnson Jacot
Production Editor: Jamie Wielgus

Production Director: Susan Beale
Production Manager: Michelle Roy Kelly
Series Designer: Daria Perreault
Cover Design: Paul Beatrice, Matt LeBlanc
Layout and Graphics: Colleen Cunningham
Rachael Eiben, Michelle Roy Kelly,
John Paulhus, Daria Perreault, Erin Ring

An Everything® Series Book.
Everything® and everything.com® are registered trademarks of F+W Media, Inc.

Published by Adams Media, a division of F+W Media, Inc.
57 Littlefield Street, Avon, MA 02322 U.S.A.
www.adamsmedia.com
ISBN 13: 978-1-59337-135-7
ISBN 10: 1-59337-135-7
Printed in the United States of America.

J I H G F E D

Library of Congress Cataloging-in-Publication Data
Marshall, Abigail.
The everything parent's guide to children with dyslexia / Abigail Marshall.
p.   cm.
ISBN 1-59337-135-7
1. Dyslexia–Popular works. 2. Dyslexic children–Popular works.
I. Title. II. Series: Everything series.

RJ496.A5M365 2004
649'.15144–dc22

2004013263

This publication is designed to provide accurate and authoritative information with regard to the subject matter covered. It is sold with the understanding that the publisher is not engaged in rendering legal, accounting, or other professional advice. If legal advice or other expert assistance is required, the services of a competent professional person should be sought.
—From a *Declaration of Principles* jointly adopted by a Committee of the American Bar Association and a Committee of Publishers and Associations

Many of the designations used by manufacturers and sellers to distinguish their products are claimed as trademarks. Where those designations appear in this book and Adams Media was aware of a trademark claim, the designations have been printed with initial capital letters.

This book is available at quantity discounts for bulk purchases.
For information, call 1-800-289-0963.

dys·lex·ia (dis lek'sē ə)

▶ *n.* **1.** a learning difficulty primarily associated with problems with written language such as reading, writing, spelling, and in some cases, working with numbers, stemming from naturally occurring variations in brain structure and function.

Acknowledgments

I would like to gratefully acknowledge the support, encouragement, and inspiration of the following people:

My son Ethan. Ron and Alice Davis, Sharon Pfeiffer, Dorothy Owen, Robin Temple, Catherine Churton, Lot Blom, Sue Hall, Mary Kay Frasier, Cyndi Deneson, Gerry Grant, Cathy Smith, Ana Lima, Larry Smith, Jr., Charlotte Foster, Olga Zambrano, María Silvia Flores, Judith Schwarcz, Raewyn Matheson, Dr. Fatima Ali, Brian Grimes, Bill Allen, A.J. and Gwin Pratt, Lexie Strain, Wendy Gilley, and 300+ other members of the Davis Dyslexia family who have led and inspired me with your dedication, expertise, and creativity. Mary W. Yohn, Sue Jones, Karen Buck, and Chris Phoenix for special help with research. Mary Ellen Schutz, Dan Willeman, Corina Salas, and all of the Board Hoggs. My daughter Elise, for her patience and understanding while I wrote this book. Special thanks to Annette Marshall and the DyslexiaSupport Egroup for the constant window into the joys and frustrations of raising and educating our extraordinary children.

• • •

CONTENTS

CHAPTER 8: *Beyond Reading—* *Therapies for Related Issues* **109**

CHAPTER 9: *Choosing a School* **123**

CHAPTER 10: *IDEA and the IEP Process* **135**

INTRODUCTION

DYSLEXIA IS NOT THE SAME AS READING FAILURE. Teachers often see only that aspect, because reading instruction is their concern. They are trained to measure a child's progress against a "norm" or "grade level" or "expected reading age." When the child does not meet the standard, they intensify early reading instruction, assuming that reading is an essential skill that must be acquired early.

Children invariably grow up, but few researchers have charted the developmental path of dyslexia over time. One who has is Professor Rosalie Fink, who tested and interviewed sixty prominent adults with dyslexia who had become leaders in fields requiring extensive reading, including medicine, law, business, and sciences. This group of adults included a Nobel Laureate and a member of the National Academy of Sciences. Each tested above twelfth grade level on word recognition, oral reading accuracy, and word meaning; more than 40 percent tested well on spelling and did not need extra time to complete reading tasks. As a group, they performed significantly worse than their controls when reading nonsense words, a test commonly used to measure decoding ability and diagnose dyslexia.

On average, these high-achieving adults learned to read at age eleven. They learned through reading about subjects that fired their imaginations and excited their passions. Their reading was supported by their intense interest, which had spurred them to develop the background knowledge and vocabulary needed to use context to help interpret the words on the page. For each, there had come a time when the thirst for knowledge simply drew them past whatever barriers to reading had existed before. That time seems to correspond with the onset of the period Piaget called the "stage of formal operations" (age eleven to fifteen-plus), and the rapid growth in brain gray matter and synapses known to occur just prior to puberty.

Children with dyslexia are capable learners who manifest some abilities well ahead of their peers, but their brains simply are not constructed for early reading. They need an enriched learning environment to fuel their inherent curiosity and thirst for knowledge. If they cannot find intellectual stimulation at school, parents should work to provide it at home.

Reading support to build foundational skills is essential and should begin early, but it should not overshadow or impede other learning opportunities, nor should it be withdrawn as the child enters her teens. The eight-year-old diagnosed with dyslexia can reasonably be expected to begin reading comfortably in her teens; she should not be deprived of educational opportunity because of her difficulties in learning. As a parent, you must shield your child from the demoralizing aspects of school failure through constant support and encouragement, recognizing that your child's optimal learning periods for certain skills will not always coincide with the "norm."

The key is in understanding your child's needs and abilities, not in trying to change the child. He can be helped, but his brain cannot and should not be "rewired" nor can his dyslexia be "cured." Through observation and open communication with your child, you can facilitate this understanding, recognizing that a misfit between child and school is a failing of the school, and not your child. Celebrate your child's talents, feed his passions, and work to cultivate his emotional as well as intellectual growth—in the end you will have raised an empowered and enthusiastic learner.

CHAPTER 1

Understanding Dyslexia

C HILDREN WITH DYSLEXIA have many strengths and talents and grow up to be successful adults with rewarding careers. However, they will most likely struggle with learning to read, write, and spell, especially in the early years. They may need specialized help and support to enable them to achieve their goals. You cannot cure your child of dyslexia, but you can guide him and help him to find his own way to succeed in school and in life.

What Is Dyslexia?

Dyslexia is a learning disability that primarily affects one's ability to learn to read and develop a strong understanding of language. It's more than just a problem with reading; your child may also have difficulties with oral communication, organizational skills, following instructions, and telling time. Sometimes the symptoms can be extremely variable. For example, your child may have problems learning basic math facts and doing arithmetic; on the other hand, he may have a special aptitude for geometry and advanced mathematics. He may be physically clumsy or have poor motor coordination or he may be especially athletic and talented at sports.

While dyslexia may present certain difficulties to children, it also seems to be associated with many strengths and talents. Your child could be highly imaginative and may excel in art, music, or drama. He might be a good problem-solver, and may be especially good with solving jigsaw puzzles, working with Legos, or playing games of strategy. It's possible that you may have noticed he's handy around the house and has a knack for fixing broken toys and other objects.

 FACT

Dyslexia is far more prevalent than was once believed. In fact, dyslexia may affect one out of five children in the classroom setting. It is estimated that 15 percent of the population has reading difficulties.

What Dyslexia Means for Your Child

Dyslexia is not something that can be outgrown. Over time, your child will gain skills that he struggled with at first, but his dyslexia will present new challenges as he grows older and school becomes more challenging. He may master reading and writing in elementary school, but have difficulty learning a foreign language in high school. He may avoid early problems with arithmetic, but struggle with algebra. As you learn more about dyslexia, you will be able to anticipate these problems before they arise and help guide your child to use study methods that are effective and useful for him.

Reading is the most significant problem area associated with dyslexia. Your child will eventually learn to read, but it will probably take her longer than most other children. It is very common for a child with dyslexia to be unable to read independently until age eight, or ten, or twelve, or even until the teenage years. Despite the delayed start in reading, your child can learn to read advanced material and can gain reading comprehension skills as good as or better than her peers. Having dyslexia, though, means that she'll be more likely to read slowly and with greater effort.

Dyslexia can also affect other areas of life. Your child is likely to have difficulty remembering and following directions and have poor time management skills. She may be tremendously disorganized, or become compulsively neat as a way of compensating for her confusion. These issues can be very frustrating for you and your child, but they are also problems that can be resolved over time by using planning and learning techniques to compensate for weaknesses. For example, as your child grows you will be able to help her become more organized by relying on calendars, planners, and lists; of course, she will need to learn to read first to take advantage of these tools.

Processing Information

Dyslexia is caused by differences in how the brain processes information. These differences don't make dyslexia a mental defect or disease, they simply mean that the child has an unusual way of thinking, learning, communicating, and solving problems.

 ESSENTIAL

Dyslexia is not caused by poor schools, bad teaching practices, neglectful parenting, or a difficult home life. These factors can explain why many other children have reading problems, but they cannot cause a child to develop dyslexia.

Before dyslexia was discovered and labeled, these differences most likely went unnoticed because it was common and acceptable for children to discontinue their education at a young age, grow up to become farmers, artisans, or merchants, or take on other jobs that did not require a formal education. With their strong ability to learn through hands-on practice and apprenticeship, young people with dyslexia probably did quite well.

In today's world, though, strong literacy skills are essential. Increasing importance is placed on school performance and standardized tests; children learn in large classrooms where the "norm" (or average) is fast becoming a minimum standard to which all students are expected to aspire. In this environment, teachers must use the methods that best reach the majority of students in their classrooms. A child with a learning barrier quickly falls behind, and so what was once merely a learning difference transforms into a learning disability.

Areas of Cognitive Weakness

Educators and researchers have isolated some factors that seem to play an important role in dyslexia. Most of these are associated with language processing difficulties or the ability to think sequentially. Mental processing speed also seems to play a part.

The most significant areas of difficulty are:

• Difficulties with phonemic awareness, which is the ability to break down and manipulate the small units of sound in words, such as the three separate sounds for the "c," "a," and "t" in the word "cat."

• Problems with word retrieval or rapid automatic naming, which is the time it takes for verbal response to a visual stimulus or cue, such as quickly saying the names of letters printed on a chart, or names of objects when a picture is shown.

• Poor digit span, which is the ability to store a short sequence of letters or numbers in short-term memory.

• Difficulties with sequencing or concepts of order.

• Visual perceptual confusion, such as the inability to distinguish letters such as "b" and "d," or perceiving letters out of order, such as confusing "was" and "saw," or "from" and "form."

Areas of Mental Strength

Even though dyslexia can cause extreme difficulties with learning, children with dyslexia are usually bright and capable. In fact, dyslexia is not really a single problem or issue, but the name that given to a certain common pattern. Individuals with dyslexia tend to be very creative thinkers, with a knack for "out-of-the-box" thinking. Many are artistically talented, and adults with dyslexia usually do well in careers such as engineering, design, or architecture. Another strength is the intuitive thought process; people with dyslexia often will know the answer to a problem or question, but have difficulty explaining how they arrived at it.

Different Styles of Learning

Instead of being viewed as a disability, dyslexia can be seen as reflecting a certain type of learning style. Your child's learning style is the way in which she perceives, conceptualizes, organizes, and recalls information. All children have different areas of strength; good teachers learn to consider these factors in designing their lessons. As you learn more about dyslexia and observe your child, you will also see that you can tie some the problems she has with a specific pattern of learning. There is no one learning style that all children with dyslexia share, but there are some common patterns that seem to be often associated with dyslexia.

Auditory, Visual, and Kinesthetic Learning

One way to think about learning is to look at it as a process that combines elements of listening (auditory), seeing (visual), and doing (kinesthetic). A child with an auditory learning style will learn best from listening to a lecture or explanation; the visual learner needs to see pictures, graphs, or films to learn; and the kinesthetic learner needs to use his hands or have active participation to learn.

Your child's dyslexia may cause conflicts with her dominant learning style. For example, a child with dyslexia often has a predominantly visual learning style. This works well when he is viewing a film or looking at a picture or diagram. However, it does not serve him when he is being taught to read. The visual learner tends to try to remember words by sight, rather than sounding them out, and can often remember information by recalling how it was set out on a page. However, your child's dyslexia will stand in the way of his reading ability. You may be told that your strongly visual child has a poor "visual memory" when in fact his memory for real world objects that he sees is quite remarkable: It is only the memory for letters and words that is impaired.

 ESSENTIAL

Your child with dyslexia will learn best with a multisensory approach that simultaneously combines auditory, visual, and tactile learning strategies to teach new facts and concepts. Methods that involve seeing, saying, listening, and doing will help your child learn faster and enhance his ability to retain new information.

In a school setting, lessons are often geared primarily to students with an auditory learning style. The teacher relies mostly on talking to convey information: She lectures, explains, answers questions. If your child is a visual or kinesthetic learner, she will miss a lot of information; she will simply not be able to learn without strategies that reach her strongest learning modes. On the other hand, if your child has dyslexia but is an auditory learner, her strengths may mask her dyslexia. She may do well in school, relying on her superior listening skills to keep up in class, and learning what is in books by listening to others read aloud. Her dyslexia may go undetected until the later grades, when she will be expected to learn more from independent reading.

Left-Brained vs. Right-Brained

Some people break down two main styles of learning as being left-brained or right-brained. Researchers know that many functions related to language use and reading are typically localized in the left hemisphere of the brain. The right hemisphere is associated more with intuitive thought and creativity. Of course, the two sides of the brain are designed to work together, and most people develop the ability to use both sides, depending on the task or activity they are engaged in.

Psychologist Linda Silverman, who has worked extensively with gifted children, describes these two styles of learning as being auditory-sequential and visual-spatial. The auditory-sequential learner thinks primarily in words, learns step-by-step, attends well to detail, learns phonics easily, and excels at rote memory. The visual-spatial learner thinks primarily with images, learns concepts all at once, sees the big picture, learns best by seeing relationships, and learns complex concepts easily but struggles with easy skills.

One possible explanation for dyslexia is that some children who are right-brained learners find it much easier to think about new information and solve problems using their visual-spatial strategies. Over time, they reinforce their own tendencies toward relying on imagery and intuitive thought processes, and fail to develop strong brain pathways for thinking with the sounds of language. Thus, when it comes time for these children to learn to read, their brains simply aren't ready.

Multiple Intelligences

Dr. Howard Gardner has proposed that there are eight different modalities of intelligence; your child will be stronger in some of these areas than others. The different intelligences are:

- Linguistic intelligence ("word smart")
- Logical-mathematical intelligence ("number/reasoning smart")
- Spatial intelligence ("picture smart")
- Bodily-kinesthetic intelligence ("body smart")
- Musical intelligence ("music smart")
- Interpersonal intelligence ("people smart")
- Intrapersonal intelligence ("self smart")
- Naturalist intelligence ("nature smart")

In schools, most instruction and testing is geared to the first two intelligences—linguistic and logical-mathematical. If your child has dyslexia, he is probably weak in those areas and could struggle in school and do poorly on standardized testing. On the other hand, dyslexia does not impair the other six types of intelligence in any way. Your child is probably strong in one or more of those areas, and these inherent strengths can help him succeed in many activities in childhood, and go on to have a successful and rewarding career.

Genetic Factors in Dyslexia

Dyslexia is partly inherited, as the tendency to develop dyslexia runs in families. By studying genetic markers in families in which there is a high incidence of dyslexia, scientists have now identified genes on at least eight different chromosomes as having some role or connection with dyslexia. No single gene is involved in all cases of dyslexia. It is probable that dyslexia is influenced by a combination of genes; these genes may also influence different aspects of physical or intellectual development. However, because your child's brain continues to grow and develop from birth through adulthood, dyslexia is also influenced by your child's learning experiences and environmental factors. This may explain why the specific symptoms of dyslexia can be so variable, and why some children have much more serious reading problems than others.

Studies of identical twins have shown that where one twin is dyslexic, the other will have dyslexia about 55 to 70 percent of the time, depending on the type of dyslexia. This research shows that there is a strong genetic influence, but that environmental factors also play a part.

Brain Research and Dyslexia

Within the past two decades, scientists have been able to use sophisticated equipment to study the workings of the human brain. With this equipment, scientists can measure electrical impulses, chemical changes, or blood flow through the brain while their research subjects perform specific tasks. This has allowed scientists to look at the mental changes associated with learning to read, and to compare the mental activity of people with dyslexia with that of people who have no reading problems.

One thing that the brain research shows is that each brain is different; not all people with dyslexia process information exactly the same way. However, by studying many individuals, it is possible to generalize and to explore common elements that may contribute to dyslexia.

 FACT

Learning new skills can alter brain structure. Researchers recently found that certain areas of the brain grew larger when they taught their subjects to juggle. When the jugglers stopped practicing and their brains were measured again, the brain expansion they had seen earlier was reduced.

Searching for Answers

Good scientific research is limited in scope; scientists are careful to study only one particular theory or question, under controlled conditions. The brain is an extremely complex system, and each research project sheds light on only a small part of the mental processes of learning, reading, and dyslexia. Thus research cannot yet provide all the answers. Instead, each new study provides an intriguing look into another piece of the puzzle. Scientists measure many different responses in children with dyslexia, such as the timing of the brain's response to external stimuli, the way that the brain recognizes letter patterns, and the pattern of activity in the two brain hemispheres associated with different reading tasks.

Speed and Response Time

Scientists have discovered that the brains of children with dyslexia take a fraction of a second longer to respond to certain stimuli than the brains of children who read well; this pattern persists through adulthood. The delayed response time is seen both in tests of listening to the sounds of language and responding to visually presented symbols. These delays could explain why individuals with dyslexia tend to read more slowly.

It is also possible that because of the problem with timing, children with dyslexia may not hear the sounds and rhythms of language in the same way that others do. This may explain why they have difficulty breaking down words into component sounds or blending sounds into words.

Visual Word Form Recognition

Researchers have also discovered that the part of the brain used to quickly recognize letters, letter sequences, and words in most people does not seem to activate in the brains of adults and older children with dyslexia. In most people, an area in the left rear (occipital) of the brain activates almost immediately upon seeing any sequence of letters; the activity is very brief, and ends within about half a second after the word or letter sequence is first seen. Scientists call this part of the brain the visual word form area.

 **FACT**

In skilled readers, most words are recognized by sight even before the person is consciously aware that he is looking at a word. This is why silent reading is faster than oral reading. Sounding out and speaking words is a slower mental process and requires involvement of brain areas involved in speech production.

People with dyslexia simply do not seem to engage this area of the brain when presented with words or letter patterns. Whatever activity takes place is stronger in a corresponding area on the right side of the brain, which is known to be involved in face recognition. Part of the problem may be timing; in most readers, the visual word form area activation is completed in the fraction of a second before the brain begins to activate in research subjects with dyslexia.

The visual word form area may function as an important sorting mechanism, where the brain quickly responds to familiar words and directs unfamiliar words to other left hemispheric areas for further processing. An inability to use this brain area may explain why people with dyslexia have difficulty with remembering and recognizing familiar words.

Right-Brain Activity

Scientists studying the process of learning to read in normal children have observed that the brain changes as children gain reading proficiency. Very young children have high levels of activity in both the right and left brain hemispheres when looking at letters and words. As children gain the ability to recognize familiar words and letter patterns on sight, the right brain activity subsides and a strong pattern of left hemispheric activity is observed.

The left hemisphere is important to reading because it contains pathways and areas in the temporal and occipital regions, near the rear of the brain, which are specialized for attending to and understanding the sounds of language. This is the part of the brain that will become specialized for connecting letters to the sounds they represent, and for connecting and blending the individual sounds in a series of letters to form a word.

Other studies have shown that adults and children with dyslexia have more right brain and frontal brain activity than good readers when performing certain reading tasks. For most people, the left brain hemisphere is also slightly larger than the right. Several studies show that adults with dyslexia tend to have more evenly structured, symmetrical brains, with the right hemisphere being about the same size as the left, and activity less differentiated between left and right hemispheres.

The child or adult who is using right brain processes to try to decipher text is probably getting mixed signals, and will understandably find reading to be a difficult and confusing task. On the other hand, the evidence from these studies helps to explain why the reading problems associated with dyslexia tend to go hand-in-hand with creativity, artistic ability, and strong spatial reasoning skills, as these are abilities associated with the right hemisphere.

How Brain Activity Influences Reading Skills

When scientists study brain activity of children and adults with reading difficulties, they do not know whether the differences they see reflect a structural difference in the brain or whether they are seeing functional patterns that could be changed with teaching or learning. Since studies show that poor readers do not seem to use the left brain areas for phonetic processing in the same way as good readers, scientists are interested in learning whether specific types of teaching or training can change brain use patterns.

A Different Pattern for Dyslexia

There are now many studies that show that children and adults with dyslexia do show changes in brain activity after receiving training geared to increase their sensitivity to phonetics. As expected, with such training, the brains of people with dyslexia begin to look more like the brains of good readers, at least when performing tasks such as identifying rhyming patterns in listening to or reading words. However, it is not clear whether such changes in brain activity actually promote overall improved reading skills, or carry over to contexts other than the specific tasks that have been studied.

 **FACT**

According to Dr. Sally Shaywitz, children with dyslexia need to be able to sound out words to decode them accurately. They also need to know the meaning of the word to help decode and comprehend the printed message. Both the sounds and the meanings of words must be taught.

One leading researcher, Dr. Sally Shaywitz, looked at the brains of young adults whose progress had been followed from kindergarten and whose dyslexia had been identified by their poor performance in reading skills in early childhood. Some of these young people had grown up to become capable readers, while others remained very poor readers. Surprisingly, the improved readers had a very different pattern of brain use, while the poor readers had brain patterns more closely resembling those of typical readers without dyslexia. When doing reading tasks involving making judgments about word meaning, these improved readers appeared to completely bypass the left temporal area used for phonetic decoding, relying mostly on right temporal activity and frontal activity in both hemispheres.

In another study, scientists with the National Institute of Mental Health used tests measuring blood flow in the brain to correlate brain use patterns with reading ability in subjects with and without dyslexia. After testing their subjects for reading ability with common skills tests, brain activity was measured while the subjects were reading sentences aloud. The researchers found that there was an inverse relationship of brain use, dyslexia, and reading ability. Among the group with dyslexia, increased right brain activity correlated directly with improved reading ability. This was the opposite pattern from the group without dyslexia, whose reading ability correlated with increased left hemispheric activity.

These studies suggest that in order for a person with dyslexia to learn to read, he must also learn to use different brain pathways, perhaps because his innate brain structure makes it inefficient to use the left hemispheric pathways typically associated with good reading.

Phonological Training and Brain Activity

People with dyslexia tend to have difficulty applying and using phonetic rules to decode words. As noted earlier, brain scans show that subjects with dyslexia have reduced activity in the left brain areas normally associated with reading and increased activity in right brain regions.

Using brain scans conducted before and after intensive, short-term training to improve phonetic skills, researchers have indeed observed that children and adults with dyslexia show increased levels of left brain activity after receiving such training. However, the brain scans have also shown that such training also results in higher activation of a number of regions not normally involved in phonological processing. These regions include parts of the right side of the brain that are mirror images of the typical left-sided language processing areas.

Thus, the research seems to suggest that while training can help children and adults with dyslexia use left-brain word processing areas more effectively, the person with dyslexia is still predominantly a right-brained thinker. While most children can become good readers by learning to rely mostly on left-brain thinking processes, a child with dyslexia will need to learn to harness his natural right-brain mental strengths to build reading skills.

This research may explain why it takes longer for children with dyslexia to learn to read; the process of developing and coordinating right brain thinking with the skill set needed for reading may be more complex and take many years to develop. This research also helps explain why children with dyslexia always learn best with multisensory strategies—approaches that integrate auditory, visual, and kinesthetic learning tools, and thus probably activate more brain regions simultaneously.

Limitations of Brain Research

As a parent, you should keep in mind that scientists still have much to learn. Each brain is unique, and even studies that report generalized findings may include some subjects with dyslexia whose brain activity did not fit the pattern that is described. Gender differences can play a part: Studies also show that many girls use their brains differently for some tasks than boys. Many of the studies of brain structure and function in dyslexia have looked at only boys and men; the findings may not apply to your daughter with dyslexia. Your child with dyslexia will need to discover her own best path to learning over the years as she grows to adulthood.

CHAPTER 2

Characteristics of Dyslexia

T HE SYMPTOMS OF DYSLEXIA are extremely variable. In fact, your child's symptoms may not even be consistent from day to day. Children with dyslexia might seem careless or as though they are not trying hard enough. At home and at play, they might be very adept, but at school, children with dyslexia might struggle to master the most basic material. This chapter will help you recognize the signs of dyslexia so that you can better understand your child's needs and take appropriate action.

Early Signs of Dyslexia

Because dyslexia is primarily associated with difficulty in learning to read, it cannot be reliably diagnosed until your child is the age at which reading typically begins. Although most children are ready to begin to read at about age six, individual development is variable. It is normal for some children to pick up basic reading skills as early as age four, and it is also normal for many children to be delayed in learning to read until age seven or eight.

Symptoms of Dyslexia

Identifying signs of dyslexia can be a difficult task. Many of the problems that are tell-tale symptoms of dyslexia in older children are part of normal development in a three-year-old. In order to assess whether

your very young child could have dyslexia, it's best to look at her overall learning pattern. The following are some common characteristics that may be signs of dyslexia in preschool-age children:

- Jumbling sounds of words in speech, such as saying "pasgetti" for "spaghetti" or "mawn lower" for "lawn mower."
- Confusing words signifying direction in space or time, such as "up" and "down," "in" and "out," "yesterday" and "tomorrow."
- Forgetting or confusing the word for known objects, such as "table" or "chair."
- Delayed speech development.
- Unusual speech patterns, such as frequent hesitations or stammering.
- Difficulty with behavior or learning.
- Difficulty remembering and following directions.
- Extremely low tolerance for frustration.
- Difficulty getting dressed, buttoning clothes, and putting shoes on the correct feet.
- Excessive tripping, bumping into things, and falling over.
- Difficulty with catching, kicking, or throwing a ball; with hopping and/or skipping.

 FACT

Studies show that if a child has a parent or older sibling with dyslexia, there is a 40 percent chance that he will also have difficulty in learning to read. If dyslexia seems to run in your family, you will want to be alert to possible symptoms before your child begins school.

Reading and Writing

If you've noticed that your child has difficulty learning to form letters or frequently reverses letters, it's understandable why there's cause for concern. However, many small children do not have the small-motor coordination needed for writing, and reversals of some letters in writing is common in many children up until age 7. Reversals of entire words—"mirror" writing—are less common, but are not significant in isolation; they are only a sign of dyslexia if accompanied by other symptoms. Although most children will learn to recognize some letters of the alphabet in early childhood, many children are unable to learn to recite or write the letters of the complete alphabet until they reach school age.

Here are some problems with pre-reading skills that may be early signs of dyslexia:

- Difficulty learning nursery rhymes and rhyming words.
- Difficulty in learning (and remembering) names of letters.
- Enjoys being read to but shows no interest in letters or words.
- Difficulty with clapping a simple rhythm.

Keep in mind that it is important to look at the overall pattern of learning, including strengths as well as weaknesses. Many children simply are not ready to read until they are somewhat older than average; that does not mean they have dyslexia.

Speech and Language

A child who shows significant language delays or difficulties with speech can and should be evaluated by a speech and language therapist. If you or your child's pediatrician suspect a possible hearing problem, you should also seek evaluation from an audiologist. These language problems can be an early sign of dyslexia; they can also indicate hearing or auditory learning problems. If a child is merely late to begin talking, perhaps not speaking or only saying a few words until age three or later, consider how he responds to language. If your child seems to understand what you are saying to him and responds appropriately to simple instructions, his delayed speech may just be part of his normal developmental pattern.

 **FACT**

> Delayed speech does not always indicate a learning problem. Research has shown that many highly intelligent children do not start talking until age three or four. Many of these children's parents are musicians or mathematicians; these children usually grow up to have similar aptitudes.

Expression and Articulation

You should be more concerned if your child has continued speech difficulties once he begins talking. Children with dyslexia or other language problems often have difficulty expressing themselves or with understanding what is said to them. Your child may have difficulties with articulation, which is the ability to pronounce specific words correctly. While all young children mispronounce difficult words at first, a child with dyslexia is particularly prone to making errors that confuse the order or sequence of sounds in a word or phrase.

Problematic Speech Patterns

Your child may stutter, hesitate, or stammer. This is called dysfluency, an interruption in the rhythm of speech. Some children have difficulties with voice tones, pitch, and volume. An odd or halting manner of speech can also be an early sign of dyslexia.

Your child may show signs of word retrieval problems. He may often hesitate or be unable to remember the word for common objects, or mistakenly substitute the wrong word, saying one thing when he means something else. He may frequently confuse words related to direction or time; for example, mixing up words like "over" and "under," or "yesterday" and "tomorrow." This word confusion may be apparent in his receptive language as well as his expressive language; that is, he may be easily confused by directions or statements that others make to him using these words.

Your child also may seem to have difficulty learning correct grammar and syntax, such as the use of pronouns. She may have a hard time learning the difference between "he" and "she," or difficulty learning to use "I" rather than "me" when beginning a sentence. All of these problems are very normal at early stages of development, but most children show steady progress and outgrow them over time.

Persistent problems can indicate that your child has difficulty understanding and processing language. These early oral language problems can indicate that your child has difficulty thinking with and understanding the meaning of words. Even though she may outgrow the speech problems, her language issues may remain, leading to problems recognizing and understanding words in print.

Your Child's Hearing

Even if your child is speaking and understanding language well, you should be alert to other signs of any difficulties with hearing. Undetected hearing problems can affect the way that your child's sensitivity to the sounds of language develops. Many children with dyslexia suffer from allergies or frequent ear infections in early childhood. Ear infections can cause impaired hearing or intermittent hearing loss, and these may be a contributing factor to later learning problems. It is important to seek prompt medical treatment for ear infections and other respiratory illnesses.

 FACT

The National Information Center for Children and Youth with Disabilities estimates that one in ten individuals is affected by a communication disorder. In other words, at least one million children are in placed in special education programs as a result of having a language or speech disorder.

Extreme sensitivity to loud noises or sounds with very high or low frequencies (such as the buzz emanated by fluorescent lights or the hum of a fan) may also indicate a problem with the way that your child hears the world around her. If you suspect a hearing problem, you can begin by consulting with your child's physician. He can examine your child and refer you to a specialist if necessary.

Your Child's Vision

Dyslexia is not caused by vision problems, but good vision is important to reading development. One in five preschool-aged children has a vision disorder. Many common vision problems are preventable if detected in early childhood. According to the College of Optometrists in Vision Development, problems in any of the following areas can have a significant impact on learning:

- Eye tracking skills (eyes staying on target, i.e., following a line of print)
- Eye teaming skills (two eyes working together as a synchronized team)
- Binocular vision (simultaneously blending the images from both eyes into one image)
- Accommodation (eye focusing)
- Visual-motor integration (i.e., eye-hand coordination, sports vision, etc.)
- Visual perception (visual memory, visual form perception, visualization, directionality)

Your child can be evaluated for possible vision problems well before she reaches school age. As a parent, you should suspect a vision issue if you observe any of the following symptoms:

- One eye drifts or aims in a different direction than the other.
- Your child tilts or turns her head to see.

- Your child's head is frequently tilted to one side or one shoulder is noticeably higher.
- Your child squints or closes or covers one eye.
- Your child seems to have a short attention span for her age.
- Your child has poor hand-eye coordination for activities like playing with a ball.
- Your child avoids coloring, working with puzzles, and other detailed activities.

It is a good idea to arrange a thorough optometric examination for your child by age three to determine whether his vision is developing normally, whether or not you suspect a specific problem. If you are concerned about your child's vision development, it is best to arrange an appointment with a board-certified developmental optometrist who specializes in evaluating and correcting these types of vision problems.

Dyslexia in School-Age Children

In most cases, you will probably not be aware that your child has dyslexia until he is in first or second grade. At that time, when reading instruction begins in earnest, your child is likely to lag behind and will begin to show signs of frustration at school. After several months, you may realize that your child simply hasn't caught on to reading in the same way as his peers. He may still have difficulty recognizing letters of the alphabet, or he may know the letters and their sounds but seem unable to put them together to form even simple words. You may notice that he seems unable to remember words that he has seen before, and struggles to sound out every word he sees.

Symptoms in Children Ages 5–12

Not all reading problems stem from dyslexia. In fact, 95 percent of children identified by school authorities as having reading problems are struggling for other reasons, such as socio-economic factors, language barriers, inadequate preparation for school, or overall low intelligence. Because so many schoolchildren struggle with reading for reasons other than dyslexia, your child's teacher may not suspect dyslexia in your child, even if clear signs are there. Unfortunately, most schools do not screen for dyslexia, and very often children are not identified until they have fallen far behind their peers. Thus, it is your responsibility to be alert to possible signs and symptoms.

ALERT!

Do not wait for the teacher to tell you she suspects a problem before seeking help. Many teachers have not been trained to recognize dyslexia, and they may not recognize the signs in a child who is bright and actively participates in many class activities that do not involve reading or writing.

Problems with Reading and Writing

The surest sign of dyslexia is simply the fact that your child seems bright and capable at home and at play, yet he struggles with reading, writing, and spelling. School-aged children with dyslexia will exhibit many of the following symptoms:

- Confusing letters with similar appearances, such as "b" and "d" or "e" and "c."
- Writing that contains frequent reversals, transpositions, or inversions.
- Difficult remembering common sight words, even after repeated practice.
- Stumbling, hesitating, or making mistakes or omissions when reading small, easy words like "and" or "from."
- Spelling phonetically and inconsistently (e.g., "foniks" for "phonics").
- Complaining that letters and words on the page move or become blurred.

- Complaining of dizziness, headaches, or stomachaches while reading.

Even when she gains the ability to decode and recognize words and sentences, your child may read and reread material with little comprehension. As she matures and reading demands increase, new problems may arise.

Dyslexia and Math

In addition to problems with reading, your child may experience problems with math. Even if his math skills are strong, your child is likely to have poor rote memory and difficulty memorizing math facts such as multiplication tables. He may be able to do simple arithmetic, such as addition or subtraction, but have difficulty applying or using math concepts when confronted with story problems. Even if your child seems to be good with math, he may often be unable to explain how he arrived at the correct answer or to write out the steps of the problem. All of these issues reflect an underlying problem with language; the child simply has difficulty understanding or remembering math concepts expressed in words.

Transposing numbers or making frequent errors with math symbols could be a problem for your child, such as confusing + and − signs, when copying from the board or textbook. This may reflect a perceptual problem or stem from the confusion over symbols that is part of dyslexia. Understanding time and time concepts might also be a problem.

Common Behavior Problems

Your first indication that something is wrong may be complaints from your child's teacher about her behavior or problems she is experiencing at school. Many behavior problems stem from the dyslexia itself; your child's teacher may complain that she doesn't pay attention or follow instructions, or that she is slow to complete classwork. These issues may be the direct result of your child's confusion and inability to understand much of what is going on around her.

Other behavior problems may be deliberate and could be an expression of her frustration and anger; she may intentionally try to disrupt the class to create distractions so as to avoid having to complete her work. She would rather that her classmates think of her as funny or bad than stupid. She may even want to incur punishment, if punishment means being sent to sit in the hallway or principal's office. To a child with dyslexia, such punishment can be a welcome reprieve from the torture of the classroom.

Some common behavior problems that your child's teacher may report are:

- Laziness, carelessness, or immaturity
- Daydreaming
- Disruptive behavior
- Being easily distracted
- Resistance to following directions
- Reluctance to work on assignments

To the teacher, all of these behaviors may seem deliberate. However, your child simply does not have the ability to conform to the expectations of a classroom when she is confused or unable to perform work at the same level and speed as the other children. You will not be able to help resolve the behavioral problem unless the learning problem is first addressed.

Social and Emotional Problems

Your child's school problems will probably also be reflected in problems at home and in interactions with his peers. Some of these issues may be directly related to his dyslexia, but many of these issues stem indirectly from the stress and frustration that is a constant part of your child's day.

From the age of seven, if not sooner, your child might be aware of her performance in comparison to other children her age. Struggling to understand concepts that other children find easy and making mistakes in schoolwork can be embarrassing. Showing your support and encouragement will help, but these problems will take their toll. Your child might complain of stomachaches or headaches in the morning, and while it may seem like an attempt to avoid school, the pain could be a very real manifestation of the stress and anxiety.

 ESSENTIAL

You can help your child deal with anger and frustration—and help yourself—by teaching him relaxation and stress-reducing techniques and also practicing them yourself. This not only will relieve tension at home, but will also help your child develop greater self-control and improve his ability to focus on his work.

It's easy to become short-tempered and frustrated at times, as dealing with your child may seem to require endless and fruitless repetition, day after day. It's tempting to shout, nag, and make dire threats of punishment. All of this, of course, will only make matters worse, as it will allow your child's dyslexia to become the focus of your home and family life. Confronting these problems will take patience, understanding, and effort on your part. If you can lay aside your own feelings of frustration and disappointment, you'll be able to provide your child with the support and guidance he needs. Try to encourage him to participate in activities he can succeed at, because his self-esteem will be crucial to his development and to peace in your household. Be prepared to set limits; your child needs understanding, but he also needs structure and support in learning to control his own behavior.

Dyslexia in Adolescents

As your child approaches the teenage years, dyslexia can present new challenges. In middle school and high school the academic demands increase tremendously. Additionally, your child will be faced with juggling a number of classes with different teachers, each with their own expectations about homework and class behavior.

Your child may need your help and support more than ever. However, your child is also feeling a natural pull toward independence. When he has academic problems, he may feel embarrassed by your attempts to confer with teachers and prefer to tough it out on his own rather than have his parents act as intermediaries.

Changes and New Challenges

As your child reaches adolescence, he may continue to have the same problems and symptoms that indicated dyslexia in his elementary school years. If a diagnosis has been made and he receives appropriate accommodations and services, you may notice some improvements. Often, after years of struggling and unsuccessful interventions, things seem to suddenly click at around age twelve. This can be a result of normal growth and development. Children at this age are developing a greater capacity for abstract and complex thought, and this very capacity may be the breakthrough your child needs in order to finally put all the elements needed for reading together.

 FACT

Educator Richard Lavoie has made several videos that are helpful in understanding your child's feelings and addressing his negative behavior, including one offering practical advice and showing how preventive discipline can anticipate many problems before they start. You can find them at *www.ricklavoie.com*.

Additionally, changed expectations at school may benefit your child. With separate teachers for most of his classes, he may finally have the opportunity to excel in his areas of strength. It will become more common for written homework to be completed with a computer and word processor, and your child may become adept at using the computer spell checker and grammar checker in completing his work. As math courses become more demanding, the use of the calculator becomes routine and expected. Your child may be able to round out his day with elective courses in art or music, and may find his niche in athletic or other extra-curricular activities.

On the other hand, if your child's needs have not been met in the past, the social and behavioral problems that result from her frustration and low self-esteem may be magnified. As a way of dealing with their problems, children may sometimes cut class or skip school, provoke conflict with teachers and administrators at school, or experiment with illicit drugs and alcohol, engage in sexually promiscuous behavior, or perform criminal acts such as shoplifting. Sometimes children show signs of serious depression or suicidal tendencies when they don't know how to handle their frustration.

These social and behavioral problems are not a direct result of dyslexia; many children who have never had school problems in the past will also rebel and break rules in their high school years. However, a child who has low self-esteem and finds school to be stressful and unrewarding is at greater risk. As a parent, you will need to be careful to watch for signs that your child may be in serious trouble, and be ready to seek appropriate intervention when needed.

The Undiagnosed Teenager with Dyslexia

Often, very bright children are able to compensate for their dyslexia in the early school years, but cannot cope with the greater intellectual demands of secondary level schooling. Some common signs that your teenager may have dyslexia are:

- Your child must repeatedly read and reread material in order to understand it.
- Your child has extreme difficulty managing and keeping track of homework assignments and deadlines for his various classes.
- Your child repeatedly reports that he was unaware of assignments and deadlines because the teacher "never told" him what was required.
- Your child has unexpected difficulty with learning a foreign language.

- Your child struggles with higher math, such as algebra.
- There is a significant discrepancy between your child's school performance and scores on standardized tests, including college board tests such as the PSAT.

If your child shows significant problems in any one of the above areas, it is a sign that he may have a previously undiagnosed learning disability. You should discuss these issues with him and also talk to parents of his classmates to find out whether their children are also having problems with the same subjects. Sometimes a problem with a math class or the first year of a foreign language can simply be the result of a poor teacher; poor grades in any subject can also occur with a teacher who is unusually strict in grading practices. If it is a "teacher" problem, usually other students and parents will have similar complaints. However, if the problems seem to be unusual or persistent, you should seek an evaluation for dyslexia or other learning barriers. The guidance counselor at school may be able to help arrange such testing, as well as help plan your child's course schedule to better meet his needs.

CHAPTER 3

Getting a Diagnosis

I F YOU SUSPECT that your child has dyslexia, you will want to seek testing and a diagnosis. Because the symptoms and degree of severity of dyslexia are variable, there is no one test or approach that will provide a definitive diagnosis. Rather, there are a variety of different approaches to measuring, defining, and understanding the learning profile and needs of each child. As a parent, you will find that a highly individualized approach is needed, depending on your child's specific symptoms and learning problems. You may need a multidisciplinary approach, such as having your child evaluated by several different kinds of learning and medical specialists.

Deciding to Seek Help

The first step in the process is to recognize that your child has a learning problem and that she will need extra help or intervention to overcome her difficulties. Coming to this point may be surprisingly difficult. Your child's own performance may be different from day to day, leading you to question whether there is any significant problem. Unfortunately, this inconsistency is part of the profile of dyslexia, as children with dyslexia are particularly susceptible to the effects of fatigue, stress, or frustration.

Fear of Labeling

Many parents are afraid that if their child is "labeled" with a learning disability, the label will do more harm than good. You may fear that your child will be placed in a special education classroom with children who have cognitive or emotional problems far worse than dyslexia, or that the diagnosis will prevent your child from having access to more challenging course and enrichment opportunities. You may also be afraid that your child will be singled out and rejected by his peers. Your child may also harbor similar fears. More than anything, she wants to be liked and accepted by her peers, and to be able to learn as quickly as they do and share in the same activities. Like you, she also fears being singled out or left behind.

Fortunately, many of these fears are unfounded. Public awareness has increased dramatically, and most people now understand that children with dyslexia are bright and capable. Teachers and school administrators will usually understand that your child may be struggling in one area but capable of doing advanced work in another. A diagnosis of dyslexia is often the first step toward structuring an educational program that will lead your child toward success. In fact, for a very bright child, testing of IQ and aptitude for dyslexia may also lead to qualification and placement in your school's program for gifted and talented youngsters. Once the learning disability is recognized, your child's innate strengths and potential might also become more apparent. In contrast, the failure to diagnose can leave your child struggling against an ever-increasing set of academic demands, with no real prospect of receiving help or understanding. Very few children can overcome dyslexia without specialized help and academic support.

Overcoming Resistance to Testing

You may find that when you discuss your child's problems with others, they may try to dissuade you from seeking a diagnosis. When you raise the issue with your child's teacher, she may try to reassure you that your child simply needs more time. She may seem to try to avoid any discussion of the subject, or actively discourage you from asking for testing, arguing that you do not want your child labeled with a disability.

You may also encounter surprising resistance from your family members. It is common for one parent to feel that the learning problems can be resolved with hard work and determination. Other family members may suggest that your child's problems stem from laziness, lack of motivation, or immaturity—and even try to blame your parenting style—arguing that your child simply needs more attention or discipline.

 ALERT!

You may be told that your child is too young to be tested for dyslexia, or that there is no test for dyslexia that can be given. If your child old enough to attend school, this is not true. Even though a firm diagnosis may not be possible, your child can be screened to determine if he has a learning pattern indicating possible dyslexia.

Again, you need to trust your instincts. Keep in mind that if you are mistaken in suspecting dyslexia, the best way to find out is through testing and diagnosis. Even if your child does not have dyslexia, an evaluation by a qualified professional may help you uncover other issues that are at the root of your child's school problems.

When an Older Child Asks for Help

In some cases, your older child or teenager may be the one who asks for testing. Your child may find the academic demands in middle school and high school overwhelming, at least in some subject areas. He may have learned about dyslexia on his own, through Internet Web sites or by talking to other kids. In any case, he knows that he is struggling with material that seems easy for his peers. Your teenager may be afraid to bring up the subject of dyslexia at home. He may be embarrassed to let you know just how poorly he is doing at school, or he may be afraid that you will be angry or upset. It is important that you listen to your child and try to understand the reasons he feels he needs extra help. You might want to take a list of common dyslexia symptoms from this book or from a Web site, and ask your child to show you which problems on the list he feels apply to him. You may be surprised to learn that your child has been struggling for years, but has managed in the past to hide his problems through sheer determination and hard work. Your support and understanding is crucial; for a child who has previously done well academically, an appropriate diagnosis can be the boost he needs to excel in high school and gain admittance into the college of his choice.

Is Diagnosis Always Necessary?

Some families are able to help their children without formal testing and diagnosis. Keep in mind that dyslexia is not a disease or mental defect, but a learning difference that usually requires that the child receive extra educational support. You don't need a prescription to enroll your child at a learning center or hire a tutor, and the same multisensory teaching methods that are best for children with dyslexia will also tend to help other children, as they are geared to reach multiple learning styles.

 **FACT**

Research shows that approximately 15 percent of all school children have dyslexia. However, only 5 percent of school children are identified as having a learning disability. The other 10 percent are missed because teachers fail to recognize that they are struggling, or that their academic or behavior problems are connected to specific difficulties with learning.

If you homeschool, or if your child is attending a school with a flexible and understanding staff, you may find that his needs can be well addressed without going through the process of a formal diagnosis of a learning disability. However, diagnostic testing will help you better understand your child and may guide you to make better choices. Ideally, testing should give you a map of your child's strong and weak points, and a set of recommendations as to how best to meet his educational needs.

A diagnosis of dyslexia or a related learning disability will also give you and your child important legal rights. If your child is in public school, the diagnosis will require the school authorities to work with you to design an Individualized Education Program (IEP) to meet your child's needs. You will be entitled to have a voice in the process and to attend regular meetings to discuss and monitor your child's progress and to make modifications to the IEP as needed.

It's possible that a diagnosis could also prompt your child's school to offer him appropriate modifications and accommodations to enable him to experience success in school. For example, he might be allowed extra time on tests or allowed to use a calculator. These modifications help level the playing field so your child is able to keep pace with his classmates.

How Dyslexia Is Diagnosed

There is no single test for dyslexia that all experts use, or a single agreed standard for testing. There is not even a definition of dyslexia that is uniformly accepted. The symptoms and characteristics of dyslexia vary significantly from one individual to the next, and the range of difficulties can vary from being quite mild to extremely severe. Some experts define dyslexia broadly to include a range of common learning difficulties, whereas others use different names and categories to describe the various academic, social, and behavioral issues that may accompany dyslexia.

Dyslexia by Any Other Name

The process of diagnosis is complicated by the fact that experts in different fields often prefer using different names to describe the symptoms they see. For a specialist, the term "dyslexia" seems overbroad when more precise terminology can be used to describe individual symptoms. Some experts might divide dyslexia into various subtypes; others might elect to call it something else entirely, such as "Developmental Reading Disorder." The specific label attached to your child's learning problems may depend on who is doing the labeling; a medical doctor, for example, is likely to use different terminology than a learning specialist at your child's school. While this can seem terribly confusing, it is important to stay focused on what the evaluators tell you about your child's learning needs.

Who Can Diagnose Dyslexia?

Dyslexia is diagnosed by a specialist who is trained and qualified in the assessment of learning disabilities. This may include:

- Clinical or educational psychologists
- School psychologists
- Neuropsychologists
- Learning disabilities specialists
- Medical doctors with training and experience in the assessment of learning problems

Your child's evaluation might also include examination by other medical specialists. An audiologist might be involved in determining whether your child has problems with hearing or processing the sounds of language. A developmental optometrist might be needed to determine whether your child has vision difficulties that are contributing to his reading problems. Even if your child has 20/20 vision, reading might be hampered because of difficulties with near point vision, tracking, or eye teaming. A neurologist may be involved to test for problems that may stem from brain damage or problems with brain function beyond dyslexia. If your child has problems regulating his behavior or sustaining attention, a child psychologist or psychiatrist may be consulted to evaluate for Attention Deficit Disorder or other psychiatric and emotional problems.

The purpose of all this testing is not only to determine whether your child has dyslexia, but also to consider and rule out the possibility of other problems that may contribute to his learning difficulties. Your child may have a number of different issues, some of which may be easier to treat than others.

ALERT!

Your child's teacher may suggest that he be tested for ADHD because of classroom behavior problems. If your child is having problems with reading or writing, it is crucial that he also be tested for dyslexia and other learning disabilities. Medication commonly used for ADHD may help your child pay attention in class, but it will not help him learn to read or resolve a learning disability.

Early Diagnosis and Screening

Because dyslexia is a primarily diagnosed through tests measuring skills related to reading and reading readiness, it is not possible to reliably diagnose a child who is too young to start school. Many common symptoms of dyslexia, such as letter reversals in writing, are also part of normal childhood development. Children grow and learn at different rates. Even though most children can learn to read at age six, many are not ready to learn to read until age seven or eight. That is why reading instruction in schools generally continues through the primary grades, from kindergarten through grade three.

This does not mean that your child cannot be helped, however. There are many reasons why a young child may be struggling in school, but extra support and reading instruction will help all children who are falling behind. A young child can be screened for early signs of dyslexia, and you can plan age-appropriate early interventions if indicated. If you are concerned about early signs of dyslexia in your preschool-age child (age three to five), you can also provide extra support at home to help build reading readiness skills. You will find suggestions for such activities in Chapter 14.

Who Pays for Diagnostic Testing

Federal law requires that all public schools provide testing whenever there is reason to suspect a learning disability. This is true even if your child is in private school, although the law is unclear as to whether homeschoolers are entitled to testing or services. The procedures for arranging testing are discussed in Chapter 10.

Your health insurance may also cover the costs of some kinds of testing, particularly medical testing, such as evaluations by a neurologist or audiologist. Your child's pediatrician may be able to assist by making a referral for testing by appropriate specialists. Each health insurance policy is different, so the first step is to carefully review your policy. You may prefer to arrange and pay for your own testing. Diagnostic testing can be very expensive, but you may feel more comfortable with the quality of an evaluation if it is done by professionals that you have selected.

Tests and Measurements

There are several different tests that may be used to evaluate your child. They are not necessarily specific to dyslexia, but when combined they help provide a good picture of your child's development.

Weschler Intelligence Scale

An evaluator will often start with an IQ test to determine your child's overall ability level. One of the most common tests used is the Wechsler Intelligence Scale for Children (WISC III or WISC IV). This test is favored because it breaks down scores into two scales, Verbal and Performance, which in turn each consist of various subtests. The Verbal Scale measures language expression, comprehension, listening, and the ability to apply these skills to solving problems. The Performance Scale assesses nonverbal problem solving, perceptual organization, speed, and visual-motor proficiency. It includes tasks like puzzles, picture analysis, imitating designs with blocks, and copying. This test is given orally, by an evaluator working individually with your child, so your child does not have to know how to read to score well on the test.

By looking at the scores on various subtests, the evaluator will see a pattern of strengths and weaknesses. This sort of testing is extremely valuable for all children and can be used to indicate a wide variety of learning disabilities. Dyslexia is indicated as a possible diagnosis if the subtests show that a child has particular weaknesses in areas normally associated with dyslexia—such as verbal fluency, short-term auditory memory (digit span), or speed of processing information.

 ALERT!

You may be told that dyslexia is a medical term and that you will need a medical doctor to diagnose it. This is not true. Your child's pediatrician may be able to make recommendations and refer you to appropriate specialists, but she will not be able to make a determination as to whether or not your child has dyslexia.

WISC testing will also provide a "full-scale" IQ—the number that results from combining the results of the Verbal and Performance scales. This is useful in evaluating overall cognitive ability and making recommendations for education and therapy. However, caution should be used in interpreting these results as a measure of your child's intellectual capacity. A very bright child may have a lower-than-expected IQ result due to poor performance on some of the subtests. If a child with a WISC IQ score in the average range scores particularly high on some of the subtests, further testing with other IQ tests is needed to assess for possible giftedness. Your child's emotional state and attitude toward testing could also result in poor performance on this test.

Achievement Tests

Your child will also be given achievement tests to measure reading performance. The specific tests will vary depending on the preferences of the evaluator and the age of your child. Younger children will be given tests that measure pre-reading and early reading skills, such as simple word recognition tests. Older children may be given tests that measure sentence reading, oral fluency, and reading comprehension.

These tests are not the same as the standardized tests that are used in schools to assess classroom performance. Group standardized tests are not valid for measuring individual ability levels because they are designed for purposes of comparing the overall achievement of large groups of children. Although your child's scores on standardized tests may be a relevant piece of information to include in an evaluation, these tests are not a reliable way to diagnose learning disabilities.

Specialized Tests for Dyslexia

There are also some specialized tests geared toward measuring problems commonly associated with dyslexia. For example, a child's ability to parse out the sounds of language can be measured with tests of phonemic awareness. Your child may be asked to read a set of "nonwords"—that is, invented words with no real meaning such as SLIMP or HIFE. He may also be asked to say whether certain words rhyme, or to break apart words by their sounds, such as to say the word "bent" without the "n" sound. There are also tests given that assess word retrieval skills and auditory and verbal processing speed, that may include tests of rapid automatic naming, which requires the child to quickly read aloud the names of letters or numbers presented on a chart or graph. Short-term memory, or digit span, might also be tested. These tests ask children to remember and repeat a short sequence of letters or numbers or to identify a sequence of letters, numbers, or pictures after briefly viewing a picture or card with such sequence.

Types of Dyslexia

When there is a diagnosis of dyslexia, it is often classified into one of several subtypes. These subtypes are basically labels for the pattern of symptoms that emerged through testing. Understanding the nature of your child's difficulty can help guide you to choosing the right program of instruction or remediation. Some of the common subtypes are:

Dysphonetic dyslexia (Also called dysphonesia; phonological dyslexia; or auditory dyslexia): This form is characterized by difficulties with word attack skills, including phonetic segmentation and blending. It can be identified by poor nonword reading skills; for example, the inability to decipher invented words with no real meaning used to test phonetic skills. Spelling is inconsistent with bizarre letter combinations.

Dyseidetic dyslexia (Also called dyseidesia, surface dyslexia, or visual dyslexia): Children with the dyseidetic form of dyslexia have a good ability to sound out words, but they read very laboriously. They have difficulty learning to recognize whole words visually, and have problems deciphering words that do not follow regular phonetic rules. Spelling is highly phonetic, for example writing "skul" for "school."

Naming-speed deficits (Also called semantic dyslexia, dysnomia, or anomia): This subtype of dyslexia is diagnosed primarily from poor performance on tests of rapid automatic naming. Children with naming speed deficits have difficulty with word retrieval. They may hesitate in speech, or frequently substitute a mistaken word for what they mean, such as saying "tornado" when they mean "volcano." They may also frequently use generic words (i.e., "thing," or "place") instead of specific nouns; or they may resort to descriptive phrases. (i.e., "the eating thing" rather than "spoon").

Double-deficit: Double-deficit dyslexia is a label attached to children who have both the phonological and the naming-speed subtypes. These children are thought to have a particularly severe and persistent form of dyslexia.

Many children have symptoms that overlap more than one of the various subtypes, and are not easily categorized. Research suggests that approximately 60 percent of children with dyslexia have the dysphonetic form, while about 10 percent have the dyseidetic form. The remaining children generally have a combination of forms and symptoms.

Overlapping and Related Conditions

The results of testing may indicate that your child has a learning disability other than dyslexia. In some cases, the learning disability may be the same thing as dyslexia. For example, the evaluation may conclude that your child has a Developmental Reading Disorder or Phonological Processing Disorder. These phrases are merely different ways of describing dyslexia or a subtype. It is also very common for children with dyslexia to be diagnosed as having Attention Deficit Disorder (ADD/ADHD), Central Auditory Processing Disorder (APD or CAPD), or a visual processing issue. These are different from dyslexia, but there is substantial overlap in symptoms. That is, in many cases diagnosis of these conditions will be made based on the same symptoms that support a diagnosis of dyslexia.

For example, dyslexia is primarily a problem with processing of language, and reading problems are often accompanied by problems with using and understanding language. It is possible for a child to have an auditory processing disorder without dyslexia, but when a child has both the auditory processing issues and difficulty with reading, they probably are simply different manifestations of the same underlying language processing problem. The real issue is that the child needs help with understanding the sounds of language.

Similarly, Attention Deficit Disorder is generally characterized by high distractibility, difficulty staying "on task," and a variety of related behavioral problems. A child who cannot read and is feeling confused or frustrated in the classroom is likely to manifest the same sort of symptoms.

However, it is also possible that a child will have additional symptoms or problems that will support a dual diagnosis. For example, difficulty with reading will not cause a child to be hyper-active, but many children with dyslexia also have the hyperactive form of ADHD. Solving one problem won't help unless the other is also addressed.

ESSENTIAL

Find out exactly what symptoms support each diagnosis, and think about what you have observed in your child. If the diagnosis does not make sense to you, it may be mistaken. Focus on what sort of help your child actually needs, not on the label that is given to his symptoms.

Dyslexia and the Gifted Child

As a result of testing, you may be surprised to learn that your child is intellectually gifted. It is very common for the difficulties associated with dyslexia to mask your child's true potential. Your child may have a brilliant mind, but his difficulties with verbal and written language have prevented him from expressing his thoughts in a way that others can understand. The combination of intellectual giftedness with learning disabilities is actually quite common. Gifted children have learning disabilities at least as often as other children. Research has shown that children who are highly or profoundly gifted often have predominantly visual-spatial or right-brained learning styles; this puts them at particularly high risk for dyslexia.

On the other hand, your child's strong intellectual abilities may also make it difficult to get a firm diagnosis of dyslexia. Test results may show that your child has some, but not all, of the common symptoms of dyslexia; or your child simply might not score badly enough on any of the tests to support a diagnosis. A close look at scores on various subtests may reveal signs of specific learning barriers that are holding your child back.

Commercial Screening

There are many private-sector or commercial programs that are geared toward treating dyslexia or related problems. If you find a program that seems to be geared toward your child's problems, you may choose to go directly to the learning center or clinic providing the program for a screening test.

These screening tests are usually far less expensive than full diagnostic testing; in some cases, the tests may be offered for free. The tests usually will give you some more information about your child; however, they are not the same as diagnostic testing. These tests are designed to determine whether the child fits whatever program or services are being offered, or in some cases to create an appropriate service plan for the child. They often use terminology that is very specific to the private program. These generally are not terms that would be accepted as a valid diagnosis by a school or qualified medical or educational professionals.

Some common screening tests for disorders are:

Concept Imagery Disorder: This describes a weakness in the ability to turn language into images. It is used by Lindamood-Bell practitioners to determine whether a child should receive their Visualizing and Verbalizing program.

Davis Perceptual Ability Assessment: This assessment determines whether a child has the ability to mentally visualize an imagined object from multiple perspectives. It is aimed at finding a strong visual-spatial skill frequently associated with dyslexia. It is used by Davis Dyslexia Correction providers to determine whether a child is likely to benefit from Davis Orientation Counseling.

Scotopic Sensitivity Syndrome: This describes a visual-perceptual problem where the child has difficulty viewing text due to sensitivity to lighting or color conditions. It is used by Irlen Method screeners to determine whether the child will benefit using special colored overlays or lenses while reading.

CHAPTER 4

Related Conditions

C HILDREN WITH DYSLEXIA often have related learning difficulties. Dyslexia itself is almost always accompanied by difficulties with expressive writing and spelling, as these are also problems with manipulation of written language. Although problems with spelling are rarely labeled as a distinct learning disability, such problems are particularly persistent with dyslexia and sometimes are apparent even when the child seems to be a good reader. In addition to differences with language learning, children with dyslexia often have academic difficulties in other areas, such as math. Dyslexia can also lead to behavioral problems that overlap with other disorders, such as ADD/ADHD; and in some cases children with dyslexia also suffer from other unrelated mental or emotional disorders that make treatment of dyslexia more complicated.

Problems with Handwriting or Expressive Writing

Dysgraphia means "difficulty with writing." Usually the term describes a difficulty with handwriting, either with printing or cursive. Sometimes this stems from physical or neurological issues unrelated to dyslexia. Some children may have difficulty with small-motor coordination that stems from other developmental causes, or from physical difficulties, which make it very hard for them to properly grasp a writing implement or coordinate their movements. These children may benefit from occupational therapy.

 QUESTION?

Can a child who is a good reader also have dyslexia?
Yes. Occasionally, a child is able to overcome or avoid issues with reading but will still have an array of related symptoms. Usually, such a child is extremely bright with a strong visual memory, allowing her to develop good sight reading skills despite having characteristic difficulty with phonetics. The dyslexia may become apparent because of problems with productive writing or spelling.

The term dysgraphia is also sometimes used to describe an expressive writing disorder: a difficulty putting thoughts to words when writing. Children with this sort of difficulty will find any sort of written composition to be a laborious process and may have great difficulty constructing sentences and paragraphs in a grammatical or logical format.

When associated with dyslexia, dysgraphia is a reflection of underlying difficulties with written language. Some common symptoms are:

- Fingers are cramped when grasping pencil or pen, or child uses unusual grip.
- Written work is marred by frequent cross-outs or erasures.
- Writing is inconsistent, with a mixture of upper and lower case letters, printed and cursive, variation in size of letters, or irregular formation and slant.
- Child has difficulty keeping writing on lines or within margins.
- Child writes very slowly and is easily fatigued.
- Handwriting is illegible.

Students with dysgraphia often have sequencing problems. Symptoms that appear to be a perceptual problem (reversing letters/numbers, writing words backwards, writing letters out of order, and very sloppy handwriting) can also be directly related to sequential/rational information processing.

 FACT

Children's writer Avi has dysgraphia. He has difficulty with writing and spelling. As a child, his teachers told him that his writing didn't make sense, and he failed most of his courses in high school. He still finds writing difficult and needs to rewrite frequently. Nonetheless, he grew up to become a prolific writer and the author of dozens of award-winning children's books.

Difficulty with Math

Dsycalculia is a learning disability with math. About 60 percent of children with dyslexia have difficulty with numbers or number relationships. However, about 11 percent of students with dyslexia excel in mathematics, while the remaining students have ordinary mathematical abilities. Thus, although strongly associated with dyslexia, dyscalculia should be considered a separate and different learning problem.

Symptoms of dyscalculia include:

- Problems with operations such as addition, subtraction, multiplication, and division.
- Difficulty learning math facts such as memorizing times tables.
- Confusion over mathematical symbols such as: + and x; –, ÷ and =; < (less than) and > (greater than).
- Difficulty with understanding words used to describe mathematical operations, such as "difference" or "sum."

- Tendency to reverse or transpose numbers in writing, such as writing 31 for 13.
- Difficulty understanding concepts related to time and learning to tell time.
- Difficulty grasping and remembering math rules, formulas, sequence (order of operations), or algorithms used for problem-solving.

Some of the problems associated with dyscalculia stem from the same underlying issues with language processing and sequencing that characterize dyslexia. Your child may be able to understand math concepts when working with math manipulatives, but may struggle working with numerals and mathematical symbols and formulas, and have difficulty understanding written procedures for solving math problems, such as "borrowing" or "carrying" in addition or subtraction. She may be able to understand math that is represented symbolically, but struggle with word problems; she may know that 3 + 2 = 5, but be unable to work out a problem like "If Mary has 3 cookies and Tim has 2, how many cookies in all?"

 ESSENTIAL

Your child will learn math concepts better using manipulatives and hands-on activities. Encourage him to use small objects such as beans or his fingers to aid in calculation. Using play money and making change may aid with understanding of addition and subtraction. Use strategies to help demonstrate patterns and relationships involved in mathematics, rather than rely on rote memorization.

Even if your child seems to have strong mathematical ability, he may use unorthodox approaches to arrive at a solution, or be unable to explain the process he uses in words. Your child may seem to know the answer to some problems immediately, but be very slow to work out pencil and paper answers. This also is a reflection of the underlying language problems, and occurs when a child relies on his stronger visual spatial reasoning skills to picture the problem and solution, rather than using orderly manipulation of numbers. Ironically, these skills may enable your child to excel later on with higher mathematics, such as trigonometry or calculus, but often hold the child back during early years when emphasis is on simple arithmetic and rote memorization of math facts.

"Clumsy Child Syndrome"

Dyspraxia is difficulty with thinking out, planning, and carrying out sensory/motor tasks. It is sometimes called "clumsy child syndrome." Your child with dyspraxia may have difficulty coordinating small-motor functions, such as learning to tie her shoes or button her clothes. There may be difficulties with balance and large-motor coordination, such as difficulty learning to ride a bicycle or catching a ball. Your child may seem particularly clumsy or accident-prone, always breaking, tripping over, or bumping into things.

Some of these issues may also be related to cerebellar or vestibular problems. The cerebellum is a section of the brain located toward the back, behind and below the cerebrum. The cerebellum is largely involved in coordination and in bodily, kinesthetic memory, which is involved in learning a new physical skill such as roller-skating. There is some research indicating the cerebellum tends to be smaller and more symmetric in children with dyslexia, who also show evidence of reduced activation of the cerebellum in small-motor tasks, such as learning and practicing a sequence of finger movements.

The vestibular system is governed by the inner ear. Its purpose is to keep tabs on the position and motion of a person's head in space. A vestibular disorder can result in dizziness, unsteadiness or imbalance when walking, vertigo, and nausea.

A child with verbal dyspraxia may have difficulty coordinating speech, which may result in stammering or garbled speech. Essentially, the brain is not sending the correct signals to the muscles to produce cognitive speech. Verbal dyspraxia is extremely frustrating, because the child knows in her mind what she wants to say, but the sounds do not come out of her mouth correctly when she tries to speak. This is different from word retrieval issues commonly associated with dyslexia, which occur when the child has an idea of what she wants to say but cannot think of the correct word. With dyspraxia, the child has the word in mind, but can't seem to get her lips and tongue to cooperate.

Attention Deficit Disorder

The letters ADD are commonly used to refer to Attention Deficit Disorder-Inattentive Type; whereas ADHD refers to Attention Deficit Disorder with Hyperactivity. Both patterns of attention deficits are very common among children with dyslexia. Also, it is very common for children with dyslexia to be misdiagnosed as having ADD because of symptoms that are common to both conditions.

 **FACT**

> Your child with dyslexia is twice as likely as other children to have ADD; about 15 percent of students with reading problems are also diagnosed with ADD. Conversely, a child with ADD is twice as likely to have difficulties with reading; about 36 percent of children with ADD also have dyslexia.

It is not clear why it is so common for children to have both ADD and reading problems. Of course, the ADD child will find it difficult to learn if she cannot focus attention in a classroom, but it is more likely that there is a common set of learning traits to both conditions. Some educators believe that, like dyslexia, ADD stems from a predominantly right-brained learning style. Like dyslexia, ADD is often seen in highly creative individuals and is common in gifted children. In many ways, the symptoms of ADD may be the result of an overactive mind and an unharnessed imagination.

Inattention-Type Attention Deficits

Because there is so much overlap between symptoms of attention deficits and dyslexia, it is important to understand how ADD/ADHD is diagnosed. The appropriate criteria for diagnosis are clearly set out in the *Diagnostic and Statistical Manual of Mental Disorders* (DSM IV), which specifies that a child can be diagnosed with ADHD (inattention type) if he has six or more of the following symptoms:

1. Fails to pay close attention to details or makes careless mistakes in schoolwork, work, or other activities.
2. Has difficulty holding attention in tasks or play activities.
3. Does not seem to listen when spoken to directly.
4. Does not follow through on instructions and fails to finish schoolwork, chores, or duties in the workplace (not because he is rebelling or has not understood instructions).
5. Has difficulty organizing tasks and activities.
6. Avoids or dislikes tasks that require sustained mental effort (such as schoolwork or homework).
7. Loses things necessary for tasks or activities (e.g., toys, school assignments, pencils, books, or tools).
8. Is easily distracted by extraneous stimuli.
9. Is forgetful in daily activities.

 FACT

Although it is estimated that 15 percent of school children have dyslexia, only 5 percent are ever identified. The remaining 10 percent have a hidden disability, but it is possible that many of these children are mislabeled as having ADD or some other behavioral or psychological problem.

However, each of the above symptoms is also a common characteristic of dyslexia. Your child's academic and language processing difficulties will simply make it very difficult for her to sustain attention, follow instructions, or complete schoolwork. Thus, you should be careful before accepting a diagnosis of "inattentive" type ADHD. In some cases, a mistaken diagnosis can lead to delays in getting help or special tutoring to address reading problems. Studies show that medications commonly prescribed for ADHD do not help children learn academic skills.

Hyperactivity-Impulsivity Type

The second type of ADHD, hyperactivity-impulsivity type, is more distinct from dyslexia. According to the DSM-IV, it is diagnosed when the child has six or more of the following symptoms:

1. Fidgets with hands or feet or squirms in seat.
2. Does not stay in seat in classroom or in other situations in which remaining seated is expected.
3. Runs around or climbs excessively in situations in which it is inappropriate (in adolescents, may be limited to subjective feelings of restlessness).
4. Has difficulty playing or engaging in leisure activities quietly.
5. Is often "on the go" or often acts as if "driven by a motor."
6. Talks excessively.
7. Blurts out answers before questions have been completed.
8. Has difficulty awaiting turn.
9. Interrupts or intrudes on others (e.g., butts into conversations or games).

Many of these behaviors may also be a result of the learning problems associated with dyslexia. A child who is frustrated or confused in a classroom will have a hard time sitting still or obeying rules. Again, it is important for you to consider the context surrounding the observed behavior.

Avoiding a Misdiagnosis

In order for attention deficit disorder to be properly diagnosed, some of the symptoms must have been present before the age of seven and the symptoms must be present in two or more settings, such as both school and home. These additional criteria help to sort out ADD from school problems, as children whose difficulties are only manifested in the classroom environment simply do not have attention deficit disorder. Many children are highly active but function normally at home or at play, where they can engage in a reasonable amount of physical activity and have freedom to choose which tasks to focus their energy on.

ALERT!

Symptoms of ADD can also be a result of physical health problems, such as vitamin deficiencies or exposure to toxins such as lead or mercury. Some children have food allergies or sensitivities that affect their behavior, including reactions to food additives and sweets or sodas.

The National Institute of Mental Health cautions that the behaviors associated with ADD may merely reflect a child's response to a defeating classroom situation. Such symptoms can stem from feelings of frustration in a child who has a learning disability or who is emotionally immature, or from boredom in a child who finds the classwork tedious and unchallenging. A child with true ADD will exhibit difficulty concentrating and completing tasks even in situations when it is clear that the child wants to participate fully, or will show signs of impulsivity and hyperactivity outside of the restricted environment of a school classroom.

Nonverbal Learning Disabilities (NLD)

Nonverbal Learning Disabilities are essentially the opposite of dyslexia. The child with NLD has early speech and vocabulary development, strong rote memory skills, attention to detail, early reading skills development, and excellent spelling skills. The learning disability is found when these strengths are accompanied by significant weaknesses in motor skills, spatial reasoning ability, or social awareness. Children with NLD have difficulty processing information which is not language-based, either spoken or in writing. They have difficulty interpreting facial expressions or body language. They have a good memory for detail, but cannot understand the "big picture" or relate the details to form overall concepts.

Although NLD is very different than dyslexia, the symptoms can be confused. For example, an NLD child may have difficulty with balance and coordination, poor handwriting, and difficulty with reading comprehension. These are all symptoms that can exist with dyslexia as well; the main difference is that the NLD child's reading problems stem from difficulties appreciating the ideas and concepts represented by the words, whereas the child with dyslexia can easily grasp complex concepts, but has difficulty making sense of the words used to convey the ideas.

Cognitive Development and Mental Retardation

Dyslexia is not related to low IQ or mental retardation of any kind. Historically, dyslexia has always been defined as existing only among children with normal or above-normal intelligence, so in theory a low IQ negates a diagnosis of dyslexia. Children with low intellectual abilities will have difficulties that are generalized to all academic areas, as well as problems with day-to-day functioning at home. In cases of moderate to severe mental retardation, parents usually will be well aware of their child's limitations long before he is ready to attend school.

Reading Problems in Children with Low Intelligence

Children who have IQs considered to be merely below average or who are borderline mentally retarded may also have reading problems. Although these children may not fit the traditional profile of dyslexia, their poor reading ability can stem from the same underlying problems. Unfortunately, it is not always easy to get a clear diagnosis.

Many educators rely on a "discrepancy" test to diagnose dyslexia: they look for a significant gap between actual reading ability and the expected ability as determined from aptitude or IQ testing. However, recent research does not support this model. There is only a moderate correlation between IQ and reading ability, far less than the correlation between reading and early language development such as phonological awareness, which is now considered closely related to dyslexia. In other words, IQ can not reliably be used as a measure to predict reading skill.

ALERT!

Your child's "potential" cannot be measured with an IQ test. Research has shown that children with visual spatial learning styles, including dyslexia, tend to be "late bloomers." Your child will become more capable over time as higher brain functions develop and he is able to better relate new learning to existing knowledge and experience.

Measurement of IQ can also be suspect in a child with dyslexia, as the tests of intelligence rely largely on the same sort of skills that are impaired in children with dyslexia, such as language interpretation and short-term memory. Many children perform lower on IQ tests because of their dyslexia. It is very common to see such children score much higher on IQ tests as they grow older, in part because over time they simply acquire the skills needed to understand the test.

Getting Help at School

The problem with comparing IQ scores to reading ability is that it leaves many children with reading disabilities unable to qualify for services such as additional tutoring or accommodations from their school district. If your child scores poorly on an IQ test, she may very well have exactly the same reading deficits as any other child with dyslexia, but be denied extra help and expected to function in the same classrooms with other children.

She may be labeled as merely being a "garden variety poor reader" or "low achiever." In essence, she may be punished because she is not considered smart enough to have dyslexia.

Most educators now favor abandoning the discrepancy model and identifying dyslexia based on the characteristic pattern of weaknesses, rather than using an artificial standard of the perceived potential of the child. Thus, if your child has low IQ scores but does not seem to be cognitively impaired in areas other than those usually associated with dyslexia, you should understand that this book is for you. Your child will need the same extra help and will benefit from many of the same kinds of educational programs as any other child who is struggling to learn to read.

Mood Disorders

Some children with dyslexia also have emotional or psychiatric problems. In some cases, the problems are caused or exacerbated by the stress or frustration experienced in connection with dyslexia and academic problems. In other cases, behavior that is a response to dyslexia may give rise to a mistaken diagnosis. Finally, of course, many children with dyslexia do also suffer from additional mental or emotional problems. Even if not directly related to the dyslexia, these issues can make it more difficult to help with academic issues, particularly if the psychiatric problems lead the child to become unmotivated or resistant to teaching.

Depression

A child may be diagnosed with depression if he has depressed mood for most of the day, for more days than not, for at least a year. His mood will be accompanied by disruptions in patterns of eating or sleeping, low energy or fatigue, low self-esteem, poor concentration, difficulty making decisions, feelings of hopelessness, or persistent irritability.

All children have feelings of sadness or frustration from time to time, but depression is diagnosed when such symptoms are continual and persistent. Depression can be treated with counseling or medications; however, if the underlying reason for depression is the child's despair over poor academic performance, it is crucial that the school situation also be addressed.

Bipolar Disorder

Bipolar disorder, also known as manic depression, is marked by extreme changes in mood, energy, thinking, and behavior. The child will alternate between periods of mania and depression. During manic episodes, a child is likely to be extremely irritable and prone to destructive outbursts. Alternatively, he may exhibit extreme elation and high energy. While depressed, the child will be extremely sad or irritable and have low energy. There may be physical complaints such as headaches, muscle aches, stomachaches or tiredness, talk of or efforts to run away from home, unexplained crying, or extreme sensitivity to rejection or failure.

 ALERT!

Bipolar disorder can be easily mistaken for attention deficit disorder. However, stimulant medications (such as Ritalin) which are commonly prescribed for ADD, can induce or worsen the manic symptoms of bipolar disorder. This can also happen with medications commonly prescribed for depression. If you observe such symptoms when your child is taking medication, you should contact your physician immediately.

Children with bipolar disorder usually experience multiple cycles between manic and depressive moods within the same day, moving from giddy, silly highs to morose and gloomy lows. Any indication of suicidal thoughts, such as a child's talk of wanting to die or wishing that he had never been born, should be taken very seriously, as even very young children may attempt suicide during depressive periods. Bipolar disorder tends to run in families, but children with dyslexia are no more at risk than any other children.

Behavioral Disorders

A child may be diagnosed with Conduct Disorder when there is a pattern of repetitive behavior where the rights of others or the major age-appropriate social norms are violated. For example, the child may frequently bully, threaten, or intimidate others; may destroy property; or may frequently lie or steal.

Oppositional Defiant Disorder (ODD) is diagnosed when there is an enduring pattern of uncooperative, defiant, and hostile behavior toward authority figures that does not involve major anti-social violations, is not accounted for by the child's developmental stage, and results in significant functional impairment. The child may frequently lose his temper, argue with adults, or actively defy rules or refuse to carry out requests from adults. He may deliberately try to annoy others or blame others for his own mistakes or misbehavior or seem angry and resentful. It can be very difficult to distinguish behavior associated with ODD from behavior that is a normal but inappropriate response to feelings of frustration and anger stemming from academic difficulties and frequent criticism encountered at school. As with other behavioral issues, it is important for parents and teachers to recognize and address learning problems as a first step toward addressing behavioral issues.

Autistic Spectrum Disorders

Autistic Spectrum Disorders include problems with nonverbal communication, socialization, and empathy. Children with an autistic spectrum disorder have difficulty understanding what other people are saying, need help to play with other children, enjoy routines, and find unfamiliar situations difficult. Symptoms can range from very mild to profound social and cognitive delays. The disorder is not associated with dyslexia, but it can coexist with dyslexia. Many children with autistic spectrum disorder also have difficulties learning to read and write.

Autism

Autism is a complex developmental disability that typically appears during the first three years of life. A child with autism processes and responds to information in unique ways. Although some can function at a relatively high level, many children with autism have serious cognitive impairments or mental retardation, and some never gain the ability to speak. A child with autism may seem closed off and shut down or locked into repetitive behaviors and rigid patterns of thinking. He may avoid eye contact and resist physical contact, such as hugging, or may have frequent tantrums or remain fixated on a single item or activity such as spinning objects. It's possible that his sensitivity to pain could be higher or lower than typical.

 **FACT**

Autism is about three to four times more common in boys. However, girls with the disorder tend to have more severe symptoms and greater cognitive impairment. Although autism is frequently accompanied by mental retardation, about one out of ten children with autism also are savants with exceptional talents in narrowly constrained areas such as drawing ability or playing the piano.

The severity of autism can be extremely variable, ranging from mild to severe. Children with mild to moderate symptoms are considered "high-functioning." Two children may share the diagnosis of autism, but behave very differently and have very different skills and abilities.

Asperger's Syndrome

Asperger's Syndrome is similar to autism, but milder in form. Children with Asperger's have normal or above-average intelligence.

They do not have language delays, but often have unusual speech patterns; they may speak formalistically or without inflection, or speak in a rhythmic nature or with a high-pitched tone. They often have a very literal understanding of language, and have difficulty understanding irony or verbal humor.

Children with Asperger's usually want to fit in and have interaction with others, but they tend to be socially awkward and have difficulty understanding conventional social rules or the give and take of normal conversation. They are often obsessively interested in particular subjects and may become proficient at knowing obscure categories of information, such as memorizing baseball statistics or bus routes. They may enjoy collecting things such as rocks or bottle caps. Although diagnosis of Asperger's syndrome does not include reading problems, the condition is frequently accompanied by symptoms of dyslexia.

Semantic Pragmatic Disorder (SPD)

Semantic Pragmatic Disorder is a communication disorder characterized by difficulties with social interaction, communication, and imagination. Autistic features are mild and concentrated in the areas of social use and understanding of language and communication. Children with SPD are unable to process all the given information from certain situations, often focusing on details without understanding the big picture. The condition is usually first identified because of marked delays and difficulty with speech and language development.

Hyperlexia

Children with hyperlexia demonstrate an early and intense fascination with letters, numbers, patterns and logos, and a self-taught, precocious ability to read, spell, write, or compute, usually before the age of five. At the same time, they have significant difficulty understanding and using oral language and with socializing and interacting appropriately with other people.

Although the early acquisition of reading ability makes hyperlexia seem very different than dyslexia, both conditions are rooted in difficulties with understanding and using language. A child with hyperlexia is often highly intelligent, learning best from visually presented information. The difference is that the child with hyperlexia can easily manipulate and understand written symbols for language and concepts, but has problems with oral language. Your child with dyslexia has difficulty with symbols but will be stronger with verbal communication skills and in understanding concepts that language represents.

It is possible for a child to learn to read early without having hyperlexia; many intellectually gifted children easily acquire reading skills as early as age three or four. Occasionally, a child with dyslexia will also be an early reader; dyslexia will be diagnosed when the child encounters problems with advanced reading skills, writing, or spelling as she grows older.

CHAPTER 5

Learning to Read

ALTHOUGH CHILDREN WITH DYSLEXIA usually have marked difficulty learning to read, the process of reading development in all children is essentially the same. In order to become a good reader, your child will need to first learn decoding and word recognition skills, and then develop fluency and comprehension skills. The specialized help he will need may vary over the years, depending on his age and reading level and specific areas of difficulty. Understanding what makes a good reader will help you understand what programs or reading methods are best for your child.

Stages of Reading Development

Some children naturally progress from preschool through primary years and beyond, easily learning to read from minimal instruction and gaining improved skills naturally through exposure to print and practice with reading. However, a child with dyslexia will not be able to learn so easily; your child will need assistance and instruction tailored to his needs and specific areas of difficulty. Your child's needs will change over time, depending on her age and reading level. You will be able to better understand what methods and programs are right for her if you understand the basic stages of reading development.

Stage 0: Reading Readiness/Pre-Reading (Birth–6)

According to renowned professor Dr. Jeanne Chall, children follow predictable stages of reading development. At the earliest stage, children first gain control of language. They begin to realize that words are made up of a series of sounds and start to recognize rhyme and alliteration. If exposed to print, preschoolers also learn to recognize the alphabet and begin to learn the sounds associated with letters. They may begin to recognize a few words, relying largely on contextual information provided by pictures and highly predictable language.

Stage 1: Initial Reading, or Decoding Stage (Ages 6–7)

At this stage, beginning readers learn to decode by sounding out words. They understand that letters and letter combinations represent sounds and use this knowledge to blend together simple words such as *cat* or *top*. This is the phase that generally is the first major barrier for a child with dyslexia. While your child will probably be able to understand that individual letters represent discrete sounds, he may find it extremely difficult to put the sounds together to spell words, and almost impossible to decode words by breaking down the component sounds.

Stage 2: Confirmation, Fluency, Ungluing from Print (Ages 7–8)

Once primary level students have become adept at decoding, they begin to develop fluency and additional strategies to gain meaning from print. They are ready to read without sounding everything out. They begin to recognize whole words by their visual appearance and letter sequence (orthographic knowledge). They recognize familiar patterns and reach automaticity in word recognition and gain fluency as they practice with reading familiar texts.

Your child will need extra help to develop the strategies that lead to fluency. Your child's ability to recognize whole words may be hampered by visual-perceptual problems; if so, she may need therapy to address these problems as well as specific instructions and methods to build the orthographic skills. It is at this phase that children with dyslexia often begin to fall seriously behind, as the skills they need are often not explicitly taught. Although a child needs to "unglue" from print in order to progress, remedial instruction or tutoring often remains focused on phonetic strategies.

 ALERT!

Because of dyslexia, your child may reach each of these stages at a later-than-typical age. Keep in mind that your child will need to move through each stage at his own pace. Use the information to guide you, but focus on your child's actual level within the progression, not on what the grade or age level is for other children.

Stage 3: Reading to Learn (Ages 8–14)

Readers in this stage have mastered the "code" and can easily sound out unfamiliar words and read with fluency. Now they must use reading as a tool for acquiring new knowledge. At this stage, word meaning, prior knowledge, and strategic knowledge become more important.

Your child will need help to develop the ability to understand sentences, paragraphs, and chapters as he reads. Reading instruction should include study of word morphology, roots, and prefixes, as well as a number of strategies to aid comprehension.

Stage 4: Multiple Viewpoints (Ages 14–18)

As opposed to the previous stage of reading for specific information, students are now exposed to multiple viewpoints about subjects. They are able to analyze what they read, deal with layers of facts and concepts, and react critically to the different viewpoints they encounter.

Ironically, when your child finally reaches the phase where reading involves more complex thinking and analysis, he is ready to shine. Your child's whole-to-part learning style is geared for the demands of dealing with shifting viewpoint and contrasting information. He may still have difficulty with some of the mechanics of reading, but his mind is well suited to sharing and manipulation of ideas. He will be well prepared to move on to the final, fifth stage of reading—college level and beyond. Fortunately, if you can successfully guide your child past the early stage barriers to this phase, he will be able to excel at understanding and integrating advanced reading material.

 FACT

About 40 percent of children with reading difficulties have problems that are not apparent until they reach fourth grade. These children often do not have difficulties with tasks such as letter and word recognition, or phonetic decoding. Instead, their problem is that they are unable to read fluently or comprehend what they read.

Phonemic Awareness

In order to become a reader at the initial stage, a child needs to develop phonemic awareness. A phoneme is the smallest unit of sound that differentiates words in a given language. There are forty-four phonemes in the English language, represented by the twenty-six letters of our alphabet. Phonemic awareness is the ability to recognize and isolate the individual phonemes in a word. For example, the word *sent* has four phonemes—the sounds represented by each of its letters. An individual with good phonemic awareness is able to differentiate among and manipulate the four sounds. Phonemes are not the same as letters: the word *toad* has only three phonemes, though it has four letters; the "oa" is a digraph that represents a single sound, the long vowel ō.

Children do not develop phonemic awareness naturally, as it is not inherent in the process of listening to sounds of words. It is not necessary to break up words into separate sounds to hear or to speak them; to the ear, a single-syllable word seems like one continuous bundle of sound. Children gain phonemic awareness through exposure to print and the concept that letters represent sounds. Most children will start to pick this up as preschoolers as their parents, older siblings, and other caregivers point out the relationship between sounds and letters. Once they begin to learn to read, their early attempts at decoding reinforces their rudimentary skills, and the level of phonemic awareness increases. Thus, phonemic awareness is a learned skill.

 ESSENTIAL

You can help your young child develop phonemic awareness skills at home drawing his attention to letters and their sounds, and playing games involving manipulation of sounds, such as pig-latin, and teaching rhyming games and songs, such as the "Name Game."

Most children with dyslexia will score poorly on tests designed to measure phonemic awareness, and they will have corresponding difficulty using phonetic strategies to decode words. Because of their reading delays, they will not be able to build skills through reading experience, and they will tend to fall farther behind their peers as time goes on. For this reason, programs to help children with reading difficulties often include specific training in phonemic awareness. These programs may be helpful to very young readers to help them with beginning reading skills.

Morphological Awareness

Morphological awareness means the ability to recognize the parts of words and word segments that convey meaning. A morpheme is the smallest element of a word that can change a word's meaning. It can be a single letter—for example, the *s* at the end of a noun such as *cat,* which converts the singular to plural: (cat/cats); or the *a* at the beginning of a word such as *atypical*, which is a prefix conveying the meaning "not."

Understanding the morphological structure of words is crucial to developing reading fluency. At around third grade, during the Stage 2 level of reading, morphological awareness becomes more important to decoding than phonemic awareness. At this point, students need to increase their reading speed, and letter-by-letter decoding is inefficient. Students who are good readers will have naturally acquired a good basic sight vocabulary of familiar words and will easily be able to transfer what they know to decoding new words using morphological analysis. Morphology is the key to decoding polysyllabic words—for example, the word *decode* is a combination of the prefix *de–* and the familiar root *code.*

 ALERT!

> Don't get stuck! Phonics programs are designed for beginning readers. When your child is able to read at about second-grade level, it is time to introduce additional strategies. The National Reading Panel found that phonics instruction is most effective at the kindergarten and first-grade level. After second grade, phonics tutoring did not help most students, and had only a moderate effect for students with learning disabilities.

Your child will probably need extra help to gain an understanding of morphology. It is important to begin to introduce these concepts to him at the age at which other children are gaining these skills, even if he is still struggling with phonetic decoding. Otherwise, he will not be able to progress beyond a second- or third-grade reading level.

Orthographic Knowledge

Orthography is the set of rules that dictates how to write correctly in a given language. In some languages, such as Spanish, those rules are essentially the same as the phonetic rules. English probably has the most inconsistent writing system in the world. This obviously creates a major barrier for your child. Studies show that dyslexia exists in all countries and all languages, but children with dyslexia in countries with phonetically regular languages have far less difficulty learning to read.

 ESSENTIAL

Good English spellers rely heavily on their knowledge of morphology and visual memory of words. They will recognize a misspelled word on sight simply because it doesn't look right.

Studies show that good readers also rely more on their orthographic knowledge as they grow older. In fact, older children and adults often do not score as well as younger children on tests of phonemic awareness, as their knowledge of orthography supplants their phonological assumptions. For example, one researcher commonly uses a nonword, *Jete,* in testing phonological knowledge of rhyming patterns, assuming it will be correctly read as jēt. Experienced readers, however, might recognize the letter sequence as being a word imported from the French, pronounced as zhété.

Your child's reading and spelling, as well as reading fluency, will improve tremendously as his orthographic knowledge improves; but unfortunately, this is another area where dyslexia stands in the way. Even if your child tries to visualize what the word ought to look like, he probably does not have a stable memory—after all, he may habitually reverse or transpose letters, and his memory of the correct spelling will tend to be obscured by his memory of all the times he spelled the word wrong. Your child will need special help to learn to correctly remember the visual appearance and letter sequence of words.

Automaticity and Fluency

Automaticity in reading is the ability to identify words fast, accurately, and effortlessly. It is the result of full mastery of the reader's sight vocabulary, so that known words are recognized at a level that requires no conscious thought. Beginning readers recognize very few words instantly. Through repeated exposure to the same words, they increase the number of words that they can recognize instantly. It is particularly important that developing readers learn to recognize words that occur very frequently in print. The twenty-five most common words make up about one-third of all reading material, so automatic recognition of those words has a tremendous impact on reading speed and comprehension. Examples of high-frequency words are *the, and, to, you, he, it, of.*

 QUESTION?

What is the Dolch Word List?
The Dolch words are the 220 most frequently found words in print. These words are usually learned in first and second grade; students who learn these words have a good base for beginning reading. Many of these words cannot be sounded out because they do not follow decoding rules, so they must be learned as sight words.

Fluency is the ability to read connected text rapidly, smoothly, and without conscious effort. Fluent readers are sensitive to the rhythm and flow of language, so they can read with expression, and their reading is enhanced by the ability to anticipate what comes next in text. Many people with dyslexia are able to become accurate readers, but are not able to gain automaticity or fluency. They are able to keep up in high school and college through hard work and determination, but their reading remains labored and slow. However, you can help your child build fluency by providing appropriate support and instruction geared to building automatic reading skills. This support with higher-end reading skills is as important to your child as learning the basics.

Comprehension

The ultimate goal of reading is good comprehension. Reading can be defined as a system of deriving meaning from print. To achieve good comprehension, readers need to have all the basic skills outlined above. Additionally, they need sufficient background information and vocabulary to foster an understanding of what they read. They also need to develop an array of good strategies to aid with comprehension. These strategies will include familiarity with the organization and structure of written language, different forms of writing, literary devices such as metaphor and allusion, and development of an ability to read critically.

Your child may have problems with comprehension because of his difficulties understanding and processing language. He may not understand what some words mean, and if he reads too slowly it may cause him to lose track of meaning before he reaches the end of a sentence. If he frequently confuses or omits small words like prepositions, the meaning of a passage can be dramatically altered.

Again, your child will need specific strategies to overcome confusion and to aid in comprehension. Most of the strategies your child needs are no different than what ideally should be taught to other students, but your child may miss the opportunity to learn if his reading instruction has focused primarily on his weak basic skills.

You can help improve your child's reading comprehension by encouraging her to use her imagination to visualize what is happening as she reads. Teach her to stop at the end of a sentence or paragraph and make a mental picture depicting what she has read. This will improve her memory of the text as well as her understanding.

Phonics vs. Whole Language

Over the past two decades, there has been a cultural war over two ideologically distinct methods of teaching reading—phonics and whole language. A phonics-based approach focuses instruction on learning to connect letters and letter combinations with their corresponding sound and provides students with specific strategies for decoding by sounding out familiar words. The teacher relies on direct instruction, using a well-developed and highly structured curriculum with carefully planned, sequential lessons.

Whole language instruction focuses on providing a literature-rich environment and emphasizing comprehension skills. Reading and writing is incorporated throughout the day in the context of lessons in other subjects. There is emphasis on both oral and silent reading and reading authentic literature. Lessons may be fluid and theme-based, rather than tied to a set curriculum.

 **FACT**

"Whole language" is not the same as whole-word teaching, which was the hallmark of the "look-say" method popular in the mid-twentieth century. With "look-say," children learned new words through repeated exposure and repetition in "Dick and Jane"-style basal readers.

Pros and Cons

Dr. Maria Carbo, founder of the National Reading Styles Institute, points out that neither phonics nor whole language will reach all children. She points out that phonics programs are good for children who have analytic learning styles and benefit from systematic teaching. Whole language programs are more suited to children who have strong visual, tactile, and global learning styles who do best in an environment emphasizing hands-on learning and peer interactions.

Your child with dyslexia doesn't fit into either of these molds. It is true that she probably has the overall learning style that thrives in the enriched atmosphere of a whole language classroom; but unlike her peers, she won't be able to absorb the tools and strategies needed for reading merely through exposure. On the other hand, as much as she needs specific help, the sequential teaching of phonics is geared to her weakest learning pathway.

Benefits of Both Methods

The debate over phonics vs. whole language makes about as much sense as arguing over whether you should feed your child only meat or only vegetables. Good reading requires that students have a variety of skills. The research is unequivocal: Students learn best when they are taught with programs encompassing both phonics and whole language. Students taught only phonics tend to have better decoding skills, but weaker comprehension skills. Students taught with whole language tend to have stronger comprehension skills, but weaker decoding skills.

Just as you need to provide your child with a balanced diet, he must also have balanced reading instruction. In fact, your child needs more than phonics or whole language; he needs instruction that covers all of the elements that are part of reading. He needs to be taught to focus on how a word sounds, how it looks, and what it means. He needs practice to develop reading automaticity and fluency. And he needs an array of strategies to support comprehension, build motivation, and to keep him engaged.

Different Needs of Students with Dyslexia

Your child with dyslexia will probably need some sort of special intervention or tutoring to learn to read. Even if your child is in a classroom with an excellent reading and language program, his dyslexia will stand in the way of his learning. He will not learn well in a group setting because his language processing issues will cause him to miss much of what the teacher says. The standard worksheets used in class will not help him learn, because he does not do well with paper-and-pencil tasks. His low tolerance for frustration and high distractibility will make it hard for him to focus sustained attention on learning, especially with tasks that are difficult for him.

In order for your child to learn to read, he will either need tutoring or therapy that replicates the instruction in the classroom in a way suited to his unique learning needs or he will need a different approach and set of strategies for reading more suited to his learning style. However, whatever the method, there are some common elements that should be part of any reading program for a child with dyslexia.

Individualized Instruction

Your child needs instruction that is tailored to his unique needs. Ideally, your child needs to have plenty of time working one-on-one with a well-qualified teacher, tutor, or therapist. He needs help from an adult who keeps him engaged and is focused. The one-on-one attention does not need to be continuous, but it needs to be regular, frequent, and sustained.

 ESSENTIAL

If your child's resource or special ed teacher seems stressed or overworked, volunteer! You can help free up the teacher's time by offering to helping correct homework or prepare materials outside of regular school hours. If you are free during the school day, offer to help supervise some children doing group work while the teacher is working more intensively with others.

If a one-on-one program is not feasible, look for as small a group setting as possible. It's simple: The larger the group, the less attention your child will get. Videos or computer software are not an acceptable substitute for attention from a skilled professional. If your child is being taught in a resource or special education classroom, the teacher should have at least one aide who can assist with classroom supervision, so that the teacher is free to move around and spend individual time with each child.

Multisensory Teaching

Your child needs a method that simultaneously engages his visual, auditory, and kinesthetic learning modes. He needs to physically participate in his learning, to touch and to move. He needs to see and to hear and to speak. It is particularly important that the senses associated with your child's dominant learning style are engaged, as for him that is the most effective path to learning.

Age-Appropriate Instruction

Your child needs a method that is appropriate to his age, to his actual level of reading development, and to the expected level of reading development for children in his grade. Age appropriate means that the program will not attempt to force learning of concepts that are too difficult or at a pace too fast for a very young child, and it means that the method will not be too boring or limiting for an older child.

Teaching must also be geared to his expected grade level, so that a foundation is laid and more advanced concepts introduced to help him catch up. So, for example, a sixth grader who reads at second-grade level may need help both with improved whole word recognition skills of basic sight words (Stage 2, "Ungluing from Print"), and strategies to improve vocabulary and understanding of word meaning (Stage 3, "Reading to Learn"). Even though he is not yet ready to read sixth-grade material on his own, he can access age-appropriate literature with the aid of audio books. A good mix of teaching strategies will help your child keep pace and catch up on as many fronts as possible.

Instruction That Builds Motivation

Your child needs a method or an environment that will be interesting and engaging for him, and that will allow him to experience success. This is accomplished by breaking down lessons and expectations into manageable segments and setting realistic, achievable goals. If your child cannot learn ten new spelling words this week, perhaps he can learn five. If he can learn five this week, perhaps he can learn six next week. The child who meets a goal of five words feels proud; the child who learns four out of five feels encouraged because he has almost reached his goal. But the child who learns the same five words when he is required to learn ten feels like a failure.

 QUESTION?

What is "learned helplessness"?
Learned helplessness is a psychological reaction to repeated frustration and failure. Research shows that continual exposure to academic failure contributes to withdrawal, unwillingness to approach new tasks, and a lack of persistence. In essence, the person simply gives up trying.

The child who only experiences frustration and failure will quickly give up. She will begin to think of herself as inept and stupid and will become fearful of facing new challenges. But a child who feels capable of learning will, over time, become more and more willing to devote sustained effort to accomplishing her goals. She discovers through experience that her hard work can pay off, so she is willing to keep on trying.

CHAPTER 6

Reading Instruction

A LTHOUGH DYSLEXIA AFFECTS YOUR CHILD in many ways, you are likely to find that learning to read is the primary and most significant barrier. Your child may be offered or exposed to a number of different strategies or methods for teaching reading. Most reading programs involve some sort of direct instruction or tutoring, and are generally geared to building skills and understanding in specific areas of academic weakness. Instruction may be one-on-one or in small groups, or it may rely heavily on videotapes or computers. Your child may receive instruction from a highly qualified teacher with a master's degree and certificates demonstrating advanced training in a variety of reputable methods; or your child may end up being tutored by a student trainee or classroom aide. Instructional reading programs do not cure or remedy dyslexia; rather, they are geared to building essential reading skills without purporting to address the underlying neurological or cognitive issues that may give rise to dyslexia.

Early Preventive Intervention

Early intervention programs are generally introduced at the kindergarten or first-grade level. They are geared to preventing reading failure by addressing the needs of "at-risk" children. "At-risk" does not necessarily mean that the child has dyslexia; reading experts believe that the vast majority of the children served by these programs do not have learning disabilities. Instead, their reading or learning problems are usually the result of social or cultural factors, such as lack of proficiency in the English language or limited exposure to books and reading before they begin school.

However, there is no reliable way of sorting out the child who is "at-risk" from one who has dyslexia at the age when early intervention begins. Educators agree that it is important to try to reach children early. For children who do not have dyslexia, early support may help them catch up with their peers with a minimum of time and effort.

While early intervention is helpful, your child with dyslexia is likely to need specialized support beyond the level provided in the preventive programs. One value of early intervention, however, is that these programs provide a better foundation for learning to read, and they can help identify the children who need further support. If your child continues to struggle despite participating in a strong early reading program, you will know that her reading problems cannot be blamed merely on poor teaching.

Reading Recovery

Reading Recovery is a short-term program of one-on-one tutoring for struggling first graders, geared to rapidly bringing students up to grade level. The program serves the lowest-achieving students, who each receive a half-hour daily lesson for twelve to twenty weeks with a specially trained Reading Recovery teacher. Lessons include reading familiar stories, working with letters or words using magnetic letters, writing a story, and reading a new book. The lessons focus on phonics as well as problem-solving strategies and reading comprehension, and are individualized for each child, building on strengths and responding to the child's growing abilities. As soon as the student is able to read independently at a level equivalent to average students in his class, he is removed from the program and another student takes his place.

Many parents of children with dyslexia feel frustrated if their children do not succeed with Reading Recovery. However, this program is not designed to help learning-disabled children, but rather to provide an effective, early way to distinguish them from children whose reading difficulties can be addressed through short-term tutoring. About 60 to 80 percent of students do become capable readers with this program, reducing the overall number of children needing further services. Even if your child is not successful with this program, the individualized instruction is helpful and will help target your child's areas of difficulty. Children who do not progress with Reading Recovery should always be referred for further testing and intervention; in no case should the instruction continue beyond twenty weeks.

 **QUESTION?**

What is Reading First?
Reading First is not a specific reading curriculum, but is a legislative initiative that is part of the No Child Left Behind Act. Reading First provides grant money to states to support programs to train teachers in the essential components of reading instruction and to assess children for reading difficulties.

Success for All

Success for All is a schoolwide reform program based on the premise that all students can succeed in the early grades. The program targets students in lower elementary school grades, providing them with intensive instruction in language arts to build early reading skills. The program includes a systematic reading program that emphasizes story telling and retelling, and uses cooperative learning techniques to integrate teaching phonics with meaning-based instruction. One-on-one tutoring is provided to children who are reading below grade level. This program has been implemented in more than 400 schools nationwide, in thirty-one states.

Early Intervention in Reading Program

Early Intervention in Reading Program (EIR) provides an in-class alternative to traditional pull-out remedial reading programs. Regular primary level teachers work for an extra twenty minutes each day with a small group of the lowest-ability readers in their classroom. The students also practice reading for an additional five or ten minutes working individually or in pairs with the teacher, a teacher's aide, or volunteer.

Instruction focuses on phonemic awareness, phonics instruction, word recognition, oral reading, and writing practice. The results of EIR are not as dramatic as those reported for other, more intensive interventions. However, the program is inexpensive and relatively easy to implement, and does result in some degree of improvement for the children who participate.

 **FACT**

Forty percent of America's children have difficulty learning to read. More than 90 percent of these children can learn to read at average levels when taught with appropriate programs in the primary grades. The key to successful intervention is to provide support to primary-grade students before they fall behind.

Davis Learning Strategies

Davis Learning Strategies is an innovative program, aimed at all learners, which implements methods geared to visual and kinesthetic learners in primary level classrooms. The program is designed to supplement a school's existing reading program by teaching attention-focusing and self-awareness techniques and uses clay modeling to learn alphabet letters and basic sight words. It functions both as an intervention program for at-risk learners and as an enrichment program that builds on the creative learning process for able students.

In pilot classrooms, where the program was implemented continuously in grades K–3, the need for special education referrals was eliminated, and there was a significant increase in the number of children who qualified for gifted education placement. Teachers reported the program easy to implement and found that the self-regulation skills taught reduced disruptive behavior in the classroom and enhanced the ability of all children to focus on classwork.

Classroom Phonics Curriculums

Many schools have adopted excellent text series that provide a strong emphasis on phonics instruction for general use with all children in the classroom. Two highly regarded examples are *Open Court Reading*, published by SRA/McGraw-Hill, and the *Houghton Mifflin Reading* series. These textbook publishers also provide extra materials or books geared for small group use with struggling readers. However, although these reading programs may provide a good foundation, children with dyslexia usually need more specialized intervention, generally in the form of individualized tutoring or placement with specially trained teachers for all or part of the school day. Most primary-level reading programs for dyslexia are based on teaching phonics more intensively and thoroughly than is done in the regular classroom. Some of these programs teach phonics in isolation, and some focus on teaching phonetic elements in conjunction with other strategies to help with word recognition, spelling, fluency, and comprehension.

Any phonics-based program will provide your child with some guidance for understanding the sounds of language, the correspondence between letters and sounds, and segmenting (breaking apart) and blending (putting together) individual sounds to make words. However, the particular approach to teaching may vary, especially with regard to the sequence and pace of instruction.

After-School Tutoring Centers

You may wonder whether you should enroll your child in an after-school tutoring center such as Sylvan Learning Centers, Kumon, or Score! Educational Centers. One advantage of such programs is simply that they are readily available and will provide tutoring directly targeted to your child's area of academic difficulty. They usually offer individualized attention within a small group environment of no more than three students per tutor.

If your child is having difficulty at school but not faring badly enough to qualify for extra services, or if you are uncertain about what sort of program is most appropriate for your child, enrollment in an after-school learning center might be a good interim approach. These centers may also provide good supplemental support in addition to other therapy or teaching that your child may be receiving, and can help your child catch up after he has achieved minimal proficiency with a more specialized program.

 ALERT!

A survey shows that 44 percent of parents waited a year or more after noticing their child was struggling at school before seeking help. You do not need a formal diagnosis of a learning disability in order to start trying to find help for your child. If your child is doing poorly or seems frustrated with school, he should have reading support or intervention as soon as possible.

However, you need to keep in mind that these centers are not geared to children with learning disabilities, and the tutors they employ do not have specific training in how to reach children with dyslexia. You should keep your expectations realistic. If your child is not happy in such a program or does not seem to be making progress, it is a good sign that more specialized intervention is needed.

Orton-Gillingham Tutoring

The most commonly used method for individualized tutoring of students with dyslexia is the Orton-Gillingham (O-G) approach. This is not a single program, but a model for teaching named for pioneering dyslexia researcher Samuel T. Orton and psychologist Anna Gillingham in the 1930s. Dr. Orton saw dyslexia as being rooted in the tendency to reverse or transpose letters and coined the term "strephosymbolia" (twisted symbols) to describe the condition. He advocated including tracing and writing practice along with teaching letters and sounds, a technique borrowed from the work of psychologist Grace Fernald, so that the child's memory of the physical movements associated with forming letters would eliminate confusion about the shape and appearance of the letters. Dr. Fernald used these techniques to teach whole words, rather than phonetics, but psychologist Anna Gillingham, working with Dr. Orton, developed an approach for teaching the entire structure of written English through systemized teaching of letters and their corresponding sounds.

Elements of Orton-Gillingham Teaching

With the O-G approach, the teacher begins by presenting the most common consonants and vowels, one or two at a time. Each letter is taught using multisensory methods, so that the child links how the letter looks with how it sounds and how it feels to form the letter. Some tutors have the child trace the letter in sand, write it in the air using large motions, or run a finger over fine sandpaper or textured carpet. After a child has learned the individual letters, the teacher moves on to consonant blends and letter combinations. Advanced students will study the rules of English language, syllable patterns, and how to use roots, prefixes, and suffixes to study words.

There are dozens of different reading methods that incorporate the basic principles of the O-G approach. Each method has differences in specific techniques and manner of presentation, but all are characterized by the following elements:

- **Multisensory teaching:** Instruction involves interaction between what the student is seeing, hearing, and feeling in forming speech and writing. Language elements are reinforced by having the student listen, speak, read, and write.
- **Phonics-based:** Instruction focuses on teaching individual sounds of letters or letter combinations rather than teaching whole words or word families.
- **Sequential:** Concepts are taught in a specifically designed order, beginning with the easiest and most basic and moving on to more difficult material.
- **Structured, systematic, and cumulative:** Lessons are organized with specific patterns and activities, following a familiar routine. Each new lesson includes review of previously learned material, and concepts are reinforced through practice or repetition.

Keep in mind that the criteria above are only used to determine whether a program fits within the definition of "Orton-Gillingham." There are other valid and emerging reading approaches that use different philosophies or strategies. Try to find the program that seems like the best match for your child's personality, learning style, and current needs.

 QUESTION?

What is a phonogram?
A phonogram is a letter or set of two to four letters representing a single voiced sound within a word. The original set of seventy-two phonograms identified by Anna Gillingham are: a, b, c, d, e, f, g, h, i, j, k, l, m, n, o, p, qu, r, s, t, u, v, w, x, y, z, sh, ee, th, ay, ai, ow, ou, aw, au, ew, ui, oy, oi, oo, ch, ng, ea, ar, ck, ed, or, wh, oa, oe, er, ir, ur, wor, ear, our, ey, ei, eigh, ie, igh, kn, gn, wr, ph, dge, tch, ti, si, ci, ough, and gu.

Finding a Tutor

Many teachers and tutors have training in Orton-Gillingham methods and can provide help to your child. Your child's school may provide tutoring without charge, or you may choose to hire a private tutor. You should ask your tutor whether she has specific training or certification, the name of the program or organization where she received her training, and the number of hours of training she has had. There are no "official" standards for teacher training in O-G methods, but there are several reputable organizations, such as the nonprofit Academy of Orton-Gillingham Practitioners and Educators, that provide professional training and certification. The qualifications of your child's tutor may range from merely having watched a training video for a few hours to having completed a short course of one or two days, to several hundred hours of coursework and practice.

Orton-Gillingham tutoring is also available free of charge in many states through 32nd Degree Masonic Learning Centers, a charity of the Scottish Rite Masons. More than 1,100 school children have received up to two years of one-and-one tutoring through this program. These centers also provide free training to teachers. To obtain Scottish Rite certification, a teacher must complete forty-five hours of coursework and 100 hours of practice work.

Effectiveness of O-G Teaching

Because there are now so many variations of O-G, and it is offered in so many contexts, it is hard to draw generalized conclusions about the effectiveness of the program. Like other methods, it will help some children more than others.

Orton-Gillingham is a method that is best introduced early. The emphasis on phonics is geared to beginning-level readers, and the program does not integrate many of the strategies that are useful to older learners. Because of the sequential, repetitive, and systematic structure of the program, O-G teaching is very thorough, but slow. It is reasonable for you to expect to see steady progress with your young child, but unlikely that he will progress by leaps and bounds. Although reports of progress rates are extremely variable, it is reasonable to expect about eighteen months of growth in reading ability for every twelve months of instruction and to expect tutoring to continue for two to three years.

 ESSENTIAL

Tutoring can be hard work for your child, but with a good teacher it can also be fun. Your child will do best with reading instruction that builds both skill and the desire to read increasingly complex materials. Look for a teacher who provides encouragement and finds ways to create successful reading experiences for your child.

The O-G emphasis on phonics means that the teacher is working to build your child's skills in his weakest area. In addition to problems with processing the sounds of language, most children with dyslexia also have difficulty with concepts of order and sequence. Even with multisensory teaching, a good deal of drill, repetition, and practice is needed to cement the knowledge, and your child may find the program frustrating if he does not have a good rapport with his teacher. Thus, it is also important that your child's teacher can work to build motivation and sustain interest.

Keep in mind that no one approach can meet every child's needs. Because O-G is so well established, parents are sometimes discouraged from seeking other help if their child does not seem to benefit from the lessons. It is important to support your child's teacher and her efforts to help your child. However, if your child seems to be making little or no progress after several months of tutoring, you may want to begin exploring other reading programs.

School Programs for Dyslexia

Ideally, Orton-Gillingham should be taught in a one-on-one setting with a well-qualified teacher who has specialized training to work with your child. However, it is not always practical or affordable for families to obtain such tutoring. There are now many reading programs designed for classroom use with children with dyslexia that incorporate the basic O-G methodology and which also include many additional techniques to support reading development. Some of the best known are profiled here.

Spalding Method

Romalda Spalding, author of *The Writing Road to Reading*, was a teacher who studied with Samuel Orton and developed her own variation of the method, influenced in part by the ideas of Maria Montessori. The Spalding Method is a total language arts curriculum and is generally implemented in a classroom setting. The method begins with phonics instruction based on fifty-four phonograms, which is integrated closely with handwriting practice. As the phonograms are learned, they are combined into words and written in a spelling notebook compiled by the student during dictation. Students also learn writing composition skills beginning with using oral sentences using words in their spelling notebooks and moving on to writing sentences and paragraphs. The Spalding Method also emphasizes early exposure to high-quality children's literature, such as Caldecott and Newberry award-winning books, which are incorporated into the teaching curriculum through oral reading and discussion.

Slingerland Approach

The Slingerland Approach was developed for classroom use by Beth Slingerland, a teacher who studied with Samuel Orton. Reading is taught sequentially proceeding from single letters and symbols to one-syllable words and then to longer words. Multisensory approaches are emphasized throughout, with each step of instruction incorporating auditory, visual, and kinesthetic channels. Writing and letter formation are taught systematically, one letter at a time, and each lesson includes emphasis both on auditory (sound-correspondence) and visual aspects of letters and words.

Slingerland includes teaching visual strategies for recognition of phonetically irregular words, and also provides explicit, systematic instruction in the development of vocabulary and reading comprehension. In addition to use in primary grades or special education classrooms at many schools, Slingerland has also been widely implemented at private schools geared to teaching dyslexic students.

The Herman Method

The Herman Method for Reversing Reading Failure, named for teacher Renee Herman, is also based on Orton-Gillingham and follows a sequence of instruction that starts each student at his point of deficit and sequentially teaches mastery of up to twenty skill levels. Students are not given reading material until they have mastered all necessary underlying skills. The program has a strong emphasis on visual and tactile exercises to aid in learning the appearance and sound of letters. In addition to decoding, the method also teaches reading strategies for sight words, contextual clues, and dictionary skills, with consistent emphasis on comprehension. Teachers trained in this method are encouraged to use creativity and develop individualized approaches for each student's needs.

Wilson Reading System

This is a twelve-step program developed especially for older children and teenagers with dyslexia. It includes many aspects of O-G teaching, including mutisensory and systematic instruction. However, the emphasis is primarily on application of concepts rather than on coding. Wilson includes a unique sound tapping system to help the student learn to differentiate phonemes and uses a simplified method of syllable division. It uses extensive, controlled text reading material, including words suited to older students, to correspond with the skills taught. All concepts are taught with manipulation of cards containing phonemes, syllables, and suffixes. Fluency is emphasized throughout the program. The program also focuses on oral expressive language development through vocabulary instruction, and building comprehension through visualization techniques.

ESSENTIAL

The full Wilson Reading System program takes one to three years to complete. Research has shown that students achieved the highest gain in word attack skills, which are measured by testing of reading lists of nonsense words. Gains in passage comprehension were more moderate.

Other Multisensory Techniques

There are several major approaches to teaching reading to children with dyslexia that are multisensory, but do not follow the precepts of Orton-Gillingham. Some of these include phonics-based instruction whereas others focus on other strategies. Two leading reading methods, Lindamood-Bell Learning Processes and Davis Dyslexia Correction, also include strategies aimed at treating underlying issues associated with dyslexia, and are covered in Chapter 7.

Phono-Graphix

Phono-Graphix is a multisensory, phonetic approach that is faster paced than Orton-Gillingham and encourages children to apply concepts quickly to reading real text. The method was developed by Carmen and Geoffrey McGuiness, authors of the book *Reading Reflex*. At the outset, children are taught that letters are pictures of sounds, that some sound pictures have more than one letter, and that some sound pictures represent more than one sound. Starting with eight sound pictures—six consonants and two vowels—the student immediately begins building and reading words. Manipulatives are used in a variety of games and exercises, along with a whiteboard and markers. During writing practice, the child says the sound of each letter as he writes each word.

A key aspect of Phono-Graphix is avoidance of drills. Rather than requiring that the child fully master every letter sound before progressing, the concepts are reinforced through the child's practice and experience with reading words in context and with immediate correction of errors by the teacher or tutor. Because of its relative simplicity and faster pace, many parents prefer to start with this approach, especially if working on their own with their child.

Simultaneous Oral Spelling (SOS)

Simultaneous Oral Spelling is a multisensory technique to reinforce the sequence of letters in a word that uses letter naming rather than relying on blending of letter sounds. The teacher says a word and the child repeats it, reinforcing the auditory component. Next, while looking at the word, the child names the letters, reinforcing both the visual component and the left-to-right sequential aspect of letter combinations. Then, the child writes the word, naming each letter as he writes, bringing in the kinesthetic element through the movement associated with writing. Finally, the child reads the word aloud, again associating visual and auditory pathways. This technique is often used in conjunction with Orton-Gillingham methods to teach phonetically irregular words, but it also may be effective as a separate technique for a child who has difficulty using or applying phonetic rules.

Developing Advanced Reading Skills

Phonetic approaches will enable a child to learn to read short, easily decodable words, but your child will need to learn additional strategies to recognize longer words and words with irregular spelling patterns. Such words become more common as a child progresses beyond primary level. The older child with dyslexia needs to have workable strategies that are aimed at higher reading levels; otherwise, the child will tend to become bogged down, habitually reading in a slow, labored, and halting manner. Such strategies include the ability to segment words into component parts, to recognize roots and affixes as well as compound words, and to combine meaning-based, contextual strategies with decoding.

One school program for teaching these strategies is called REWARDS. REWARDS is an acronym for Reading Excellence: Word

Attack and Rate Development Strategies. Geared to children in fourth through twelfth grades, it consists of twenty classroom lessons, usually given over the course of five weeks. Students are taught to use and combine several alternative strategies to analyze word structure and segment words into parts, including phonetic blending strategies and recognizing affixes, helping them learn a flexible approach aimed at more efficient word recognition.

 FACT

> One of the most powerful predictors of reading comprehension abilities is the speed and accuracy of reading single words. In addition to being able to quickly recognize words, the students must also know the meaning. Knowledge of word meanings is the most important single factor in reading or listening comprehension.

Dr. Virginia Berninger of the University of Washington has reported impressive gains with a program geared to fifth graders with dyslexia that uses high-interest materials to teach words using visual, auditory, and morphological strategies. Students focus on learning what the word looks like, what it sounds like, and what it means. According to Dr. Berninger, learning all three elements of the word together builds brain connections that foster a "jump-start" in reading.

Building Fluency

Once your child is able to recognize words in print, it is crucial that she also gain an ability to read smoothly and at an efficient pace. If she continues to hesitate and stumble during reading, her slow pace undermines comprehension—by the time she gets to the end of a sentence she will have forgotten what was at the beginning. The best way for a child to develop reading fluency is through practice, both through oral and silent reading. As with other reading skills, however, your child may need specialized help via a more structured program.

Great Leaps Reading

Great Leaps is a one-on-one program designed to be taught in short five- to ten-minute practice sessions. The child completes several timed one-minute readings under the direct supervision of the teacher or tutor. The goal is that the child will have no more than two errors per reading; correction of errors is through immediate feedback and modeling of the teacher. As soon as the child meets the goal with one passage, he "leaps" to a passage written on a slightly more difficult level. One unique aspect of the program is that it focuses on teaching sight words via small phrases, such as "when we try" or "who is that," with the idea that reading phrases in context will work around the common tendency of struggling readers to skip or stumble over small function words, like "the" or "from." Studies suggest that it is possible to gain two to three reading levels with a year's instruction with this program.

 ESSENTIAL

Listening to stories read aloud or on tape can help your child build fluency, as it helps the student gain a better sense of the structure and flow of written language and enhances vocabulary.

Guided Oral Reading

Another approach to building fluency is for the student to repeatedly read the same passage or short story under the guidance of a tutor, or with a computer or tape recorder, or with peer assistance, or a student partner or buddy. Reading can be done in a timed context to build speed and the teacher, peer, or recording device promotes accuracy. Computer-assisted programs include *Failure-Free Reading,* and *Read Naturally.* Computer software offers the benefit of instant feedback in a setting that can be controlled by the child. Alternatively, the child may be encouraged to read along with tape recorded passages of a book. For example, with the Carbo Recorded-Book Method, the teacher records small segments of a few minutes each of high-interest reading materials onto tape cassettes in short phrases, at a slightly lower speed than normal, to allow the child with reading difficulties to follow along while looking at the same passage in print. The student listens repeatedly to the recording while reading along, later reading the passage unassisted to the teacher.

Visualization and Reading Comprehension

One of the most effective ways to help improve reading comprehension is to encourage the child to form mental pictures of the events described in the stories she reads. This is especially useful for children with dyslexia, who tend to be highly imaginative and visually oriented. Studies consistently show that children who are encouraged to use visual imagery have improved performance on tests of comprehension and recall of materials. Although your child may be a daydreamer who finds mental imagery natural in contexts other than reading, she may struggle to relate the words on the page to mental pictures. When she does try to visualize the story, she may get lost in her thoughts and lose track of the words on the page. She will benefit from a teaching method geared to make sure that she understands and thinks about word meaning as she reads and that provides a specific scheme for visualizing. For example, the Davis Picture-at-Punctuation technique encourages students to stop to form a mental picture whenever encountering punctuation signaling the end of a clause or sentence; this allows the child to build imagery directly related to the concepts conveyed in the reading and at the same time to continue to focus on the printed symbols on the page.

Mental imagery can also be promoted through modeling by the teacher and use of open-ended questions during and after reading.

Integrating the child's own artwork with story reading, such as having the child draw a map or diagram of events, or represent the story in cartoon form, is also useful. However, illustrations in text generally do not promote the formation of a child's own mental images; while richly illustrated text is very appropriate to build interest in young children, studies show that older children report forming fewer, not more, mental images when text is illustrated.

CHAPTER 7

Dyslexia Treatment Programs

A DYSLEXIA THERAPY IS AIMED primarily at treating either the underlying causes of dyslexia or specific skill deficits that are seen as precursors to developing the ability to read and write. It differs from tutoring because the goal is to find ways to enhance your child's ability to learn. Some therapies are based on novel theories as to the causes of dyslexia and some are controversial; however, all the therapies profiled in this chapter are now well established and widely used. These treatments cannot cure dyslexia, but a single program or a combination of approaches may eliminate or minimize many of the symptoms of dyslexia. You will need to carefully evaluate your child's needs and the focus of any treatment program in order to decide which is best for your child.

Choosing a Program

In choosing a dyslexia program for your child, it will help to understand the various categories or types of programs. Some programs are geared toward building on your child's academic and intellectual strengths, whereas others are focused mostly on addressing weaknesses. The programs that focus on weaknesses usually offer some sort of skill-building exercises or training. Many do not include specific instruction on reading; these programs are either based on the assumption that acquisition of the underlying skills taught will enable your child to learn to read well on his own, or that the treatment program will be followed by appropriate tutoring.

Questions to Ask

When considering a program for your child, you should start by determining what specific problem or symptom will be treated, and what the expected outcome of such treatment will be. You also need to consider whether you will need to supplement the program with additional tutoring or therapies for your child, and if so, what sort of extra support is recommended.

 ESSENTIAL

Your child's age and level of functioning are important factors to consider. Your teenager may do better with a flexible approach that allows him to actively participate in choosing the direction of the program. Your younger child may benefit from a more structured approach and may be less resistant to programs that rely heavily on repetition to build skills.

Some factors to consider are:

Expected outcomes. Find out what the expected or usual outcome is of the program for children the same age and with similar difficulties as your child. No one can guarantee success in all cases, but you should be able to get a general sense of what the typical results are for most children. Ask what kind of children do best with the particular therapy, and what kinds of issues cause children to have difficulty.

Program history and success rate. Find out how long the particular therapy has been used and what the reported rate of success is. Be sure you understand what "success" means for each program; successful acquisition of specific skills does not necessarily transfer to improved reading ability. Be sure to ask what sort of evaluation is done to screen prospective clients to determine whether they are likely to benefit from the particular therapy.

Duration of program and time commitment. Find out how long you can expect your child to continue with the program. Ask whether there are specific activities or practice that must be done at home during the program or after its completion. Consider whether you and your child are willing and able to make the required commitment. Beware of costly programs that are open-ended as to the amount of time you will need to pay for professional services.

Qualifications of therapist. Find out what sort of background and training the therapist who will be working with your child has that is specific to the program being offered. If your child will be at a clinic with many staff members, find out whether your child will be working with the same person at each visit and what sort of training and supervision the support staff has.

Program reputation and references. Learn what you can about the reputation of the program you are considering, and ask the therapist you will be working with for references. Most qualified professionals will have a list of former clients who are willing to talk about their experiences.

 **FACT**

You may be able to find parents with experience with particular therapies on Internet discussion boards and mailing lists. This is a valuable source of information, but try to get feedback from a number of different sources. Make sure the person giving you information is relying on personal knowledge or experience, rather than rumor.

The best place to start learning about a program is by critically reading information available from the program providers, such as in books, brochures, or on their Web sites, with the above questions in mind. Once you have a basic understanding of what the program claims to offer, you should explore other sources of information, including contacting references.

Understanding and Evaluating Research

Many programs claim to be supported by scientific research, but such claims may be exaggerated or overstated. Research that has been conducted or funded by individuals with a financial stake in the program can also be biased; researchers may be tempted to report or manipulate their data to present it in the light most favorable to the program. Do not rely merely on summaries or news articles about research; try to get a copy of the actual journal article describing the research.

Many excellent programs do not have a lot of research support but are grounded on well-established scientific knowledge about the process of learning or on long-term experience by clinicians or teachers involved in developing the methods. Anecdotal evidence or testimonials can provide excellent insight into a program, but they can also be unreliable and may present only a carefully selected view. In reviewing evidence of any kind—whether in the form of published research, news articles, or personal accounts—focus on the actual facts and details presented, not on adjectives or superlatives used to describe the program.

Quantitative vs. Qualitative Research

Quantitative research is research based on measurements of objective facts, usually with group studies, and often includes comparison of a treatment group with a control group. Generally, all members of the treatment group will be exposed to an identical, tightly controlled therapy, and standardized assessments will be used to measure results. Such research is useful for determining overall effectiveness of a program, but it can be misleading when applied to individual cases. Although the overall validity of the research is improved when researchers are able to work with a large sample group, larger samples also tend to obscure individual variations. It will not help you to know that a program helps 80 percent of participants if your child is one of the 20 percent who cannot be helped by that approach.

 ESSENTIAL

Improvement in skills that is statistically significant for research purposes may not be particularly unusual or reflect better results than comparable programs. When looking at research, keep in mind how much time and effort was involved in producing the gains reported.

Quantitative research is also extremely difficult to conduct when studying behavior and learning in children, as it is not practical in most cases to arrange truly randomized groupings and extremely difficult to control for outside influences on the children. Studies of children are particularly prone to a placebo effect or "Hawthorne Effect"—improvement that results primarily from the psychological effects of participating in a study as opposed to the specific program being implemented. A study comparing students receiving a specific therapy with a control group of children receiving no therapy at all is also prone to be misleading; it may simply mean that a given program is better than doing nothing at all.

Qualitative research involves the very close study of a number of cases, with research generally reporting detailed subjective observations of highly variable circumstances. It is more probing and comprehensive at an individual level and is likely to be presented in the form of a collection of case studies or clinical observations. It provides better insight into how an individual child might fare with a given program, and what factors influence failure or success; at the same time, it produces few hard facts that can be generalized across all cases. It is also difficult to verify or replicate observations and prone to the same potential bias in reporting as quantitative research.

In addition to providing insight and information about a program, qualitative research helps practitioners improve delivery of their program over time, as they can use such research to better tailor their programs to the needs of different individuals. It also can help improve the process of identifying which students are likely to do best with the program.

All Kinds of Minds

All Kinds of Minds is a unique approach that helps children achieve success through diagnostic services and guidance. Pioneered by Dr. Mel Levine, this is not a specific method for treating learning disabilities but rather a framework for planning interventions based on understanding the complexities of your child's learning process, with an emphasis on identifying your child's individual strengths. With this approach, your child receives an in-depth evaluation at a Student Success Center, beginning with an assessment that looks at underlying factors that influence the learning process, such as attention, memory, language, and cognition. Standardized IQ or achievement tests are not used, and labels such as "learning disabled" or "dyslexia" are avoided; instead, the goal is to provide a complete picture of your child's unique pattern of learning.

Your child will also be involved in a dynamic process called demystification, where your child interacts with a therapist in order to better understand her own learning needs. This process helps your child gain insight and learn the language needed to chart her own learning path and interact more successfully with teachers.

Working with you and your child, the clinicians help develop a learning plan that includes accommodations (or "bypass strategies") to work around weaknesses; specific interventions targeted at areas causing breakdowns in the learning process; strategies to enhance inherent strengths; and "affinity development," a process to help your child recognize and deepen areas of high interest. In the end, you will have an action plan geared to making your child a successful and empowered learner, rather than merely helping him overcome weaknesses. Because of his own role in the process, your child will have a sense of control and an increased level of confidence and motivation.

 FACT

> According to Dr. Mel Levine, the biggest mistake we make in life is treating every child equally when it comes to learning. All children have strengths; the job of parents and teachers is figure out what those strengths are and develop them in our children. It is not fair to expect every child to be good at all subjects.

This approach gives you a roadmap, but does not implement the specific steps. Your child will have support to help forge a path to success, but a good deal of responsibility for arranging and negotiating interventions and modifications remains on you.

Davis Dyslexia Correction

Davis Dyslexia Correction is a unique approach geared to the creative thinking strengths of individuals with dyslexia. It combines specific techniques to resolve perceptual problems and attention focusing issues with a method for mastering sight words and improving reading fluency and comprehension that is geared to creative thinking strengths that accompany dyslexia. It is a two-stage program beginning with a one-week, intensive program of counseling and guidance that breaks down major learning barriers and often results in dramatic reading improvement. The second stage is practice and implementation of the Davis methods at home, mostly through a systematic program of clay modeling, and generally takes between six and eighteen months to complete.

Description of Program

The Davis program was developed by an adult with severe dyslexia, Ron Davis, author of the book *The Gift of Dyslexia*. The program always begins with Orientation Counseling, a type of mental training that will help your child recognize and eliminate visual perceptual distortions such as letter transpositions or the false sense that letters are moving on a page, as well as resolve auditory perceptual confusion. Your child will also learn specific strategies to regulate her energy level and to improve balance and physical coordination.

The Davis program also includes a set of strategies for reading. The primary strategy, Davis Symbol Mastery, is based on the idea that a child with dyslexia thinks primarily in pictures rather than words and needs to create mental pictures for words before he can read or understand words in print. While your child probably understands nouns such as "dog" or "lion," he may stumble over words like "for" or "in" because he has no clear mental image to go along with the word. The focus of the Davis program is to help the child supply his own pictures for each word.

 FACT

The Davis methods were developed in 1981 and were used in a clinical setting with more than 1,000 students before a program of professional training was created in 1995. Because the reading techniques can be easily transferred to different languages, the program has grown rapidly and by 2004 was offered in twenty-nine countries and nineteen different languages.

The primary tools of the Davis program are a dictionary and clay. Your child learns how to look up words, how to use the pronunciation key to find out how each word sounds, and how to use the definition and example sentences as a starting point for mastering the meaning of the word. Your child will then use clay to form the letters of each word and also makes a three-dimensional model to depict the word's meaning. The child will model small, abstract words such as *the* or *and*, and may also use this approach to understand larger words or concepts such as *sequence* or *time*. Reading practice also includes a technique called Spell Reading, which builds visual tracking, sequencing, and whole word recognition skills, and Picture-at-Punctuation, an approach using visualization to build comprehension skills.

Program Outcomes

The Davis program is geared toward children aged eight and over and often produces very rapid reading gains, especially with older children. It is common for word recognition and reading fluency skills to jump by three to five grade levels during the initial week with children or teenagers aged nine and over. However, the Davis techniques must be practiced after the program in order for progress to continue and initial gains to be sustained; thus, the program requires that you and your child be ready to follow a recommended schedule of reading practice and continue with the clay modeling until a word list of almost 220 words is fully mastered.

Davis providers can work with almost any child who has symptoms of dyslexia, but the program is particularly appropriate for children who have difficulty gaining reading fluency, who have difficulties with letter reversals and transpositions, or who tend to stumble over or omit small words when reading. It is also an excellent choice for multilingual children, as the methods can readily be transferred from one language to another. Often, children who have been labeled as unteachable with phonics-based reading tutoring are the ones who report the most dramatic gains with the Davis methods.

Students who complete the Davis program often become very capable and enthusiastic readers, often gaining proficiency at or above grade level. This may be partly attributable to the fact that the program is aimed at higher-order reading skills rather than at early-stage decoding strategies. However, because the program de-emphasizes phonics, it remains controversial among many educators who prefer traditional tutoring. Also, a Davis provider will screen carefully to evaluate your child's learning profile and level of maturity and motivation. Because the program emphasizes mental strategies for self-awareness and control, it is not recommended for children using medications such as Ritalin to regulate attention level or behavior.

Fast ForWord Language

Fast ForWord Language, a product of the Scientific Learning Corporation, uses specially developed computer software to stretch out the sounds of language and provide children with listening practice in order to build phonological understanding and awareness. Your child plays a series of computer games, and as her ability to distinguish sounds improves, the software gradually increases difficulty and rate of speech until your child reaches a plateau in development or attains the highest level of mastery built into the software program.

 FACT

An alternative approach to building listening skills is Earobics, which also uses a computer game format. This software is available for home use and does not require special training to use, and it is less intensive and time-consuming. This program will also provide your child with extra practice learning to distinguish language sounds and relate them to letters and words.

The program is very intense; students work with the computer for 100 minutes a day, five days a week, for four to eight weeks under the guidance of a trained clinician. Research shows that the program produces significant gains in phonemic awareness among children with weak skills at the outset of training, but results are mixed as to how well these gains transfer to other reading skills such as word recognition or whether children do better with this approach over time than with more conventional teaching methods.

The Fast ForWord Language program itself does not include reading instruction, so it must be followed up with other teaching. However, the developers of Fast ForWord have also created a series of supplemental software-based learning programs that include specific exercises for reading. Like the initial program, the supplemental software packages are intended to be used intensively over a period of four to twelve weeks, depending on the total time spent each day.

Lindamood-Bell Learning Processes

Lindamood-Bell Learning Processes is a set of specific programs geared to addressing different types of underlying weaknesses associated with reading difficulties through a program of intensive therapy and practice.

The most well-known program is Lindamood Phonemic Sequencing (LIPS), which builds phonemic awareness skills through developing awareness of the mouth actions which produce speech sounds. The process uses Socratic questioning, mirrors, mouth pictures, and descriptive labels such as "lip popper" for the sound /p/ to help your child connect the sounds of words with the process of producing each sound in speech.

A second program, Nancibell Seeing Stars: Symbol Imagery, develops the ability to mentally visualize the identity, number, and sequence of letters for the sounds within words. This strategy may help your child to improve word recognition and spelling skills.

A third program called Nancibell Visualizing and Verbalizing builds reading comprehension and critical thinking skills by enhancing a child's ability to create mental images related to language and reading and to describe the images in words. The therapist uses a systematic series of questions such as asking about color, size, shape, or movement to stimulate detailed and vivid imagery.

Lindamood-Bell is very highly regarded but does require a substantial commitment of time; the recommended intensive format for each program involves one-on-one therapy four hours a day for four to six weeks. An alternative format of one hour a day over 4-6 months may fit better within your child's schedule. If you work through an authorized Lindamood-Bell learning center, the program can also be very expensive, especially if you need to enroll your child in two or three separate program series. A modified version of the program may be available through your child's school or through a private tutor who has attended a workshop or received related training; however, the quality of such instruction may vary.

 FACT

More of a good thing is not always better. The National Reading Panel evaluated fifty-two separate programs for teaching phonemic awareness skills and found that training programs lasting from ten to eighteen hours were almost three times as effective in building reading skills as programs lasting twenty to seventy-five hours.

Audiblox

Audiblox is a system of exercises aimed at developing foundational learning skills. It was developed by Dr. Jan Strydom, a South African educator. The goal is to improve cognitive abilities such as concentration, perceptual skills, memory, number concepts, and motor coordination.

One advantage of the Audiblox program is that it is designed primarily for home use. Although it is possible to hire a therapist to work with your child, the materials are designed for ease of use and are sold in kit form. The kit comes with ninety-six colored blocks, a set of cards printed with colored patterns, and an instruction book detailing a series of games and activities to be practiced with these materials. The kit also includes a student reading book with a story made up of the 800 most commonly used words in English, and a set of colored word cards and word lists to be learned by memory in conjunction with reading the book. Although geared for all ages, Audiblox can also be started with children as young as age three. The program developers recommend that your school-age child practice the exercises for about three hours a week; you should expect to see improvements within six weeks to three months of sustained practice.

PACE and BrainSkills

Processing and Cognitive Enhancement (PACE) is an intense program of exercises designed to strengthen weak skills such as difficulties with memory or processing speed. BrainSkills is a simplified version of the PACE program developed for home use. Both programs are done with the parent or tutor working one-on-one with the child, usually for an hour a day over the course of twelve weeks, with sequenced and repetitive activities that become progressively more difficult as the child's skill level increases. The program can address skills such as processing speed, working memory, visual processing, auditory analysis, and logical reasoning. A related program, called *Master The Code*, is specifically geared toward reading skills.

Irlen Lenses

Pyschologist Helen Irlen, author of the book *Reading by the Colors*, found that many children she worked with were able to improve reading fluency when using colored lenses. She coined the term Scotopic Sensitivity Syndrome, or Irlen Syndrome, to describe the condition that her approach proved effective in treating. Some symptoms of Irlen Syndrome are discomfort working under bright lights or fluorescent lights, problems with reading print on white or high gloss paper, or perceiving print as shifting or blurring.

If you choose to have your child evaluated at an Irlen Center, your child will first be screened to determine whether reading improves with use of a colored overlay; if this seems to help, your child will work with a diagnostician using a wide array of colored lenses to determine the precise color that seems to work best for your child.

You can also achieve some of the benefits of this approach by buying colored overlays from an art or theatrical supply store for your child to use. Although this is not as precise has having your child evaluated at an Irlen Center, it may afford some relief.

 ESSENTIAL

Keep in mind that the Irlen program is aimed at addressing a particular problem with vision; it may help your child comfortably focus his eyes on a page, but this program does not address other symptoms of dyslexia or include strategies to teach reading. This approach is probably best used in combination with other educational therapies.

Vision Therapy

Many of the symptoms of dyslexia may be caused by problems with vision, including the way that your child focuses on print and her ability to shift focus from one word to the next. These problems can cause blurred vision, eyestrain, headaches, and double vision when reading. Your child may frequently lose his place, omit words, close one eye, or show difficulty sustaining reading for long. It is very possible for your child to have 20/20 vision but still have undetected vision problems that impact her ability to read.

These problems are correctable, sometimes with specialized lenses or prisms or with specific exercises and practice geared to help your child learn to use his eyes effectively. Some of the visual skills that may affect reading are the ability to quickly locate and inspect a series of stationary objects, such as moving from word to word while reading (fixation); the ability to clearly see and understand objects at near distances, such as print on a page (near vision acuity); the ability to shift focus from near to far quickly, such as looking from a chalkboard to a book (accommodation); and the ability to keep both eyes eyes aligned on a book or other near-point work (binocularity). Different approaches and exercises are tailored to various problems; for example, your child may practice shifting focus from a near to far object and back with one eye covered, and then repeat the exercise with the other eye covered.

A developmental optometrist will develop an individualized program for your child; treatment may be from several weeks to several months depending upon the condition. Some insurance plans may cover vision training.

DORE Achievement Centers

The DORE approach is an individualized exercise program aimed at improving balance and coordination. The program begins with an assessment to determine whether the child has problems with balance or coordination. After the assessment, the child is given a set of exercises to do at home for five to ten minutes twice a day. A typical exercise is to stand on a cushion on one leg while throwing a beanbag from one hand to another for one minute. Every six weeks, the child returns to the DORE center for a follow-up assessment, and a new or revised set of exercises is prescribed; the program typically lasts about twelve months.

ALERT!

Beware of hype! No program for dyslexia is effective for all learners, and professionals who care about your child's needs will want to screen carefully to make sure that your child will benefit from their program. Always try to match the program to your own observations about your child's learning style and preferences.

The DORE program is very new; it was established in 2002. It is based on the theory that dyslexia and related learning problems stem from a delay in development of the cerebellum, an area at the base of the brain that is important to developing physical coordination and automatic motor skills. The program does not include any specific instruction or techniques geared to reading or other academic skill areas.

Because the program is new, there is no long-term data or information available for whether claimed improvements are sustained over time. Although the DORE program itself is new, the concept of using training to improve balance and coordination of children with dyslexia is not. In the past, such approaches have proved to be helpful to many children, but they are not a complete solution or a substitute for other educational interventions. Some other approaches that include training geared to improving both small- and large-motor coordination, balance, and cross-lateral movements include Balametrics, which uses a special board set on rockers called a Belgau Balance Board; the Davis Dyslexia Correction program, which integrates Orientation training with practice exercises with tossed Koosh balls; and various exercises commonly used with vision therapy.

Levinson Medical Center

Dr. Harold Levinson is the author of several books about dyslexia, including *Smart But Feeling Dumb* and *The Upside-Down Kids*. Dr. Levinson believes that dyslexia stems from a disturbance in the inner ear, which is critical for maintaining balance; he theorizes that this disturbance causes the brain to receive scrambled signals, which in turn produces the symptoms commonly associated with dyslexia. Dr. Levinson treats patients with a combination of medications, using a combination of anti–motion sickness antihistamines and medications commonly used to regulate attention, such as Ritalin.

Although Dr. Levinson has published a number of books describing his approach, his theories are unorthodox and have not been accepted by other medical professionals. Most educators and therapists do not feel that prescription medications should be used to treat dyslexia, and all medications can produce unwanted side effects in some individuals. Talk to your child's regular pediatrician before considering this approach.

CHAPTER 8

Beyond Reading— Therapies for Related Issues

D YSLEXIA SHARES MANY SYMPTOMS with other learning or behavioral problems, particularly attention deficits, auditory processing problems, and motor coordination issues. There are many therapeutic programs geared primarily to these related issues, rather than dyslexia, that may also prove helpful to your child. You may want to explore using these approaches either in conjunction with other tutoring or therapy for your child, or as a foundation to enable your child to gain necessary skills before receiving instruction more targeted to academic skill areas. The therapies summarized in this chapter are all geared to addressing issues such as attention focus or motor coordination that play a part in your child's ability to learn.

Occupational Therapy

Occupational therapists (OTs) help children who have difficulties with tasks requiring small- and large-motor coordination. An OT can help your child overcome practical challenges such as difficulty using scissors, pens, pencil and paper, or self-care such as tying shoelaces, or with hand-eye coordination needed to catch a ball or copy from a blackboard. An OT can also work with your child to help overcome problems with handwriting.

If your child has qualified for services under the Individuals with Disabilities in Education Act (IDEA), the school will provide OT services to the extent they are required to meet your child's educational goals as set forth in his Individualized Education Plan. The scope of the school-based therapy is limited to your child's functioning within the educational environment and his ability to perform tasks or participate in activities required of him at school. These will ordinarily be typical classroom objectives such as improving handwriting or learning to work with tools such as scissors or other classroom materials. The OT may also suggest modifications to the classroom environment or the use of assistive technology, such as a keyboard, to help your child achieve success.

Sensory Integration Therapy

Sensory Integration (SI) therapy is a specialized form of occupational therapy aimed at helping your child to better integrate and manage sensory input. It is based on the work done in the 1950s and 1960s by Dr. Jean Ayres, an occupational therapist who believed that many learning and behavior problems arose from difficulties children had in responding and reacting to stimuli such as noises, light, touch, and movement.

 **FACT**

Research has found that up to 70 percent of children identified as having learning problems also have sensory integration problems. These problems are also seen in children with learning disabilities and attention deficits.

Sensory integration plays a part in how well your child develops her motor and speech skills, emotional stability, attention, and behavior. Your child experiences the world through her senses such as hearing, vision, and touch. She needs to be able to accurately perceive and interpret what is going on around her, and screen out irrelevant distractions. When she cannot do that, it indicates a problem with sensory integration.

Signs of a Problem

The most distinctive symptom of a sensory integration problem is over- or undersensitivity to touch, movement, sights, or sounds. Your child may recoil from being touched, or avoid textures, certain types of clothing, or foods. He may be so sensitive to light touch that routine self-care becomes difficult; for example, he may fight having his hair cut or washed as though it caused excruciating pain. He may exhibit fearful or aggressive reactions to ordinary movement of other children in play, or be easily frightened by loud noises.

On the other hand, your child may seem to crave enhanced sensory experiences. He may seek out intense physical experiences such as body whirling, falling, and crashing into objects. He may seem oblivious to pain or danger.

 **FACT**

If your child complains that he cannot concentrate on reading or school work because of distractions in the classroom, or says that bright lights or glare from the paper interferes with his ability to focus on print, he may have sensory integration issues. SI training may improve his ability to function in the classroom environment.

Many other symptoms of sensory integration dysfunction overlap with symptoms of dyslexia or attention deficit disorder. These overlapping symptoms include unusually high or low activity levels, problems with balance and coordination, problems with handwriting, poor organization, difficulty following directions, and low self-esteem are all characteristics. Because of these issues, you may find SI therapy useful in helping your child with dyslexia overcome behavioral or motor control issues that are problems at home or at play.

What Therapy Entails

SI therapy is given by a specially trained occupational therapist or physical therapist. The goal is to help your child overcome his aversions and become more tolerant of his environment through exposure to stimuli through play and physical activities. Techniques may include deep brushing, swings for vestibular input, contact with various textures, bounce pads, scooter boards, or weighted vests and other clothing.

The therapy is always highly individualized and child-directed. The therapist will allow your child to select among activities and tailor the program to your child's response. To your child, a therapy session or practice activities at home will seem like play. The therapist gently guides your child toward activities geared to improve his processing and organization of sensations.

Brain Gym

Brain Gym is a series of twenty-six exercises designed to help learners coordinate their brains and their bodies better. It consists of simple movements similar to natural movements, such as crawling, that are part of early childhood development. The goal of the program is to improve your child's sense of balance and ability to focus, as well as to relieve stress. Many of the movements can be done while a child is seated, and the exercises can be easily incorporated into a classroom setting. It is not usually used as a specific therapy for learning disabilities, but rather as an approach to enhance the learning process for all children; however, it often is very helpful to children with attention focus problems and learning disabilities. This program will not resolve all problems, but it is a simple and easy-to-learn approach that may provide a needed boost to your child's overall readiness to learn.

Neurofeedback

Neurofeedback, also known as brain-wave training or EEG Biofeedback, is a learning technique that helps your child become aware of and learn to regulate his own brain wave activity. This technique has been used primarily with children with attention deficits, but some therapists are exploring applications to dyslexia as well.

Studies have shown that children with ADHD have higher theta (slow brain wave) activity and lower beta (fast wave) activity when compared with control subjects. Theta activity is associated with daydreaming and other distractions. Children who receive neurofeedback training are able to decrease theta activity.

Neurofeedback training is given through the use of specially designed computer games. Your child sits a few feet away from a computer monitor displaying a computer game; painless electronic sensors are placed on his earlobes and scalp to monitor brain wave activity. As your child relaxes and focuses his mind, the computer responds by moving elements on the computer screen; the game is programmed so that the child will be rewarded as he achieves set tasks by focusing his mind in the desired manner.

 ESSENTIAL

Neurofeedback may seem like science fiction, but it is not difficult to learn to use the mind in new ways. Researchers have even been successful in training cats and monkeys to control their brain waves, and are working on applications to help severely disabled persons, such as quadriplegics, learn to use their minds to control electronic devices such as prosthetic limbs or to work with computers.

This therapy is often effective in helping children with attention deficits learn to regulate their own attention and behavior. This technique is now also being applied to help with dyslexia, by setting the computer to encourage the production of a left hemispheric brain wave state known to be involved in reading. Neurofeedback does take time and can be expensive; generally, your child will need twenty to forty sessions before you can expect to see significant changes. It is also still should be considered an experimental therapy; it may not be effective or helpful for all children.

Interactive Metronome

Interactive Metronome (IM) uses special interactive equipment in order to improve your child's sense of rhythm and timing. This is a form of occupational therapy that enhances the mental ability to plan, sequence, and process information; it has been shown to be effective with many children with ADHD and various learning disabilities.

With this program, your child performs a set of repetitive hand or foot exercises in time with a computer-generated beat; he wears headsets to listen to guide tones, and sensors attached to his hand or foot send signals back to the computer. If your child hits ahead of the beat, he hears an auditory guide tone in the left side of his head; if he hits after the beat, the tone comes from the right. When your child is able to hit on the beat, a reward tone is heard simultaneously through both ears. The computer records reaction time in milliseconds and provides a score; the goal is to reduce the time interval to optimum levels.

 ESSENTIAL

Research shows that children with dyslexia have difficulty detecting beats in sounds with a strong rhythm. Awareness of beats may influence the way young children assimilate speech patterns and affect their ability to break down the sounds of words. One dyslexia researcher has found that classroom music lessons help build phonologic and spelling skills.

By learning to keep the beat, your child becomes better able to sustain focus, disregard distractions, and stay on task for longer periods of time. This program is done under the guidance of a specially trained therapist, and takes about three to five weeks to complete, with three- to five-hour-long sessions each week.

The Tomatis Method

In the 1950s, Dr. Alfred Tomatis developed the first listening training device using progressively filtered sound, specifically sounds rich in high frequencies, to address learning problems. Dr. Tomatis found that children with learning disabilities often have difficulty distinguishing between low- and high-pitched sound frequencies, and do not perceive high frequencies sounds well. He also theorized that language problems could be caused by an inefficient pattern of dominance. Sounds captured by the right ear are directly transmitted to the language center in the left brain. On the other hand, sounds captured by the left ear go first to the right brain before being transmitted to the language center in the left brain; this more circuitous route is less efficient for listening to the sounds of language.

Dr. Tomatis developed a device to retrain the ear by switching constantly between two channels, one emphasizing low-pitched sounds and the other accentuating higher frequencies. The switching forces the ear to adjust continually to changing sounds. Your child listens to electronically filtered recordings of Mozart, the mother's voice, and Gregorian chants through headphones that have a special bone conductor on the top. The listening exercises are gradually combined with active exercising using the voice to maintain learning. Through this training, your child essentially relearns the listening process.

Berard Auditory Integration Training

The goal of Berard Auditory Integration Training (AIT) is to help your child overcome hypersensitivity or difficulty hearing sound at certain pitches and frequencies through listening practice geared to building his tolerance to sounds and listening acuity. The program can help children who have attention deficits, autism, or central auditory processing disorder, as well as dyslexia. Your child may benefit from this approach if he appears to have difficulty listening to or following directions, if he seems to have a tendency to zone out or daydream, or if he is unusually sensitive or distraught by loud noises or sounds within certain frequencies.

Dr. Guy Berard, the developer of AIT, believes that auditory processing problems are caused by hypersensitive hearing. He developed a special electronic device, called an Audiokinetron, that randomizes and filters music frequencies. The theory behind the program is that the acoustic reflex muscle can be exercised by listening to varying pitches and frequencies, and that through such exercise, pain or sensitivity to loud noises or certain frequencies is reduced, and the pathways in the brain that transmit and respond to sound are stimulated. Your child listens to electronically altered pop music over the course of twenty sessions, each involving thirty minutes of listening time; ideally this is done in two daily sessions over the course of ten consecutive days. At the end of the training, your child's hearing should show significant improvement, with most frequencies being perceived within normal ranges. This should be reflected in behavioral changes, some of which may be observed immediately. Other changes will become evident over a period of 3 to 6 months following treatment, as your child's overall functioning improves in response to his improved hearing ability.

 **FACT**

The goal of AIT is to exercise the acoustic reflex muscle, which a muscle connected to the tiniest of three bones located in the air space behind the eardrum. These bones help transfer sound vibrations to the cochlea, where the hearing nerves are located. The acoustic reflex muscle contracts involuntarily in response to loud noises; the lowest level at which this occurs is called the acoustic reflex threshold.

The LCP Solution and Essential Fatty Acids

There is some evidence that a nutritional or dietary deficiency of long chain polyunsaturated fatty acids (LCPs) or Essential Fatty Acids (EFAs) may play a part in attention deficits or learning disabilities.

This evidence has in turn led to various nutritional supplements containing these essential nutrients being promoted heavily as a potential cure for dyslexia or ADHD. The truth lies somewhere in the middle: Evidence is still mixed as to whether these supplements are likely to provide significant help to your child, but it is true that your child's overall nutrition and health will benefit if you ensure that his diet provides an adequate source of these important nutrients.

 **QUESTION?**

What is the value of Evening Primrose Oil?
Evening Primrose Oil is an ingredient of Efalex, and is a source of omega-6 fatty acids. Although these are also important to your child's health, there are many other sources of omega-6 fats in your child's diet, such as vegetable oils commonly used in salad dressing or mayonnaise, and it is less likely that he needs extra supplementation.

Alphabet Soup

In order to understand which nutrients your child needs and what supplements may be best, it helps to know what all the abbreviations for various chemical names mean. Here is a list of the most important:

- **EFA:** Essential fatty acids (fats which cannot be manufactured by the body and must come from the diet).
- **LCP:** Long-chain polyunsaturated fatty acids (necessary nutrients that are described by their chemical composition).
- **LA:** Linoleic acid (an omega-6 fatty acid found in many vegetable oils).
- **ALA:** Alpha-linolenic acid (an omega-3 fatty acid found in vegetable oils and dark-green leafy vegetables).
- **DHA:** Docosahexaenoic acid (an omega-3 fatty acid needed for brain function, found in oily fish).

- **EPA:** Eicosapentaenoic acid (an omega-3 fatty acid needed for cardiovascular function, found in oily fish).

LCPs are the "good fats" that your child needs to help growth and learning. These are needed for visual functioning in the retina of the eye, in the synapses of the brain, in nerve tissues, and in the adrenals for regulating stress. They are called "long chain" polyunsaturated fatty acids because they are made up of molecules that consist of chains of twenty or more carbon atoms. ALA, DHA and EPA are three types of LCPs needed by the body, but only ALA is deemed "essential," because the body can produce DHA and EPA on its own.

Increasing ALA in the Diet

The two essential fatty acids are ALA (alpha-linolenic acid) and LA (linoleic acid). ALA falls into a group of fatty acids known as omega-3s. The typical American diet is deficient in omega-3s, so it is very likely that your child is not getting enough of this important nutrient in his diet. There is some evidence that children with dyslexia or ADHD may be more likely to have low levels of EFAs, even if their diets are adequate. It is possible that this is an effect, rather than a cause, of their symptoms; children who are unusually active or under a lot of stress may simply "burn through" fats and other important nutrients at a higher than average rate.

 FACT

An Oxford University researcher conducted a trial with forty-one children with reading problems. Half were given fish oil supplements, a good source of omega-3 fatty acids, and the other half were given a placebo containing olive oil. After six months, the children receiving the fish oil supplements were able to concentrate better and had reduced anxiety levels.

Even if it is not connected to her dyslexia, ALA's are connected to your child's health in a number of ways. There is nothing to lose and everything to gain by feeding your child a diet rich in EFAs. Some of the benefits of adding ALA to the diet are smoother skin, higher energy levels, stamina, performance and recovery, better insulin sensitivity, lowered inflammation, improved mood, and better ability to handle stress.

ALA sources

The best source of ALA is flax or flaxseed oil. It is also found in smaller quantities in walnuts, cold-pressed canola oil, wheat germ, and dark-green leafy vegetables.

ALERT!

Although fish is an excellent source of omega-3 fatty acids, some types of fish have dangerously high levels of mercury and should not be fed to your child. It is safe to give your child canned light tuna, but avoid white (albacore) tuna or fresh tuna. Do not feed your child shark, swordfish, king mackerel, or tilefish, as these fish all have very high levels of mercury. As a rule of thumb, choose smaller fish that are low on the food chain.

ALA is not only an essential nutrient by itself, but it is vital to the production of the two LCPs, DHA (docosahexaenoic acid) and EPA (eicosapentaenoic acid). DHA is crucial to brain function; the brain is about 60 percent fat by weight, and DHA is the most abundant fat. The fat in the brain is contained in cell membranes of neurons and in the protective myelin sheath that covers them. The highest concentration of DHA is in the forebrain, the brain area used for concentration and higher-order thinking. DHA is also needed by the rods in the retina of the eye for normal ability to adapt to see in the dark and to adapt to bright lights. A deficiency in these fats can impair the ability of the brain cells to communicate and may affect overall brain development.

Although your child's body can manufacture DHA on its own, it requires an abundant supply of ALA as well as other nutrients, vitamins C, B$_6$, B$_3$, zinc, and magnesium. DHA can also be obtained through the diet; the best source is oily cold-water fish like salmon, trout, sardines, herring, tuna, and eel.

EFA Supplements

Because of the clear benefits of adding EFAs to the diet, supplements are readily available. As noted above, the most readily available and inexpensive source of ALA is flaxseed oil. DHA and EPA can be obtained through fish oil capsules.

There are several commercial formulations specifically targeted toward children with learning disabilities. Some of the brand names for such supplements are Cormega, Efalex, ProEFA, and Equazen Eye Q.

Keep in mind that although these supplements may help your child, they are not a cure for dyslexia, attention deficit disorder, or any other learning disability—no matter what the manufacturer may claim. However, these supplements do provide nutrients that are known to be necessary to your child's overall health, and so they probably do boost performance for many children.

The Feingold Diet

Dr. Benjamin Feingold, a pediatrician and allergist, believed that hyperactivity and related learning problems in children were caused or influenced by sensitivities to certain natural food substances as well as to artificial food additives. He developed a program to test for such sensitivities through a diet that eliminates all synthetic colorings and flavorings, certain preservatives, and salicylates (chemicals similar to aspirin that are found in a wide variety of foods).

The Feingold program consists of two stages. During the first stage, the chemical compounds found in certain food additives and the salicylate compounds found in certain foods are avoided. Certain fragrances and nonfood items which contain the chemicals listed above are also eliminated. The artificial additives that are avoided include artificial colorings and flavorings, and preservatives such as BHA, BHT, and TBHQ. Salicylates are found in a wide variety of fruits and nuts, so the first stage of the program requires elimination of foods such as almonds, apples, berries, cherries, grapes, oranges, plums, and tomatoes. During the second stage, the salicylates are tested by adding them one at a time back into the diet to determine which can be tolerated.

The Feingold program is controversial, in part because research findings are mixed, and in part because it is difficult to follow. At best, this program may help about 20 percent of children who appear to be sensitive to the foods targeted by this diet; it is not difficult to see why there is skepticism over a diet that only helps a small fraction of children. However, if you suspect your child is one of the small number who will be helped, you may find it worthwhile to try this approach. Because the goal of the program is to test for food sensitivities, it does not need to be followed long-term if it does not seem to be helping.

CHAPTER 9

Choosing a School

AT SOME POINT YOU MAY REALIZE that your child will not do well in a traditional, public school environment. Perhaps you are concerned about large classes, overburdened teachers, outdated textbooks, and other issues that plague many urban schools. Even if your local school has a good reputation, you may realize that your child needs a more specialized program. If another family member has dyslexia, you may be thinking about choosing a specialized school even when your child is still a toddler or preschool age. If your child is older, he may already be struggling and failing in school, and you may be seeking an alternative placement. Since children with dyslexia tend to struggle in traditional classroom environments, this chapter focuses on a variety of alternative approaches you may consider in choosing the best educational path for your child.

Charter and Alternative Schools

Many public school districts offer parents excellent choices in addition to the regular schools. These may be labeled as charter schools or alternative schools; in general such schools receive public funding and must meet some guidelines of your district, but are free to use different curriculums and strategies for teaching. The philosophies and programs of these schools cover a wide spectrum, ranging from schools that are highly structured and offer a challenging academic curriculum to schools that are innovative and focus on creating a hands-on, child-centered environment. Some schools are parent co-ops, with a high level of parent involvement in the classroom and in planning outside activities.

 QUESTION?

What is a charter school?
A charter school is a publicly funded school that is typically governed by a group or organization under a contract with the state, which exempts it from selected rules and regulations. In the year 2001, there were almost 2,000 public charter schools in the 37 states that allowed them.

Your district may also have magnet schools. Magnet schools generally are schools with a special focus, such as arts or science and technology. You are more likely to find magnet schools at the middle school or high school level. Some are open to all students in the district whereas others may require that the child demonstrate a special aptitude or talent.

In considering a school, focus on your child's personality and his strengths. Of course you will also want to consider what services each school offers for children with dyslexia and whether the curriculum used will fit your child's needs. But it is a mistake to focus exclusively on your child's areas of weaknesses, because ideally you want to select a school where your child will be happy, will be able to make friends, and will enjoy participating in school activities beyond the classroom.

As with choosing a specific program for dyslexia, there is no one best answer for choosing a school. Part of your choice will be based on your own preferences and expectations for your child, and part will be based on your child's wants and needs. Thus, it is important for you and your child to visit a prospective school rather than rely on the school's local reputation or factors such as standardized test scores. The "best" school in the district may not be best for your child—it may be a place where your child simply encounters demands that he cannot possibly live up to, whereas a school with a lesser reputation may be a place where he can shine and receive far more attention and support from his teachers.

Private Schools

There are many good reasons to choose a private school for your child. You may feel that a private school can better meet her unique learning needs, or you may prefer private schools in general. There are a wide range of choices and types of programs and many ways that private schools can help meet your child's needs.

However, in choosing a private school for a child with dyslexia, there are a few things to keep in mind. Unlike public schools, private schools are under no legal obligation to provide special educational services for your child. Teachers at a private school with a strong academic program may be unwilling to make special accommodations for your struggling child, and if your child is unable to keep up with the work, you may be asked to withdraw your child. You may still be eligible for services via the public school district, but you may find it impractical to arrange for your child to receive those services while attending the private school.

 ESSENTIAL

You naturally want the best for your child. However, even if it is clear that your child is exceptionally bright, you should avoid placing him in an academically demanding private school unless it is clear that the school will be sensitive to his learning needs and provide extra support where needed. Your child will do better in the long run if he learns in a nurturing environment where he can experience success.

Some of the social and emotional issues that accompany dyslexia may manifest as classroom behavioral issues. Your child might be a physically active, kinesthetic learner, always on the move—but to a teacher, he may seem like a troublemaker who refuses to stay in his seat and obey the teacher. Again, unlike the public school, a private school is not legally obligated to retain students whose behavior is disruptive. Whereas in public school you could arrange via an IEP for specific classroom modifications to address your child's unique learning needs, in a private setting your child may simply be subjected to repeated discipline and eventually asked to leave the school.

Of course, not all private schools are insensitive to the needs of children with learning differences. In fact, a private school may offer exactly the supportive environment your child needs. Some things to look for in a private school are:

Small classes. Many private schools offer smaller classes and a higher teacher-to-student ratio than public schools. Your child with dyslexia will do better in a smaller group setting, where the teacher has more time to focus attention on her.

Flexible educational approach. It is important that the school administrator and teachers show a flexible attitude and a willingness to consider individual needs. Your child can do well in almost any environment if the adults who work with her are willing to adjust their expectations and modify teaching when appropriate.

Enrichment and special-interest programs. A private school may offer enrichment or special instruction in areas of high interest to your child, including many where your child shows a strong aptitude or talent. This may include instruction in the arts or music, athletic programs, or enrichment activities geared to gifted students.

When choosing a school, be sure to ask whether there are other students with dyslexia or learning disabilities enrolled, and what type of support can be given to such students.

Montessori Schools

Montessori is a child-centered, individualized approach to learning following the philosophy of Maria Montessori, an Italian physician and educator. In the early part of the twentieth century, Dr. Montessori developed a set of hands-on, self-correcting materials to assist children with severe learning disabilities. At the time, the children were labeled as mentally defective and relegated to asylums, considered wholly uneducable. Yet Dr. Montessori was able to teach these children to read; in only two years, her pupils were able to pass standardized tests given by the public schools for their age level. Dr. Montessori had invented the first "multisensory" approach to teaching; the handicapped children that she worked with would likely be diagnosed with dyslexia, high-functioning autism, or related learning disabilities by today's standards.

 **FACT**

Maria Montessori believed that every human being went through a quantum leap in learning during the preschool years. She also believed that children experience sensitive periods in their development, during which they seek certain stimuli with immense intensity, to the exclusion of all others. These are transitory periods in which they develop specific mental functions, such as: movement, language, order, refinement of the senses, and social awareness. If a child's need for specific stimuli is not met during the sensitive period, learning will be more difficult later on.

Soon after this success, Dr. Montessori was asked to open and administer a day care center for working class children in the slum district of Rome. She found that the children, ages two to five, were fascinated by educational devices she had developed for use with mentally handicapped children, and she allowed the youngsters to explore the materials, following the same progressive approach she had developed for teaching the asylum children. By age four, most of the pupils in her "Children's House" were reading, writing, and performing four-digit mathematics calculations.

The Montessori approach is based on providing children with access to specially developed materials that allow each child to discover basic concepts on his own, through self-guided work with the materials, and to use knowledge gained to move on to progressively more advanced concepts. Classes are typically large, with twenty to thirty students and two to three teachers per room. Children work individually with materials that are kept on low, open shelves; the teachers are trained to observe each child carefully and introduce new materials when the child appears ready to move on.

Children are introduced to the letters of the alphabet by learning the sounds of each letter and by running their fingers over sandpaper cutouts of the letters. They prepare for writing by tracing insets or stencils of simple shapes, like circles and triangles, until they have the manual dexterity to manage letters as well. Most will learn to write before they can read, encouraged by the teacher to piece together letter blocks or cutouts on their own to form words. This phonetic approach begins at age two; a child is never pushed or prodded by the teacher, but simply allowed to progress at his own individual pace, under the watchful eye of the teacher.

Children in a Montessori environment are kept in mixed-age groups, such as ages two to five or six to nine. This allows younger children to learn from observation of their older peers, and also provides a classroom that will be well-stocked with materials appropriate for many different ability levels. At the elementary and middle school level, Montessori continues to be highly individualized, allowing each child to work at his own level, but there is more focus on group work as older children are better able to work and learn cooperatively with their peers.

If you are fortunate enough to recognize your child's unique learning style when he is still a toddler, you may find the Montessori classroom to be a place where he will flourish and build a strong foundation for learning. Many of the skills and concepts that are emphasized in remedial programs for dyslexia are included as a natural part of the Montessori child's world from the start. For example, your child will be learning to recognize letters and associate them with their sounds long before the typical age when "early intervention" to teach phonemic awareness begins for children in traditional schools.

However, if your child is older, it may be difficult for her to integrate into a Montessori environment. The Montessori classroom has its own set of norms and rules; it is an orderly, clean, and quiet environment that depends on the cooperation of children who have grown up with the concepts of self-care and responsibility inherent in the approach. An elementary school-age child may have a hard time fitting in, especially if she has come to rely on the teacher-directed instructional methods used in traditional classroom settings.

Even if your child has been in a Montessori environment since preschool, he may not be able to successfully become a reader without extra support and intervention. The individualized, child-led approach of the Montessori method will serve your child well in most cases, but it may not give him all he needs to learn to read. You may need to supplement your child's schooling with specialized tutoring or programs to help him fill some of the gaps left by the self-guided approach of his school.

Waldorf Schools

A Waldorf school follows the philosophy of Rudolf Steiner, who felt that schools should cater to the needs of children and encourage creativity and freethinking. A key element of Waldorf schooling is a strong emphasis on arts and music, with formal reading instruction delayed until second- or third-grade level. During the early years, emphasis is placed on developing oral language skills through storytelling.

During the elementary years, the students have a class teacher who stays with them from year to year. In early grades, all subjects are introduced via artistic mediums. All children learn to play the recorder and to knit; children also spend time gardening and usually study two foreign languages. Math instruction relies on developing a conceptual understanding. Textbooks are avoided, but children maintain their own workbooks for each subject, recording their experiences and what they have learned. No grades are given at the elementary level; instead, the teacher writes a detailed evaluation of each child at the end of each school year.

ALERT!

Because your child will not be expected to read until about age nine, it is unlikely that dyslexia will be detected in the early years. This is a mixed blessing: while your child will be develop and learn in a supportive environment, it will be harder for you to know when extra help is warranted.

A Waldorf school can provide a safe and nurturing environment for your child with dyslexia, where the child grows and learns in a supportive, family-like atmosphere. The emphasis on art projects and imaginative play provides a realm where your child can flourish emotionally and learn through the sensory pathways that best fit his learning style. On the other hand, few Waldorf teachers will be prepared to help your child if he does not naturally transition into reading at age nine or ten; the teachers are not trained in methods for dyslexia, and the practice of having your child with the same teacher can backfire if that particular teacher is not skilled at guiding children toward reading proficiency.

Democratic Schools

Some children do best if they are allowed to be the captains of their own ships, charting their own paths by exploring their interests and pursuing their passions. If you favor this approach, you may want to choose a private school following a "democratic" philosophy, such as the Sudbury Valley model, where students of all ages determine what they will do, as well as when, how, and where they will do it.

The theory behind the Sudbury approach is simply that all children are curious, have an innate desire to learn, and that the most effective learning takes place when it is compelled by the intrinsic motivation of the learner. This approach can provide significant emotional benefits for a child with dyslexia, as the child will naturally tend to utilize his strengths and talents, and over time will gain confidence in his own ability to seek and explore new information. It can also provide a welcome respite for a child who has come to feel demoralized and discouraged in a conventional school setting.

On the other hand, your child will naturally tend to avoid tasks that are difficult unless they clearly lead to a desired goal. A child with good reading skills can use books to learn about almost anything, but the child with dyslexia who is unable to read is unlikely to be able to teach himself. There seems to be little harm done when a bright and active nine-year-old has not yet mastered the basics of reading, but the situation may be very different when the child is fifteen and still unable to read. Thus, at the very least, a child with dyslexia needs access to a good teacher or tutor when he is ready and asks for help on his own. As with other alternative approaches, if you choose the Sudbury model, you should be prepared to supplement your child's education with private tutoring or outside services if necessary.

Specialized Schools for Dyslexia

There are a number of excellent private schools geared to students with dyslexia—in fact, far too many to list or describe them all in this book. However, a brief profile of some of the schools will help you get a sense of what you might look for. Most schools offer remedial teaching based on traditional Orton-Gillingham principles as well as providing a full academic curriculum. Some of the schools are geared primarily to helping their students gain sufficient proficiency in reading and other academic skills to reenter mainstream schools; others are intended to provide a comprehensive and high-quality education with the expectation that they will retain students through completion of their educational program.

Assets School

The Assets School in Honolulu, Hawaii, is a combined K-12 day school for gifted children and/or children with dyslexia. The curriculum is individualized and matched to meet each child's specific needs. Faculty are specially trained to provide acceleration, remediation, and enrichment. The school provides a model for providing an environment that nurtures the strengths and gifts of children with dyslexia while at the same time providing support and specialized teaching to assist them in areas of weakness.

The Lab School of Washington

The Lab School of Washington is a K-12 day school with campuses in Washington, D.C. and Baltimore, Maryland, that offers innovative teaching to students with learning disabilities. The curriculum emphasizes hands-on experimental learning and the use of the arts to teach academic skills. Elementary education incorporates work with computers and storytelling as well as art, with a continual emphasis on project-based learning through junior and senior high school levels. More than 90 percent of Lab School students go on to college.

 **FACT**

Many private schools also offer summer sessions that are open to children who are not enrolled during the school year. This may be a good alternative if you are reluctant to enroll your child in a specialized school full time. There are also many summer camp programs for children with dyslexia or related learning problems. Some focus on providing a fun environment to help build self-esteem, but others include extensive tutoring and support.

The Landmark School

Located in Massachusetts, the Landmark School offers both day and boarding programs for children in grades two to twelve. The Landmark academic program emphasizes achievement rather than grade placement levels, with a primary emphasis on development of oral and written language skills at all levels. The elementary program provides a daily one-to-one tutorial for children aged seven to nine; class size is limited to a maximum of six. Middle school children up to age fourteen continue with the daily individual tutorial and receive rigorous remediation in language and other skills in classes of six to eight students. The high school program continues with the same format, but provides a full college preparatory curriculum as well as elective courses and classes in visual and performing arts.

Boarding Schools for Boys

Two boarding schools for boys with dyslexia are the Greenwood School in Putney, Vermont, and the Gow School, located in upstate New York. Both schools offer remedial teaching based on the Orton-Gillingham model, as well as a full academic curriculum.

The Greenwood School is a prepreparatory program for boys aged nine to fifteeen who need special help mastering grade-level skills in reading, writing, spelling, or mathematics. Most Greenwood graduates go on to attend mainstream private and public high schools; only 20 percent continue their secondary studies in specialized remedial schools.

The Gow School offers a college preparatory curriculum to boys in grades seven to twelve. With a 4 to 1 faculty/student ratio, the school provides instruction in classes with three to six students, allowing individualized attention to all students.

Tax Deductions for Specialized Teaching

If your child's doctor recommends tutoring by a teacher who is specially trained and qualified to work with children with learning disabilities, you may deduct amounts spent on such services from your taxes as a medical expense. If the doctor recommends that your child attend a school that provides specialized services for learning disabilities, and if the principal reason for your child's attending such a school is to overcome his dyslexia, you can deduct the costs of his tuition, meals, and lodging at that school.

Because these costs are treated as a medical expense, you can only deduct amounts that exceed 7.5 percent of your adjusted gross income. Tax laws are always subject to change; if you are planning to deduct expenses associated with your child's dyslexia treatment, consult IRS Publication 502 (Medical and Dental Expenses) for the current tax year.

CHAPTER 10

IDEA and the
IEP Process

Y OU ARE LEGALLY ENTITLED to get help for your child, without charge, through the provisions of the federal Individuals with Disabilities in Education Act (IDEA). The process will begin with an evaluation of your child to determine whether he has a learning disability and needs special education services. Once your child qualifies for services, you will attend a formal meeting with your child's teacher and school administrators to create a written plan for addressing his educational needs, called an Individualized Education Program (IEP). This chapter will help you understand the process and prepare for your child's IEP meeting.

Qualifying for Services

Your local public school district must provide a free evaluation of your child if there is reason to suspect a learning disability. In many cases the evaluation will be initiated at the request of a teacher or school administrator familiar with your child. However, if you suspect that your child has dyslexia, you can request testing directly. Be sure to put your request in writing and send it to the school principal.

You should not limit your request to a test for dyslexia, as the law requires that your child be assessed "in all areas related to the suspected disability" and it is possible that some of your child's problems may stem from another related condition. Rather, your letter should briefly state the reasons you suspect a learning disability, and then request full evaluation of your child. The letter should also say that you consent to evaluation under the terms of the Individuals with Disabilities Act. Be sure the letter is dated and is signed by you, and keep a copy for your records.

 FACT

The school must obtain your consent before evaluating your child for learning disabilities. If you are opposed to such evaluation for any reason, the school is legally prohibited from proceeding with an evaluation unless it is ordered after an impartial hearing, called a "due process hearing."

The law requires the school to complete an evaluation of your child within a reasonable time after you make the request. Unfortunately, federal law does not specify exactly how much time that is; the time frame may be set by regulations in your state. If not, it is generally assumed that sixty days would be considered reasonable.

If the evaluation shows that your child has dyslexia or a related disability, the law requires that the school provide whatever special education services are needed because of the learning disability. You are legally entitled to inspect and review all educational records that the school relies on in making its determination, so you will be able to see the specific results of whatever diagnostic testing is completed by the school.

Requesting an Independent Educational Evaluation

If you are not satisfied with the results of the school's evaluation, you may request an Independent Educational Evaluation (IEE) by a qualified evaluator of your choosing. The school must provide you with information about where the independent educational evaluation may be obtained. The IEE will be done at public expense, unless the school initiates a proceeding before an impartial hearing officer to oppose the second evaluation.

 ESSENTIAL

If you are confused about procedures, you can get assistance from your state's Parent Training and Information (PTI) center. Every state has at least one PTI; these are agencies funded by the US Department of Education to provide training and information to parents of children with disabilities.

The school may ask you the reasons that you object to the initial determination; however, you are not required by law to give an explanation. Of course, like the initial request, you should make any request for an IEE in writing and keep copies of all correspondence.

The Individualized Education Program (IEP)

The primary mechanism for ensuring that your child's needs are met is the Individualized Education Program (IEP). The IEP is required by the provisions of the Individuals with Disabilities Education Act (IDEA); your child's first IEP meeting must take place within 30 days of the time your child is determined to be eligible for services. Your child qualifies for services if he has been found to have dyslexia or any other learning disability, and if his disability impairs his school performance.

An IEP has two purposes. First, it sets reasonable learning goals for your child. Then, it outlines the services that the school district will provide and specifies where they will take place.

The IEP Meeting

As a parent, you are entitled to have input into the entire IEP decision-making process. The school must take steps to ensure that one or both parents are present at each IEP meeting and are given the opportunity to participate. This includes notifying you of the meeting early enough to enable you to attend, scheduling the meeting at a mutually agreed-upon time and place, and providing you with all the necessary information regarding the meeting and your rights as parents. Your child may also attend the meeting if you wish.

 FACT

You can improve the quality and effectiveness of your child's IEP meetings by bringing a buddy. Bring your spouse or a close family member if you can. Consider pairing up with another parent of a special needs child—offer to attend her IEP meetings if she will attend yours. Don't forget your child—he can learn useful self-advocacy skills by being an active participant in the IEP process.

The IEP team will also include your child's regular teacher, a special education teacher, a person who is qualified to interpret the instructional implications of your child's evaluation results, a school system representative who is qualified to provide specialized services to your child and is knowledgeable about the general curriculum and availability of resources, and other individuals who have special knowledge or expertise about your child.

The school must initiate and conduct a meeting to review your child's IEP at least once every twelve months to determine whether the annual goals are being achieved, and to revise the IEP as needed to address any lack of expected progress. You can ask for more frequent meetings if you feel they are needed to address concerns or issues that arise with your child.

Contents of IEP

The IEP should begin with a statement of your child's present levels of educational performance and explain how your child's learning disability affects his involvement and progress in the general curriculum.

The IEP should then specify a set of objectively measurable annual goals, including benchmarks and short-term objectives. These goals should be related to your child's needs regarding the learning disability specified in his evaluation, and should enable your child to be involved in and progress in the general curriculum. The IEP goals should focus on reducing or eliminating your child's academic problems.

ALERT!

The IDEA was amended in 2004; the amendments may change some of the ways that IEP short-term objectives are set, as well as affect the means for you to appeal or challenge a decision by school authorities. As of the time of writing this book, the law had not been finalized by Congress, so it is not possible to explain the changes. Be sure to check the legal resources in Appendix B for up-to-date information.

IEP goals should be specific and directly related to your child's learning needs and achievement levels. For example, "Robert will increase oral reading skills to fifth-grade level as measured by the Gray Oral Reading Test" is measurable and specific; "Robert will work to improve reading fluency" is not. Make sure that goals are both reasonable in light of your child's present level of functioning and his expected grade level.

The IEP must also specify how your child's progress toward the annual goals will be measured, and the means by which the school will keep you regularly informed of the degree of progress. You are entitled to regular progress reports at least as often as school report cards are regularly issued.

Finally, the IEP must specify the services and modifications that will be provided to address each of your child's needs. The actual availability of services has no bearing on the IEP. That is, if a service is needed it must be written in the IEP; if the school district cannot directly provide the service, it must arrange for and fund the service to be provided by another agency.

The IEP must be individualized. It is not appropriate for the school to present you with a form IEP that is used for all children with similar learning issues; your child is entitled to a unique plan to meet all of his specific needs. The plan may address his non-academic as well as academic needs. For example, if your child has social or behavioral issues that are connected to his dyslexia, the plan should specify those and provide for appropriate interventions.

Preparing for the Meeting

It is important for you to prepare in advance for the IEP meeting, so that you can advocate effectively for your child. If you are unprepared, you are likely to find the process intimidating—you may arrive to find yourself confronting a roomful of teachers and school administrators, and find it difficult to express yourself or hold your ground.

Start by talking to your child. Ask her what is going well in school and what she would like to do better. Explain the purpose of the meeting, and ask your child whether she would like to attend.

Write a short description of your child, including a list of her strengths and weaknesses.

Include such items as: hobbies, behavior at home, and relationship with family and friends. Focusing on your child's strengths, interests, and preferences will help develop an IEP that best meets her needs. Write out a list of your specific concerns and questions, and list your own recommendations or ideas for how to best meet your child's needs.

Write down some goals you would like to see your child achieve in the coming year.

Be sure that you know your options. Gather information about various programs offered within your school district, as well as any privately provided programs that may be appropriate for your child.

Talk with your child's teacher, the district special education administrator, and other parents. Visit your child's classroom so that you can observe her present learning environment. As much as possible, visit potential programs that might be indicated for your child before the IEP meeting.

 ESSENTIAL

> The IEP meeting is a time to use teamwork to help your child, and create goals for the future—not to revisit or argue over past mistakes. At the meeting, show a positive outlook. Start by talking about some areas you know everyone will agree with. Avoid speaking in absolutes, such as "always" or "never." Focus on your concerns about your child and specific needs, and use questions ("What if we tried . . . ?") to elicit suggestions from other IEP team members, rather than a declarative statement of a firm position.

Use this information to develop your ideal IEP to present at the meeting. Gather all available information that supports your position and your child's ideal IEP. This can include new information, such as an evaluation by someone outside the school district or a statement from your child's pediatrician.

Ask for a written list of the people the school plans to have at your child's IEP meeting. Let your school contact person know if you plan to bring others to the meeting as well. Try to find out in advance what school staff members are likely to recommend at the meeting. It is especially important for you to know what to expect from your child's teacher, as her opinions and suggestions will usually be given great deference. If possible, meet with the teacher in advance to go over your mutual concerns—things will go better if you and the teacher present a united front.

Invite appropriate people who can support your position to speak at the IEP meeting. This can be an experienced advocate, a professional who has worked with your child, or someone who provides services that you would like your child to receive. If a key person cannot intend, have her prepare a written statement for you to read at the meeting. It is also a good idea to bring a support person, such as a friend or another parent, who can assist you by taking notes and helping you stay focused at the meeting.

Organize your materials in advance and make photocopies of any important documents or exhibits (such as samples of your child's school work) that you are bringing, so that you can distribute these to the other people at the meeting. You may want to assemble a portfolio of your child's work, and keep a binder with all school documents, reports, and information related to the IEP process. These can be updated from year to year.

FAPE—Free and Appropriate Education

As a parent, you naturally want what is best for your child. You want your child to receive the best education possible; your goal is to maximize his learning potential. You may have a specific program or therapy in mind that you think your child needs. However, the law does not require that school administrators provide the best possible interventions for your child; rather, the law requires only that the school provide your child with a "free and appropriate education"—commonly designated as FAPE.

FAPE means that the school is required to provide individualized instruction with sufficient support services to enable your child to benefit educationally from the instruction. In other words, the school must provide the minimal level of support that is adequate to allow your child to learn. The Supreme Court has held that this standard is met with services that are reasonably calculated to enable the child to achieve passing marks and advance from grade to grade.

Many children with dyslexia are extremely bright, and often their pattern of weaknesses and strengths leaves them highly functional in many areas, even though they struggle in others. For example, your child may read very slowly, but with excellent comprehension, and she may have a strong ability to retain information learned from oral instruction and class demonstrations. Through hard work and determination, your child may be able to keep up in class and generally earn B's and C's in classwork. With such a child, you may find it difficult to qualify for school services, even with a diagnosis of dyslexia—the school may take the position that the dyslexia is mild and does not affect her ability to learn.

 **FACT**

Dyslexia is as likely to be found among gifted children as any other group, but the IDEA does not provide for services for giftedness. However, 9 states—Florida, Kansas, Kentucky, Louisiana, New Mexico, Ohio, Pennsylvania, Tennessee, and West Virginia—currently require IEPs for gifted students. In these states, FAPE may be construed to include enhanced educational goals via an accelerated and enriched curriculum.

Even if your child does qualify, you may find that the services offered are not adequate. Through formal testing or your own observations, you may realize that your child is intellectually gifted and capable of learning at an accelerated pace, if only the reading barrier were addressed. You will want to find a corrective approach to dyslexia—one that is geared to eliminating barriers and employs a fast-paced instructional methodology—but the school will see its obligation to be far more limited in scope. In fact, if your child does receive special education services, you may find that as soon as he progresses to what you consider to be a level of minimal proficiency, the services are withdrawn.

You can't change the law, but understanding the concept of FAPE will help you know how to frame your arguments when dealing with school authorities. Use language like "appropriate" and "adequate" when asking for services, and highlight your child's weakest skill areas. For example, if your child is earning B's in the regular fourth-grade classroom, but standardized tests show that he is reading on a first-grade level, work toward an IEP that will specify efforts to be taken to help him learn to read at grade level. Do not let your child's strong compensation skills overshadow his need for specific remediation in areas of weakness.

Special Provisions in Texas

Under Texas state law, public schools must have procedures for early identification, screening, intervention, and support for all children with dyslexia and related disorders. Screening must be performed by individuals or professionals who are trained to assess for dyslexia. Each school must provide the services of a teacher trained in dyslexia to each identified student, on the school campus. The school may also offer optional additional services at a centralized location.

Because federal law also applies in Texas, the provisions of the Texas law can be used to develop a strong IEP for any student with dyslexia; however, the provisions of the law apply even if your child does not fall within IDEA or have an IEP. There is no requirement under Texas law that your child have any specific academic deficiency; that is, even a child with mild dyslexia who is reading close to grade level should be entitled to appropriate services under the law.

 ALERT!

Although a strong law is on the books, many parents in Texas report that the law is not well implemented or enforced. It is important to know your rights. The exact legal requirements are set forth in Texas Education Code, Section 38.003 ("Screening and Treatment for Dyslexia and Related Disorders") and Texas Administrative Code, Section 74.28 ("Student with Dyslexia and Related Disorders").

Typical Special Education Services

Usually, a child with dyslexia will have an IEP that will provide that she will spend most of her day in the regular classroom, but also spend part of her day in a resource room with a special ed teacher. Resource rooms provide support for children for a small portion of the school day. Class size is typically limited to eight to fourteen students, allowing individualized attention and small group instruction. The resource room typically serves the needs of children with a variety of learning difficulties. Your child may also spend a specified amount of time each week working with a speech and language therapist or an occupational therapist.

 **FACT**

Research shows that children placed in special ed often fare worse over time than their counterparts in regular classrooms, often showing an overall deterioration in reading skills rather than an improvement. This may stem from practices that deprive children of exposure to grade-level language arts instruction while they are receiving remedial reading instruction.

If warranted, the IEP may specify that your child be placed in a special education classroom for all of her studies. The IDEA requires that services be given in the "least restrictive environment," meaning that your child should not be removed from the regular classroom for more time than absolutely necessary to provide supportive educational services. Full-time placement in a special ed class is rarely a good choice for children with dyslexia, as it often segregates them to learn with children with much more severe intellectual and emotional problems. If such a placement is being considered for your child, be sure to visit the special ed classroom; although rare, there are some special ed or LD classrooms with skilled and innovative teachers who are able to bring out the best in their students. Some schools may have specialized classrooms for dyslexia. While you should be wary of a full-time special ed placement, keep an open mind until you have met the teacher and seen for yourself what type of students will be in the classroom with your child.

Payment for Private Services Under IDEA

You may feel that that the services provided by the school will not meet your child's needs. Based on your own observations and exploration of various methods, you may have decided on a specific method or program that you would like your child to receive. Unfortunately, the provisions of IDEA do not allow you to choose or specify the method of instruction as part of an IEP.

 ALERT!

If you do not understand or agree with your child's IEP, you do not have to sign it. Alternatively, attorney Pete Wright suggests to preserve your objections by writing a statement on the IEP above your signature, saying "I consent to this IEP being implemented but I object to it for the reasons stated during the meeting."

However, in many cases school districts will pay for private services, including placement in private schools. Initially, you may be able to convince the school to provide such services with a strong presentation at the IEP meeting; if not, you may ultimately succeed in obtaining such help by demonstrating that your child is not receiving the promised FAPE. The best way to do this is to show that your child has either not received promised services or that the services provided by the IEP have not been adequate to help your child attain the specific goals set by the IEP. So if your fourth grader who was reading at first-grade level shows no significant gains after a year of services via the resource room, you have a good case for convincing the school to try something new.

Your first step should be to prepare to request the placement or service you want at your child's next scheduled IEP meeting, or to request that an additional IEP meeting be scheduled. If the school does not grant your request and does not provide an alternative that appears to meet your child's needs, you may choose to enroll your child in the private program at your own expense. If you provide the school with written notice of your intent to do so, clearly stating why you feel that the school has failed to provide a FAPE for your child, there is a good chance that you will be able to later obtain reimbursement from the school at a due process hearing. To do this, it will be important to keep good records of your child's progress in the alternative placement, so that you will later be able to clearly demonstrate to a hearing officer that your privately funded services were more effective in assisting your child to meet stated IEP goals than the services directly provided by the school.

Appeals and Due Process Hearings

If you are unhappy with the determinations that have been made at your child's IEP meeting, ask what the procedures are in your district for administrative review. Sometimes a higher level school district administrator brings a new perspective to the issue or has the ability to authorize resources that can help resolve the issue. You may also be able to request mediation.

If you still cannot reach an agreement with your school district, your next step is to request a due process hearing. This is a proceeding before an impartial hearing officer who has the power to consider evidence presented by both the parent and school district, and then render a decision to resolve the dispute. The cost of the hearing officer is paid for by the school district. It is a good idea to seek advice from a lawyer or special ed advocate to prepare for this hearing.

CHAPTER 11

Additional Legal Protections

O NCE YOUR CHILD HAS BEEN DIAGNOSED
with dyslexia or a related learning disability, federal law
provides a number of additional protections. Whether or
not your child qualifies for special education services, your child
has the right to receive whatever accommodations or modifications
are necessary to provide equal access to educational services. Your
child also shares in the same legal rights that apply to other children, and your child may be protected by special legislation that
applies to schools in your state. As a parent, it is important for you
to understand what your child's rights are and how to make sure
they are enforced.

ADA and 504 Accommodations

In addition to the provisions of IDEA discussed in the previous
chapter, your child may also be entitled to accommodations or
classroom modifications under the Americans with Disabilities Act
of 1990 (ADA) or Section 504 of the Rehabilitation Act of 1973.
These laws protect your child from discrimination on the
basis of her learning disability. This may be a good alternative if your child has been diagnosed with dyslexia but
has difficulty qualifying for services because she is not
"behind enough" and does not seem to need tutoring
or special education in order to keep up in class. Even

if your child does qualify for services, you might also prefer the ADA/504 protections if you do not agree with the educational plan and goals specified by the IEP, but still want to obtain modifications for your child.

 FACT

Some common 504 accommodations are: extended time on tests or assignments, peer assistance with note-taking, extra set of textbooks for home use, computer-aided instruction, enlarged print, rearranging class schedules, preferred seating assignments, oral testing, or use of a tape recorder in lieu of taking notes.

The difference between protections under the ADA/504 and the IDEA is that your child does not have to demonstrate a need for special education services in order to receive ADA/504 accommodations. On the other hand, with ADA/504, he will not have an IEP or be given specialized tutoring or educational services. What your child can get via the antidiscrimination laws is the right to use assistive devices, such as a calculator or keyboard, or modifications such as extended time on exams or an exam reader. Of course, you need to be able to show that your child needs these services to overcome his specific disability-related limitations; however, usually the diagnosis of dyslexia will suffice.

Although your child is legally entitled to "reasonable" accommodations, the law does not specify what is reasonable. This is something that may be determined by the school in accordance with its practices in similar cases, or it may be developed over time through trial and error.

Suggested Classroom Modifications

Modifications should be tailored to your child's specific needs, and they may vary in different settings or with different classes. For example, if your child has auditory discrimination problems, she may need to be seated closer to the front of the room in a class with a soft-spoken teacher, but may have no problems in another class where the teacher has a louder and more commanding demeanor. A child who has difficulty writing may need extra time to complete written essays or exams, but have no difficulty with worksheets or multiple-choice exams that merely require checking or circling the correct answer.

Some common accommodations are:

Extra time. Your child might need extended time on just about anything: on written homework, on oral tasks requiring a rapid response, or simply moving from one task to another in class.

Alternative assignments. Your child might need to substitute all or part of an assignment with an alternative project or task; for example, a science project could be modified to allow your child to build a model in lieu of writing a paper.

Assistive technology. Your child may do better on written assignments if she is allowed to use a laptop computer or keyboard to type them, rather than turn in handwritten work. In addition to utilities like the spell-checker that are standard on all computers, your child may benefit from more sophisticated software like predictive-text programs, text-to-speech utilities, dictation software, or handheld devices like an electronic spelling dictionary or calculator.

E-books, recorded books, and multimedia. Your child may do better if some or all of his assignments can be accessed through audio or visual formats. In some cases, equivalent information in textbooks may also be available in video or computer CD-ROM format.

Changes to classroom seating arrangement. Your child may do better if seated closer to the teacher or in an area that is shielded from distractions.

Modifications to curriculum. Your child may need modifications to the expected curriculum such as a shorter spelling list or a spelling list made up of easier words.

Keep in mind that the ultimate goal is to maximize your child's ability to learn by eliminating learning barriers and to make sure that assignments are within his capacity to complete and to master. You do not want to make things too easy for your child, but your child will be discouraged and soon give up if every assignment ends in frustration and failure.

 **FACT**

> Dr. Martin Kutscher, author of *The ADHD e-BOOK*, suggests these strategies to teachers to improve communication with a child who has difficulty following directions: Establish good eye contact, use a cue such as tapping on the desk to bring the child back into focus, alert the child's attention with phrases such as "This is important", and break down longer directions into simpler chunks.

Audio Books and Visual Aids

Your child may also be able to keep up with assigned reading and improve his own fluency and comprehension skills by listening to books on tape or CD, or reading e-books along with a text-to-speech device. A wide variety of literature is available in audio format; your child can improve fluency and reading speed by reading the text while simultaneously listening to audio, or he can keep up with grade-level reading that is beyond his own reading capacity by relying on listening alone. For books that are not available commercially in an audio format, including assigned textbooks, your child may qualify for services from Recording for the Blind & Dyslexic. This requires a small membership fee and use of a specialized listening device.

Your child may also find it helpful to watch use videos or DVDs to supplement classroom reading, watching movie versions of novels and plays that are assigned reading. Educational videos or CDs with multimedia content may also supplement the content of textbooks on any number of subjects; your highly visual child is likely to learn, retain, and understand far more from watching a documentary about the Civil War than by reading a chapter in his history book. Keep in mind that if your child does not read comfortably at grade level, audio-visual media is his primary means to access more advanced topics and subject matter. Your child is a capable learner; while reading remediation is important, his reading difficulties should not prevent him from studying and learning advanced materials when he can get information from alternative sources.

 **FACT**

> Recording for the Blind & Dyslexic (RFB&D) was established in 1948 to provide recorded textbooks to veterans blinded in World War II. Today, RFB&D has a catalog of more than 98,000 titles. More than 70 percent of its members have been identified as having a learning disability.

Accommodations on Standardized Tests

If your state uses standardized tests to determine your child's eligibility to advance to another grade or to graduate from high school, you need to plan ahead to make sure that your child will have appropriate support and modifications. Make sure that your child's IEP contains goals that will meet the content requirement for such tests; your child cannot reasonably be expected to pass a test on material he has never been taught. If your child is in a resource or special ed class even for only part of the day, he may be missing instruction that is important to meet grade-level standards.

Dyslexia and Standardized Tests

Students with dyslexia tend to have difficulties particularly with standardized tests, and their scores often do not accurately reflect their level of achievement. One problem is simply that these tests are written, and your child has a disability affecting reading. Your child is likely to have more difficulty deciphering the questions and the set of answers given and is likely to read more slowly, or need to reread questions several times. Typically, the "right" answers to a multiple-choice question are dependent on very specific words in a question, often phrased in the negative. For example, the question may ask the child to choose the one answer that is "not" correct; the child who misreads the question or skips over the word "not" will be confronted with a list of several correct answers. Since other test questions may ask the child to choose the "best" answer, he may assume that he is again being asked to choose the "best" correct statement, rather than the one incorrect statement. Alternatively, he may compensate for his poor reading speed by adopting a strategy of choosing the first correct answer that he reads—again, resulting in an incorrect choice if there is more than one correct answer listed. If your child focuses on being extra careful in reading each question, his slower reading speed means that he is likely to run out of time and leave many questions unanswered.

 FACT

Your child may also have perceptual and motor coordination problems that work against him. He may correctly see that the correct answer is choice "d," but then mark "b" on his answer sheet. In filling in bubbles on a scantron form, he is more likely than other students to have difficulty lining up the row of answers with the number of the question, and thus may simply mark a series of answers on the wrong lines.

Finally, your child's intellectual strengths and her creativity may work against her. Children with dyslexia simply tend to have more unusual ideas and different reasoning strategies than children who are primarily left-brained, analytical thinkers. Given a set of five responses to choose from, where the fifth choice is "none of the above," an imaginative child is likely to think of obscure or trivial reasons why each of the first four choices are flawed. If asked to choose the "best" of several flawed options, your child's definition of "best" is likely to be quite unconventional. In a classroom setting, your child's originality may delight her teachers, who recognize some of her ideas as being ingenious—on the standardized test, her novel approach will simply be deemed an incorrect response.

Arranging Testing Accommodations

It is important that your child's IEP specify the modifications and accommodations to be provided during administration of standardized tests. This may include extended time for testing or provision for oral administration of the tests. If your child does not qualify for an IEP, make sure that your child's 504 plan clearly specifies the accommodations that will be allowed during standardized testing. Many students have encountered unexpected barriers when they simply assumed they would be allowed the same accommodations that were usually provided in class.

 ALERT!

> Testing accommodations will not be allowed if they would invalidate the test, making the results meaningless. For example, if a test of reading comprehension is read aloud to your child, then it doesn't measure his ability to understand what he reads. Instead, it tests his understanding of what he hears.

Finally, make sure that your child's IEP provides for multiple or alternative forms of assessment in making any decisions about grade retention or advancement. Again, even if your child has met the educational objectives set forth in the IEP, the standardized test used by your state may not be an accurate or valid measure of his achievement. Your child should be afforded the opportunity to demonstrate progress through other means, such as teachers' assessments of classroom performance or a portfolio of his work.

Informal Accommodations

You may be able to arrange modifications for your child without using the formal IEP or 504 process. Often, accommodations can be arranged informally with the teacher simply by making a request or suggestion. You can arrange this by meeting with the teacher, or via a telephone conversation, written note, or email; or you can guide and encourage your child to make suggestions on his own.

 ESSENTIAL

If your child has not yet been diagnosed with dyslexia, or does not have severe enough problems to qualify for school services, informal modifications are the best way to tailor the school curriculum to your child's needs. If your child attends a school which follows a philosophy of individualized education, you may be able to rely solely on the informal process to arrange needed modifications

Of course, for informal arrangements to work, you need a cooperative and supportive teacher. Many teachers will be happy to work with you and your child, and may come up with many helpful ideas of their own. Even with an IEP in place, you will probably find it more efficient to work out many issues as they arise through informal discussions with the teacher. Some advantages of the informal process are:

Greater flexibility. You cannot anticipate all possible problems in an IEP. Classwork and homework assignments change over time and are likely to present new and unexpected barriers. Informal modifications can be implemented immediately, revised by trial and error, and changed, extended, or abandoned as circumstances warrant.

More choice and control. You and your child will have more control of the process and are more likely to have your suggestions implemented by working with a single teacher, rather than by trying to convince a group of teachers and administrators to agree to something that must be reduced to writing at an IEP meeting.

Improved implementation. No teacher likes having a committee tell her how to do her job, and busy classroom teachers may forget or ignore many specifications of an IEP. By working directly with the teacher, you will be able to arrange modifications that you know the teacher is willing and able to implement.

Increased self-advocacy skills. Your child will learn continually from the informal process. When very young, he will learn that it is acceptable to ask for changes to meet his learning needs, and he will learn problem-solving and communication skills by observing how you work with the teacher. As he grows, he will be able to follow your lead and handle the task of arranging modifications on his own.

Wider range of modifications. You and the teacher will be free to try new things and make revisions as needed. Changes do not need to be tied directly to your child's learning disability but can simply be implemented with the stated goal of helping your child learn or improving classroom behavior.

Ability to enhance the curriculum. The modifications provided by the IEP or 504 process are geared to helping your child over-come areas of weakness; however, with informal arrangements, you can use the process to also substitute or add to the curriculum to enrich your child's education or add challenge in areas of strength. This approach can improve the overall quality of your child's schooling and also increase his sense of accomplishment and self-esteem.

The drawback to relying to informal accommodations is that the teacher may later refuse or fail to implement agreed-on changes. Since you are working with individual teachers, you will have to renegotiate with each new teacher. In some cases, a school principal or other staff member who disagrees with the plan may intervene to prevent implementation of the modifications, perhaps citing concerns of fairness or discipline.

 ESSENTIAL

If you arrange informal modifications without an IEP, try to get something in writing to record the arrangement, especially if it may affect your child's grades or likelihood of promotion at the end of the year. Make sure that the teacher or school district will not later penalize your child and that you and your child clearly understand any possible negative consequences related to uncompleted work.

If your child qualifies for an IEP, the best approach usually is a combination of both formal and informal changes. Use the IEP or 504 process to negotiate and enforce the most important and generalized modifications or to obtain some broad standards; use informal negotiation and discussion to deal with less-important matters or issues specific to a particular teacher and aspect of the curriculum.

No Child Left Behind

The No Child Left Behind Act of 2001 (NCLB) also has some important provisions that may benefit your child. Unlike IDEA or ADA/504, your child does not need a formal diagnosis of a disability in order to gain the protection of this law. The overall purpose of the law is to improve the academic achievement of all students in public schools; the law also puts a high priority on promoting reading achievement.

Rather than focusing on your child's disability, the NCLB essentially provides a mechanism to evaluate the quality of the public school your child attends. If your child's school is designated as "in need of improvement" because of general poor performance of its students on standardized achievement tests for two consecutive years, the district must offer all children in the school the opportunity to attend a different school with a better performance record.

Additionally, students from low-income families who are in schools that have failed to meet state standards for three or more years are eligible to receive supplemental educational services at the expense of the school district. These supplemental services are tutoring programs often given by private providers, including some who may offer reading programs geared to students with dyslexia. Thus, in some cases families may use NCLB to obtain private tutoring that is not being made available via the IEP process.

 ESSENTIAL

The higher standards imposed by NCLB may also have an indirect impact on developing IEPs and defining FAPE under IDEA. Your school needs to set IEP goals that will help your child perform within acceptable ranges on standardized tests of achievement in mathematics and science as well as in reading and language arts.

Finally, NCLB requires that the school test all students, including most students receiving special education services, using standardized measures of achievement, and that the results of your child's individual tests be reported to you. In the past, in some schools, special ed children were allowed to lag far behind, due to a remedial curriculum with significantly lowered expectations as to course content or individual achievement. By measuring the schools' progress in part by the ability of its special ed students to meet state curriculum standards, NCLB creates a strong incentive for each school to explore and develop high quality programs for students with learning disabilities. As a parent, you also will have better information about how your child measures up compared to others at his grade level.

Florida McKay Scholarship Program

The State of Florida has special provisions that may provide funding for your child to attend a private school. Under the John M. McKay Program for Students with Disabilities, if your child is enrolled in a Florida public school, has an IEP, and you are dissatisfied with his current school, you may transfer him to another public school in the same district or an adjacent district, or you may apply for a state-funded voucher to use any participating private school. To be eligible, your child must also have completed a year of kindergarten. The McKay program will pay an amount up to the level of state-generated funding the student would have received if remaining in public school; this can be applied toward the total tuition amount charged by the school.

 ALERT!

> If you transfer your child to a private school under the McKay program, you may lose some of the other legal protections described in this chapter. Once your child enters the private school, he will no longer be entitled to an IEP and may lose the protections available under the ADA and Section 504.

A similar program, called Opportunity Scholarships, provides funding to enable school choice for students who would otherwise be enrolled in schools identified as failing under the No Child Left Behind Act. If your child does not yet have an IEP or if he is entering kindergarten for the first time, you would be eligible for this program rather than the McKay scholarship.

CHAPTER 12

Working with Your Child's Teacher

W ITH CAREFUL PLANNING, school can be a rewarding experience for your child despite his learning barriers. You can help pave the way for a successful and enjoyable school experience by anticipating possible problems, by building strong relationships with your child's teachers, setting clear expectations at home, providing consistent emotional support, and becoming an able advocate for your child. By working closely with a teacher, you can become allies in the mutual effort to help your child.

Be the Teacher's Friend

It is important for you to be able to communicate your concerns to the teacher without engendering hostility. The first step toward good communication is to make an effort to understand the teacher's point of view. Remember, your child is not the only student in her class. The regular teacher may have twenty or thirty children to worry about. She must manage the classroom and structure lessons and activities. She cares about your child, but there may be other children with equally or more severe learning problems or disruptive children who need to be monitored and limit the amount of attention she can devote to your child.

If you have the time and your school permits it, offer to volunteer in the classroom. Even though you are concerned about your own child's welfare, use your time assisting the teacher to get to know and observe the other children and develop a sense of the classroom dynamics, as well as a typical day's schedule. When you think about accommodations for your own child, ask yourself how these will fit within the environment you observe.

Try to establish a friendly relationship with the teacher. If you cannot volunteer in the classroom, ask the teacher if there are other ways you can help or if she needs any classroom supplies. An inexpensive purchase for the classroom, such as a few reams of binder paper or a extra boxes of pencils, may win the teacher's appreciation. If the teacher's first contacts with you are as an involved and helpful parent, she will be more open to suggestions about your child.

Focus on Actual Needs

Do not assume that your child will have problems in class before they arise. Parents can sometimes make the mistake of worrying too much and having too little faith in the teacher. Many teachers are keen observers and know to make changes and adjustments on their own. Some may challenge and motivate your child in ways that surprise you, and encourage your child to succeed in ways that you would not have expected.

Ask your child how things are going at school—ask him if he likes his teacher and what his favorite class activities are. If your child complains about problems, ask him to elaborate, and ask what kind of changes he would like. Your child may come up with some sensible suggestions, or he may ask for the impossible—but even the impossible requests will give you an idea of what areas need adjusting.

If your child does not have an IEP or a formal diagnosis, you may simply want to describe your child's problems to the teacher in terms of learning style or personality quirks: "Sam is a strong visual learner. It helps him to learn if he can see pictures or diagrams illustrating the point." Or, "Megan is a bit of a daydreamer. You may need to call her name or tap her gently on the shoulder to make sure she is paying attention before you start giving instructions."

Resist the temptation to educate the teacher by supplying her with books and long articles about dyslexia, unless she asks for such information. A very short article or bulleted list, perhaps copied from a brochure or Web site, is a more efficient way to get the point across.

Support the Teacher's Goals

When you first talk to the teacher about your child's needs, start by asking whether the teacher has any concerns about your child. Children with dyslexia often have issues with communication or attention focus that cause problems for teachers; the teacher may be frustrated because your child has difficulty following directions or is slow to obey instructions. It is also quite possible that your child is disruptive or argumentative with the teacher or has other behavior problems in class.

 ESSENTIAL

Special education expert Richard Lavoie says, ""The pain the learning different child causes at home and in the classroom is never greater than the pain he feels." He explains that any child would rather look bad than look dumb. Disruptive or disobedient behavior may simply be an attempt to distract attention from the embarrassment of not being able to complete an assignment.

If the teacher complains about your child's behavior, do not argue or try to defend or excuse your child's conduct. Instead, use this as an opportunity to begin to show the teacher the connection between the learning problems and behavior, and start by suggesting strategies with the dual goal of meeting your child's needs and helping the teacher improve classroom management. Ask for more detail about the setting and circumstances that accompany behavior problems; this may be a key as to how to go about eliminating the problem.

Avoid using the diagnostic label that has been given to your child and focus instead on descriptions of precise areas of difficulty. If the teacher complains that your child ignores her directions, it will not help to simply say, "He can't follow directions because he has dyslexia." The teacher may not understand why a reading problem would affect your child's ability to participate in class or listen to her oral instructions. Don't expect the teacher to become an expert on dyslexia. Instead, say something like, "James has a problem processing the sounds of language; it takes him longer to make sense of the words and it is hard for him to remember several steps at a time." Then you can work together to think of ways to help address the problem.

You may be surprised to learn that a new teacher is unaware of your child's learning disability, or that she has not seen or read the IEP. You may want to give the teacher another copy of the IEP, with a cover page that has a summary of the major points that apply to her classroom.

Leave the Teacher in Control

Compliment the teacher. Take note of her good qualities as a teacher whether you observe them in the classroom or hear them from your child, and remark on ways that she has helped your child. It is always easier for a person to accept suggestions if you have started by showing that you appreciate her abilities and the things she has been doing right. Ask the teacher what she thinks of your suggestions, rather than make demands. Say, "Do you think it would help if we tried . . . ?" rather than "I want you to . . ." or "You have to . . ." If the teacher seems resistant to implementing items that are on your child's IEP, you could point out the specific IEP modification or goal, and then ask, "What are some ways we could begin implementing this?"

If the teacher does implement some of your suggestions and it seems to help your child, be sure to let the teacher know that things are going well. Send a note or a thank-you card with a brief statement mentioning the improvement you have seen in your child.

ESSENTIAL

Most schools regularly schedule one or more teacher conferences in the year. You do not have to wait until the first teacher conference to raise your concerns; in fact, it will probably be easier to arrange modifications separately as issues comes up. If modifications are already in place, the teacher conference is a good time to review them and assess how they are working. It is also an ideal time to consider new modifications.

Building Self-Advocacy Skills

Ultimately, your child will do better in school if he is able to advocate for himself. This is especially important as your child grows older, but even a kindergartner can be encouraged to speak up for himself when appropriate. Most modifications can also be arranged through informal, direct negotiation with the teacher. In a classroom, this can also take place in the course of normal communication; if your child learns to raise his hand and explain when he is having a problem, many issues may be resolved instantly.

Begin by helping your child understand his own learning style. Explain that every person is good with some things and has difficulty or needs to try harder in other areas. Use examples, mentioning some things that are hard for you or someone else he respects. Encourage your child to think about what strategies help him learn new material or what types of learning activities he enjoys.

Help your child learn how to approach her teacher and ask for specific changes or adjustments. Make sure your child knows the importance of speaking courteously and choosing an appropriate time to talk to the teacher. If your child has an IEP that lists specific modifications, make sure that your child knows what is in it, in language she can understand.

Your child may have better luck arranging modifications to assignments if he learns to offer something in exchange. For example, if the teacher has asked for a five-paragraph essay about a geography topic, your child might say, "I have dyslexia and it is hard for me to write, but I draw well. Can I write two paragraphs and draw a map?"

 FACT

> One tool that many teachers are comfortable with is an independent learning contract. This is an agreement between student and teacher that specifies the work that the student needs to complete in order to earn an agreed-on grade. This creates an opportunity for extensive modifications and adjustments, but at the same time holds the student responsible for completing assigned tasks.

Help your child learn to state things positively: "I usually learn better if I . . ." He should try to avoid the appearance of making excuses for himself or trying to simply avoid work; "I can't" or "I don't want to" are not phrases that go over well with teachers.

Your child may find it helpful to volunteer to do tasks that are easy for him, such as running errands for the teacher or passing out and collecting classroom supplies, simply to demonstrate to the teacher that he is an eager participant. This will help avoid problems that arise when a teacher believes a child to be lazy or uncooperative.

When your child has difficulties with a teacher at school, go over the events and conversation at home. Try to draw your child's attention to points where he might have said the wrong thing; ask him, "How could you have said things better?" Have your child try out strategies you suggest, and report back later on whether the problem has been resolved.

As your child grows older, try to encourage her to resolve issues directly with the teacher as much as possible, continuing to offer helpful suggestions and guidance at home, if your child asks for your help. Resist the temptation to take over or contact the teacher if your child seems satisfied with the arrangement, even if you feel that expectations are set too high or too low. Your child will always have dyslexia; its important that she develop the ability to advocate for herself and to exercise good judgment in making decisions. The skills she learns at school will later be crucial to success at college or in employment.

Assessment and Grading

Your child may be able to learn most of the material covered in class, but may still face barriers when it comes to the way that his work is assessed and grades are assigned. Traditionally, grades are assigned based on uniform criteria for all children in a class, often reflecting how a child measures up to his peers. It is a competitive process that may give little information about what the individual child has actually learned. It sets up children with learning difficulties for repeated failure, because no matter how hard they work, they are unlikely to be able to earn high marks. This system not only undermines your child's self-esteem, but also contributes to behavior problems.

Along with modifications to curriculum, suggest and encourage the teacher to use alternative forms of assessment. The best approaches will factor in your child's demonstrated effort and her level of improvement over time. The teacher can use records of past performance, such as with spelling or arithmetic, as a way of determining the level of performance that can reasonably be expected of your child. Improved performance should result in an improved grade—for example, if a child who usually gets seven correct answers out of twenty problems is able to increase performance to ten, the child's improvement should be recognized and rewarded.

Ask the teacher to mark your child's paper in a positive way, noting correct answers prominently. The teacher can score the papers by simply counting the number or percentage of right answers on homework assignments or quizzes, recording those in her gradebook. If a pattern of improvement is seen, the teacher can help your child chart his progress; at the end of the term, a grade can be assigned that is consistent with the level of improvement.

 ESSENTIAL

Busy teachers often ask classroom aides, student teachers, or parent volunteers to help with grading papers and exams. If you have worked out special modifications for your child, make sure that the teacher will personally mark your child's work or communicate the arrangement to whoever is helping with the grading.

The teacher can also modify grading practices to specifically exempt certain considerations for your child. For example, the teacher can agree to disregard spelling mistakes in all subjects other than spelling. Thus, your child would be graded on the content of his written essays or answers to questions, not on the mechanics of producing them.

Once the teacher has agreed on modifications for your child, it is helpful if the teacher can create a specific rubric for grading his work. A rubric is a set of written requirements that sets forth requirements to earn each passing grade. Usually it can be set out on a grid, listing the specific criteria for an A, B, C, and so forth. If the teacher generally uses a rubric for the whole class, modifications can simply be noted on your child's copy.

In addition to guaranteeing that agreed-upon modifications will be considered in assigning a grade, a well-drafted rubric will also help improve your child's performance. For example, a rubric that indicates that writing two paragraphs will earn a C, but writing three or more paragraphs will earn a B, might provide your child with the incentive to work hard to complete an extra paragraph, as he can clearly connect his extra effort to the reward of a higher grade. It also gives your child a greater sense of control and enables him to better understand how the grade relates to the quality of his work.

Dealing with a Problem Teacher

Sooner or later, you will encounter a teacher who is inflexible and unwilling to make changes or adjustments to benefit your child. Even if modifications are required under a written IEP or 504 plan, the teacher may be unwilling to implement them, resulting in conflicts when you or your child attempt to enforce the rules. There may simply be a personality conflict; for example, a teacher who places a high value on maintaining an orderly classroom may have little patience for a child whose learning difference leaves him prone to a messy desk, lost paperwork, and constantly dropped pencils.

You may become aware of the problems from your child's complaints, or from your own contact with the teacher. The first thing you should do is to try to get a better sense of what is going on. If possible, volunteer to help out in class or at the school so that you will have an opportunity to observe how the teacher generally interacts with students. Seek out parents of your child's classmates or parents who have experience with the teacher from previous years to learn whether other students have similar problems. Talk to other school staff members, such as a guidance counselor or the school principal, to see whether they can offer any insights.

Handling a Personality Conflict

If the problem seems to be unique to your child, keep in mind that your child's own behavior and response to the teacher may be part of the problem. There are many unintended behavioral aspects of dyslexia that teachers may wrongly attribute to insolence or disobedience. Behavior quirks such as classroom fidgeting, a speech impediment, or regularly forgetting to turn in homework may frustrate the teacher.

In some cases, you may be able to help by recognizing these issues and providing the teacher with information showing how the problems relate to your child's learning disability, as well as suggesting strategies to help address the issues. If the teacher won't listen to you, try to find someone else who may be able to approach the teacher in a nonthreatening manner. This may be another teacher in the school who knows and likes your child and who can offer the problem teacher some helpful hints.

Your child may not be aware of how his own behavior is affecting the teacher. If the teacher is not willing to change expectations, you cannot change your child, but you can help your child to develop greater insight. Talk to some of your child's classmates about specific incidents that your child has mentioned; the kids may be able to fill you in on missing details. Even if your child cannot change behavior that stems from his learning difference, it may help him to better understand why it is upsetting the teacher.

If you cannot resolve problems with the teacher, consider whether you and your child can live with the situation. If so, you can help your child develop better coping skills and show your child that you support him and sympathize with his predicament. Sometimes your child simply needs a sympathetic ear. If your child generally has a good attendance record, consider allowing him a few "mental health" days—days when you let him stay home from school and plan some fun activities together.

The Verbally Abusive Teacher

If your child seems very upset, or actively tries to avoid school, complaining of stomachaches or headaches or crying on the way to school, it may be a sign that the teacher is behaving in a verbally abusive manner. Although most teachers care about their students and treat them with respect, a few use emotional abuse as a means of exerting control. An abusive teacher may repeatedly threaten to tell parents of misbehavior or unsatisfactory work, reject your child or ridicule his work, allow other children to tease or harass your child, label your child as "dumb" or "stupid," or provide a continuous experience of failure by insisting that your child complete tasks that are beyond his capacity to fulfill.

 ESSENTIAL

The most common and pervasive effect of verbal abuse is negative self-image. Your child may say things like, "I'm stupid," or, "Nobody likes me." Or he may simply seem withdrawn, sullen, or depressed. The National Committee for the Prevention of Child Abuse defines emotional abuse as a pattern of behavior that attacks a child's sense of self-worth.

If you have reason to believe that the teacher is behaving in a verbally abusive manner toward your child, then you may simply need to find a way to get your child away from the teacher. These problems could arise with any child, but a child with learning differences is particularly vulnerable to suffering emotional damage from a teacher who treats her harshly. In some cases, you may be able to bolster your child's sense of self-worth with outside activities; perhaps help foster a positive relationship with another adult authority figure such as an athletic coach.

Don't be afraid to ask the school principal to intervene. If other parents have witnessed your child being mistreated, ask if they will write a letter for you to help document it—that way, it won't simply be your word against the teacher's. The principal may be able to arrange to transfer your child to another classroom for at least part of the school day. If not—or if the principal is not helpful or supportive—you may need to consider homeschooling for the remainder of the year or transferring your child to another school.

If it is not possible to get your child away from the teacher, try to arrange counseling for your child. There are many charitable organizations and agencies that can arrange free or low-cost counseling if you cannot afford to pay for a therapist. It is not your child's fault that he is subject to abuse; counseling can help build his self-esteem and develop better coping strategies. A therapist who understands the effects of emotional abuse on children will be able to help your child recognize what is happening and help him overcome some of the ill effects.

Fortunately, you will find that situations like this are rare. Although many teachers are far from perfect, most are willing to work with you if you treat them with respect and show a willingness to understand their needs and to compromise. It is far more common for problems to arise from honest misunderstandings than from ill intent. While you and your child may continue to feel frustrated, you usually can work toward improvements that will at least make the classroom tolerable for the remainder of the school year.

CHAPTER 13

Academic Barriers

E VEN THOUGH YOUR CHILD IS LEGALLY entitled
to protection from discrimination and may also qualify for
special education services, you will find that over the
years he will encounter many academic barriers at school. Some
will be major barriers, such as requirements that he perform successfully on standardized tests. Others will be less significant, and
focus on single or short-term classroom assignments, but may
nonetheless cause considerable frustration. This chapter will help
you anticipate some common problems and plan for them.

Speed Contests and Rote Learning

Unfortunately, a good deal of teaching in elementary school and
middle school involves rote memorization, often with an emphasis
on speed. Your child's dyslexia is not merely a reading issue; it
also is reflected in the speed with which he processes linguistic
information or translates his thoughts into written or oral expression. Even when your child knows an answer, he is likely to
freeze up, become forgetful, or make many mistakes when
under pressure to answer quickly.

Typically, your child will be expected to memorize
math facts and multiplication tables, usually quizzed in a
format emphasizing speed, such as the "mad minute"
where children are assessed based on how quickly they

can solve simple math problems. Your child will be given weekly lists of ten to twenty spelling words to master; as he grows older these will be replaced by vocabulary lists, with word definitions to memorize. Your child will be expected to memorize facts such as historical dates, state capitals, or lines of poetry or famous speeches.

 ESSENTIAL

Work with your child's teacher to help her understand that assignments which call for rote memorization of isolated facts are particularly difficult for your child. Your child will learn much better if she can study subjects in depth, and can relate facts to other knowledge that explains their significance. Encourage the teacher to provide alternative assignments related to the subject area that will give your child an opportunity to shine.

All of these tasks rely on strong verbal and linguistic skills. Even the rote memorization of math facts is a linguistic, not a mathematical, skill. None of these tasks is particularly important to your child's ultimate educational success: not only can your child figure out or look up this information if memory fails him, but the need to memorize many of these facts has been rendered obsolete by modern technology. This doesn't mean that these skills shouldn't be taught to those children who can easily master them—but it does mean that you should arrange modifications such as alternative assignments or extended time for your child.

School Privileges and Punishments

Even if your child has an IEP or a written 504 plan, you may find that he is denied privileges or punished in subtle ways at school because of his learning problems. For example, a teacher may allow all children who have finished all their classwork free time to play games every Friday afternoon; the other children may be sent to the library or a study hall to finish their assignments. Of course, your child never gets any free play time, as his slower reading speed and labored writing makes it impossible for him to complete assignments early. Similar difficulties may also lead to specific punishments, such as being held inside for recess, denied permission to attend a school assembly, or held after school. You may even find that your child is being punished or denied privileges by being forced to make up assignments that he missed because he was pulled out of class to work with the resource teacher.

 ESSENTIAL

Your child may not tell you about the day-to-day slights and inconveniences he suffers because of his dyslexia. He may not understand himself that many of his difficulties are directly related to his learning differences, and he may feel embarrassed about the treatment he endures at school or fear your disapproval if he confesses additional failings. Although frustrated, he may perceive the teacher's rules as "fair" because they are equally applied to other students, and may be reluctant to ask for special treatment.

In some cases, your child may suffer negative consequences because of problems that are not directly related to her reading ability. Many children with dyslexia have poor organizational skills; your daughter may habitually misplace her homework or forget to write down assignments. Her language processing issues may lead her to frequently misunderstand instructions or miss "hearing" them altogether. Your child's teacher may not understand how the reading problem relates to problems with focusing attention, listening, following instructions, or keeping track of deadlines and paperwork. You will need to work to educate the teacher about your child's limitations, and arrange for appropriate modifications in your child's IEP or 504 plan. You might point out to the teacher that her "rules" end up singling out the same students week after week for punishment or denial of privileges, and thus are not effective as incentives to change behavior. Arrange informal modifications that will give your child a chance to rectify the problems, such as reduced volume of work or the opportunity to work on finishing assignments over the weekend.

Helping with Organizational Skills

You should also work at home to help your child develop stronger organizational skills—an area often missed at school. Provide your child with a planner than he can use to track assignments; ask the teacher to check his planner each day or week to make sure that he has everything correctly noted. If the teacher is unwilling to help your child this way, help your child find a classroom buddy who can help track the homework—pick a child who is reliable, has good attendance and grades, and encourage your child to regularly check with his buddy to make sure he is on track. If your child is embarrassed to ask or has a hard time making friends, consider hiring the other child to be your child's "secretary"—for a few dollars a week you may gain a trusted ally for your own child.

 FACT

Your child may find an electronic diary or PDA more to his liking. You may be able to save money by buying a used model. Your child doesn't need a device with all the latest features—he just needs something that allows him to keep track of his work.

Help your child keep organized at home as well. Use a huge wall calendar in a prominent place in your home, such as the kitchen or dining area, to track appointments and events, including homework deadlines and reminders. Create a filing system using colored folders or binders to keep track of your child's work; keep this near his regular study area, and help him learn to keep his papers filed in the appropriate "to do" or subject folder, rather than left loose in his backpack or bedroom.

Also encourage your child to keep graded papers that have been returned to him in a file or folder for each subject, so he can review the papers later when preparing for exams. Sometimes teachers make mistakes and fail to record grades from completed work; when this happens, they often will not believe the protestations of a child who claims to have turned in work when there has been a history of missed assignments.

Use incentives at home to help keep your child on track, filling the gap where he may be denied privileges at school. Set more reasonable and smaller, short-term goals for your child. Organizational skills are partly a matter of habit, and habits must be practiced repeatedly over time before they become ingrained.

Grade Retention

If your child struggles in school, it is likely that at some point a teacher or school official will recommend that he be retained and repeat a grade. Grade retention is almost never a good idea for a child with dyslexia, as the possible negative consequences far outweigh the benefits. Dyslexia is not something that can be outgrown or cured by waiting for a child to mature; repeating the same curriculum a second time around will not help your child improve his basic skills.

What the Research Shows

Retention is far more likely to hurt your child than help him; this is especially true in the early elementary years. Dozens of research studies conducted over 25 years show that students who are retained because they are performing poorly usually fall even further behind over time. Children who are promoted despite concerns about their academic skills may still have difficulties, but their performance is usually somewhat better than their counterparts who have been retained.

Of course, statistics don't tell the whole story—some children do benefit from retention. However, researchers have found that the students who benefit usually have mastered reading skills and had been held back for other reasons, generally because of a large amount of absenteeism or a mid-year transfer to a new school. In other words, a student who is a capable learner but needs to make up for missed instruction may benefit from repeating a grade; a student with learning difficulties needs a different sort of help.

The long-term effects of grade retention can be devastating. Students who are retained for a year are more likely to drop out of school, even when compared to students with equally poor performance. Retention can also be emotionally traumatizing. In one study, 84 percent of retained first graders said they felt "bad" or "sad" or "upset" about the retention and many reported being teased by their peers. In another recent study, children indicated that they believed grade retention was the worst thing that could happen to them, even worse than losing a parent or going blind.

 FACT

Studies show that grade retention increases the likelihood that your child will not complete high school by as much as 40 percent; if your child is retained more than once, there is an almost 100 percent likelihood that he will later drop out.

Studies of middle and high school students also demonstrate a high social cost of retention; students who are old for their grade level reported higher levels of emotional distress, substance abuse, involvement with violence, and suicidal thoughts. No matter how well-intentioned, holding a child back a year can send the message that he is a failure and that the teachers do not believe him capable of keeping up with his peers.

When Retention Is Appropriate

The only time you should favor retention is when you have positive answers in your own mind to the questions "What will be different in the coming year?" and "What plan is in place that will help my child learn in the coming year?" If retention will make your child eligible for services that she cannot receive with promotion—for example, if promotion means moving on to a different school site or if there is a specialized program only available to children in certain grade levels—the prospect may be more appealing.

One consideration that may favor retention is if your child will be placed with a specific teacher that you feel is particularly well-qualified to help your child, either because of the teacher's reputation or because of specialized training she may have. Consider your child's feelings as well: in some cases, a child may prefer retention because of fears or uncertainty about her ability to perform in the next grade. While such fears should not be the sole consideration, often children have a valid basis for their concerns that should be explored.

You may also consider retention if your child is moving to a new school where the curriculum or standards are somewhat different—in that case, while the child may stay at the same grade level, he is not truly "repeating" a grade. This situation is common when children move from public to private schools, as many private schools have a more demanding curriculum. Some parents have also found it valuable to delay entrance into middle school or high school for a year, home schooling their child in the interim. Because of social ramifications, this choice should only be made when the child agrees to the plan.

Alternatives to Retention

The best alternative to retention is appropriate, specialized help for your child's learning difficulties combined with appropriate modifications and support to enable your child to keep up in academic subjects other than reading. If your child already has an IEP, it may be appropriate to review the IEP and reconsider the goals set and the specific educational services being provided, rather than hold your child back.

Kindergarten and Entering First Grade

If retention is suggested because of your child's poor reading skills or apparent lack of reading readiness, you should immediately ask that your child be assessed if she has not already been diagnosed with a learning disability. Do not accept the teacher's opinion that your child is merely immature or needs an extra year—even if the teacher turns out to be right, the apparent need for retention is a red flag that your child should be evaluated. Follow the procedures outlined in Chapter 10 to request and obtain special education services through the school.

If your child is still in kindergarten, consider both his actual age and social fit. Although the practice of holding children back to repeat a year of kindergarten is very common in many districts, there is no research evidence proving that this well help. However, many of the studies reporting long-term deleterious effects of retention focus on the child being old for his grade. If your child is one of the younger children in his class, there may be no harm in repeating kindergarten, particularly if he seems socially immature or unready for the behavioral expectations of first-grade.

However, it is still important that your child be evaluated for learning disabilities. Keep in mind that some early intervention strategies—particularly phonemic awareness training—seem to lose effectiveness if delayed past the age of seven. Find out what services your school offers to first-grade students, and ask whether your child can receive the services with a repeated year that he might also get if promoted.

Beyond First Grade

At first-grade level and above, you should not agree to retention based on concerns about your child's academic skill level if your child will simply be repeating the same curriculum in the same basic setting. Your child does not need more of the same instruction; he needs a different approach. Tutoring and remedial teaching can be provided to a promoted child as easily as it can to a retained child, and your child is likely to be more motivated and engaged in school if being introduced to new material.

One alternative to retention is to place your child in a transitional classroom with an enriched curriculum designed to lead to double promotion, with the intent that after the transitional year she will catch up with her age cohorts. It is possible that even without such a classroom, an IEP could be written to effectively serve the same goals.

 FACT

The National Association of School Psychologists strongly cautions against grade retention, and recommends that struggling students be promoted along with a plan of special interventions, accommodations, and services geared to the specific academic areas where they are struggling.

In some schools, you may be able to arrange partial acceleration or retention—that is, a combined approach where your child moves on to the next grade for some or all subjects, but leaves the classroom to work with the lower grade for areas where there are specific skill deficits, usually reading or arithmetic. This should not be used in lieu of specialized remedial help, but is something to consider if it is clear that your child will not be able to keep up even with accommodations with isolated subject areas.

Some elementary schools have mixed-age, ungraded or combined grade classrooms. Often, such schools have overlapping grades—for example, one classroom may have a grade 4/5 combination, with a 5/6 grade combination in another classroom. In such a setting, the decision to keep your child with the "lower" graded combination is not the same as retention—teachers in this environment are used to having students for more than one year and to teaching a varied curriculum. If your child has been doing well with a particular teacher in this type of environment, he may benefit from staying with that teacher another year. Conversely, if he has not been doing well, it may be time for a change, even if it seems illogical to push the child into the more difficult level.

High-Stakes Testing

High-stakes testing is the practice of using a single, standardized test to make important decisions about a student's education, usually whether the child will be promoted to the next grade or be allowed to graduate from high school. Such tests tend to work in a discriminatory fashion against students with dyslexia, both because of the content of the test and the method of assessment. At least through eighth-grade level, these tests almost always are focused largely on appraising reading and math skills; by definition, a child with dyslexia can be expected to have poor reading skills. But even after gaining skills, the timed, multiple-choice format works against students who have a history of dyslexia; many such students become capable readers and strong students but continue to perform poorly on standardized tests. Thus, the high-stakes test is a double barrier for your child.

School Pressures for Testing

Many states and individual school districts impose strict testing and grade retention policies because of political or social pressure to increase standards among their students. The practice of social promotion—promoting children to maintain age/grade level regardless of level of achievement—can lead to children being passed from one level to the next in school without learning anything. Obviously, this is not an acceptable outcome for any child. However, retention policies do nothing to improve the quality of teaching.

The federal No Child Left Behind Act creates additional pressures that may tend to encourage schools to retain children who perform poorly on standardized tests. The law is intended to provide greater opportunities to children in failing schools. In order to measure school performance, the law mandates nationwide annual standardized testing in grades three through eight. Schools are penalized and parents gain the right to transfer their students from schools that fail to meet yearly progress goals. Unfortunately, these penalties increase the pressure on schools to raise test scores by any means necessary; one way to do this is to hold back the students who do not test well. This tactic may not help the child, but it will ensure that he isn't in the testing pool of the promoted class to bring scores down the following year.

Misuses of Standardized Tests

Unfortunately, schools often misuse standardized tests to make grade retention decisions, applying their results for purposes where they are not valid. The most common problem is using the same norm-referenced test geared to test school performance to measure individual achievement. These tests are designed to provide a good statistical sampling of how a particular school's students score when measured against typical students. However, the norm-referenced tests developed for assessing school performance are not valid as a measure of individual achievement. In some cases, they may contain questions about material that has not been covered in your child's school. While it is valid to criticize the school for failing to teach content appropriate for each grade level, it is not appropriate to draw conclusions about your child's abilities based on subject areas where he may not have received adequate instruction.

 **QUESTION?**

What is a norm-referenced test?
A norm-referenced test compares a student's score against the scores of a group of students who have already taken the same exam, called the "norming group." Some widely used tests are the California Achievement Test (CAT); Comprehensive Test of Basic Skills (CTBS); Iowa Test of Basic Skills (ITBS) and Tests of Academic Proficiency (TAP); Metropolitan Achievement Test (MAT); and Stanford Achievement Test (SAT).

Even on subject matter that has been covered in class, the group norm-referenced test is ordinarily not designed to measure individual ability or achievement. In many cases, missing a single question can cause a big change in an individual student's percentile rank. The designers of these tests try to choose questions that are useful to sort students along a curve. Many items that most students in a grade level would be expected to know are not tested, and questions may be deliberately designed to focus on more obscure knowledge, in order to help rank the students. Thus, there is too much left to chance—and too much material that is not included in the test—for the test to give a good picture of your child's abilities.

When the test results of many students are considered cumulatively, as is done to measure school performance, individual variation loses significance and the tests can give a good general picture of how well the students at the particular school perform in comparison to nationally expected averages. But when the same test is used to measure your child, the test is simply being misused.

Further, on a test of reading achievement, it is unfair and unreasonable to expect your child with dyslexia to score well against a norm-referenced standard. By definition, children with dyslexia will score significantly below average for reading skills—in fact, it is likely that your child only qualifies for services at your school by virtue of such low skills. The concept of "grade level reading" is by itself an expression of a norm, or average; it reflects what the typical, or midrange, student is expected to be able to achieve at each grade. It is neither reasonable nor possible to expect that every child will perform at or above average; statistics make that goal impossible.

It is a reasonable goal to expect a child with dyslexia to eventually achieve reading proficiency; many will, in fact, become good readers. It is not reasonable to expect your child to read the same as a "normal" child at the same age or to somehow radically increase his performance when measured against other students within a single year.

Thus, your child's reading achievement should be measured using criterion-based tests—that is, tests that measure many skill areas without referencing how your child's performance compares with others.

CHAPTER 14

Teaching Reading at Home

Y OU MAY WANT TO TRY TEACHING your child at home. This may be a good choice if you feel that his school provides a positive learning environment, but you feel that the reading instruction is not enough. Alternatively, you may want to homeschool your child, perhaps for a short period to help him catch up in school or as an alternative choice to formal schooling. This chapter will provide a guide to some of the issues you will face and includes additional suggestions for helping your child become a reader.

Deciding to Homeschool

Many parents feel they can best meet the needs of their children through homeschooling. If you choose to homeschool, you will be able to provide your child with the individualized attention that is so important for a child with dyslexia, and create an educational plan that fits his needs exactly. You will be able to afford your child the extra time he needs to master subjects and skills that are difficult for him and allow him to forge ahead in his areas of strength. Your child will not face the humiliation or daily frustration of classroom failure. However, homeschooling takes work, and it isn't the ideal situation for every family. For your child with dyslexia, you will need to consider carefully whether you can successfully take on the dual role of parent and teacher, knowing that your child may present some unique challenges.

If you did well in school as a child, and are the type of person who enjoys reading and solves problems in a logical, rational fashion, you may find that it sometimes seems as if your child with dyslexia comes from another planet. Your child's style of learning and communication may be very different from yours, and you may find that your attempts to explain new concepts in the simplest, most direct fashion you can imagine leave your child totally baffled.

 FACT

In 1999, an estimated 850,000 students nationwide, or almost 2 percent of all students, were being homeschooled. Four out of five of these students were homeschooled only, and one out of five were enrolled in public or private schools part time. Homeschooling families have a greater percentage of both gifted students as well as students with learning disabilities than the national average.

Ingredients for Success

In order to succeed in homeschooling your child with dyslexia, you will need to live by three rules: patience, flexibility, and fun. Patience means the willingness to give your child the time she needs to explore and master a subject, even if that means that a lesson you think should take twenty minutes ends up spread over many days or weeks.

Flexibility means the willingness to learn new things and change approaches. You may have decided to homeschool out of dissatisfaction with the reading methods or curriculum used in the local public school. Perhaps after doing your own research, you think you have figured out what type of instruction your child needs, and realized that you can do a better job than the school is doing. Armed with your knowledge and your firm commitment to help your child, you purchase the books you know he needs and get to work . . . only to find that your home-based lessons are a disaster, invariably ending in shouting and tears. Flexibility means simply that you must be ready to change course, to try new things, to back off at times, to listen to your child, and observe him in an effort to let his interests and inclinations guide you, until you discover your own child's best learning strategies and ways to accommodate them.

Fun means that you need to always keep your sense of humor, and always mix the work of learning with play. Be creative: Use games, puzzles, songs, rhymes, or physical activity. You are bound to have good days and bad days. If you can't see the light side of things, the task of helping your child on the bad days may simply overwhelm you. Your child is entitled to have a parent who provides unconditional love and support; he will not be helped by seeing disappointment or anger in your eyes when he falters or stumbles.

Have Faith in Yourself

Once you decide to homeschool, you will need to have faith in yourself. Invariably, if your child's reading is delayed, you will encounter criticism from friends, neighbors, and other family members. Some may blame you for your child's difficulties, suggesting that it is your bad teaching or overindulgence of your child that has caused him to lag behind. Others may offer well-meaning but misguided advice or suggestions. If you decide to delay reading instruction until you feel your child is developmentally ready, someone is bound to admonish you, citing the importance of early intervention. On the other hand, if you decide to start very early with a structured approach, you are sure to hear from someone that you are pushing your child too hard. You need to understand simply that these sorts of comments come with the territory of homeschooling, and learn to graciously ignore unwanted advice.

However, don't be afraid to seek help or advice with your child's reading problems from an outsider. If you feel that you are overwhelmed or have reached a wall trying to teach your child, it may be time to seek professional therapy or tutoring. In some communities, your child may be eligible to receive home-based services from the local school district or to participate in remedial reading programs at the school; policies vary considerably from one state to another with respect to homeschoolers. Sometimes it helps to pool resources with another homeschooler, who may be able to help your child with a fresh approach. Even a tutor with minimal experience, such as a high school student in your neighborhood, may give you and your child a welcome break from each other and help build your child's motivation.

Choosing a Curriculum

There is a wide array of educational and curriculum materials available to homeschoolers. In planning for your child, keep in mind the importance of teaching to your child's strengths through multisensory and participatory methods. It may be tempting to purchase textbooks and workbooks specifically designed for homeschoolers, but most of these materials are not designed to reach children with divergent learning styles. You will either want to supplement such materials or focus on using materials geared for children with visual or kinesthetic learning styles.

 ALERT!

Before you start, check to find out what the legal requirements are in your state for homeschooling. Some states have strict requirements about teaching qualifications, have strict recordkeeping requirements, require you to adhere to specific curriculum requirements, and/or require you to report on your child's progress using standardized tests; in other states, regulation is minimal.

When it comes to teaching reading, there are many methods, kits, and books to choose from. Homeschoolers of struggling readers report a high level of success by following the approaches outlined in the book *Reading Reflex*, by Carmen and Geoffrey McGuinness, which details the PhonoGraphix approach to teaching reading; or *The Gift of Dyslexia*, by Ron Davis, which explains the key elements of the Davis Dyslexia Correction program. These are two very different approaches, but both books provide detailed instructions for how to use and apply the methods.

Many homeschoolers like Avko Sequential Spelling, which teaches spelling patterns through a word-family approach, such as a beginning lesson including the word set: *in, pin, sin, spin, kin,* or a word-building approach that lets a child progress from *all* to *tall, stall, install,* and *installment*. A popular program for teaching math concepts is the manipulative-based Math-U-See curriculum.

 ESSENTIAL

Don't allow your child's reading problem to monopolize your time at home. Even if you have decided to homeschool only for a short time, in order to work on building your child's reading skills, be sure that your lesson plans include plenty of opportunities to explore other areas of learning, especially those that are of high interest to your child.

If possible, it is best to integrate different types of skill learning with in-depth exploration of a topic or subject area, also including fun activities such as art or construction projects. Cooking projects are a great way to introduce and apply basic math concepts (counting and measuring) and to start learning about science. Literature can be enhanced with projects, play-acting, and activities geared to exploring history, geography, and science themes raised in the book.

Motivating Your Child

At its best, homeschooling is a rewarding experience for both parent and child, allowing your child the opportunity to fully explore his interests and develop his potential. You may prefer to "unschool"—to follow your child's lead, allowing him the opportunity and resources to learn in his own way and in his own time, without trying to set external goals, stick to a predefined curriculum, or use formal instruction to teach skills. Unschooling can be a welcome break for a child who has been under stress and has lost confidence in himself because of negative school experiences, but in some cases, it can also allow a struggling reader to fall further behind. In a home where information is readily available through TV or multimedia Internet formats, your child may have little inclination to put in effort to learn a skill that is elusive.

Some children simply lose interest in gaining skills without the external pressures of deadlines, assigned reading, tests, and grades that might compel a school child to put in extra effort to develop reading, writing, and spelling skills. Each child is different; some thrive in an atmosphere where they are free to follow their own inclinations, but others simply need more structure and external prodding. To be successful at homeschooling, you need to make sure that your own parenting style meshes with well with your child's personality. Observe your child and his progress. Be ready to allow him to follow a different path, but at the same time be willing to add structure or increase demands if your child seems unfocused.

Building Early Literacy Skills

Before your child begins to read, he must know what the words mean, and he needs to have a sense of the grammatical structure and flow of language. Because children with dyslexia tend to be highly visual learners, they often miss the finer points of language as they are growing up. Your child may seem to speak well and easily understand what you say, but most oral communication is also accompanied by gestures and other visual clues; conversation involves an exchange of ideas often communicated in short bursts or partial sentences, and adults are careful to use a simplified vocabulary, with short words and active sentence structure, when talking to children. So, your child may very well grow up with very strong communication skills but nonetheless have weak language skills. The best thing you can do to help your child to prepare for reading is to help boost both understanding of language and encourage development of stronger listening skills.

Read to Your Preschooler

You should begin reading to your child as early as possible, and continue the practice for as long as your child is willing to sit still and listen to you. When you read aloud, you help your child develop a love of literature; you model the process of reading for her and you expose her to an enriched vocabulary and more sophisticated and complex language structures. Even after your child begins to read on her own, you will be able to enhance her enjoyment of reading and improve motivation by continuing to read aloud, allowing her to share in reading some selections along the way.

Read from a variety of children's books, and include classic stories such as *The Velveteen Rabbit*, fairy tales, picture books, and poetry. Make reading a regular part of your day, perhaps as part of a bedtime ritual. Hold your child in your lap or have her sit next to you on a couch or large chair so that you can see the book together.

 ESSENTIAL

When reading a book where the print is large, point at each word as you read. This will help your child learn that reading goes from left to right and understand how the printed words correspond to the words you speak. Answer any questions your child has about the words and letters.

As you read, take the time to discuss the meanings of new words and to point out an interesting use of phrasing or elements such as rhyme or alliteration. Encourage your child to talk about the events of the story and to predict what may happen next. Read some books written in verse to focus your child's attention on the rhythm of language as well as rhyme. Choose some books with repetitive phrases or themes; read your child's favorite books over and over again. Help make the stories come alive for your child. If you can instill a love of literature, your child's strong motivation to read will help overcome difficulties that may be the result of dyslexia.

Limit TV

Limit your young child's exposure to TV, and monitor what he watches. Unfortunately, TV does very little to help small children with language, and too many hours in front of the TV can undermine development of strong language skills. A small child is much more likely to pay attention to images on screen and follow the action by focusing on what the actors or cartoon characters do, rather than attending to dialogue. The rapid pace and frequent scene changes, along with frequent commercial interruptions, conditions your child to respond quickly to stimulus, which does little to help lengthen attention span. Since he cannot talk to the actors on screen, your child does not get any of the feedback or practice that he might have with ordinary conversation with an adult or older child.

 **FACT**

Programs like *Sesame Street* are fun for a child to watch, but will not promote literacy in a child prone to dyslexia—the rapid-fire presentation of letters in isolation and in random order simply sends the wrong message about words and print. You can help your child by watching programs together and then discussing the story lines and events you see.

Teaching Pre-Reading Skills

Help your child focus on the sounds of words through nursery rhymes and song lyrics. Introduce your child to the idea of rhyming, and encourage him in playful conversation to make up his own rhymes. Sing songs like "Down by the Bay" ("Did you ever see a moose / Kissing a goose?") and help your child invent his own lyrics. Help your child focus on smaller word segments and phonemes by playing games with the sounds of the words; teach songs like "Apples and Bananas" ("I like to eat, eat, eat, eat / apples and bananas / I like to ate, ate, ate, ate / ay-ples and bay-nay-nays").

Include songs and games that involve clapping, jumping, and other movements to music. This will help your child develop a stronger sense of the rhythm of language and may help development of skills related to right/left bodily coordination or timing that are implicated in dyslexia.

 ESSENTIAL

Encourage games and activities that involve sorting and organizing items, as well as practice with order and sequence. Help your child develop an awareness of temporal sequence (beginning/middle/end), as well as spatial relationships (above/below, over/under, in/out, left/right). Your child can explore these concepts while playing with blocks, putting away toys, or helping to set the table.

When your child is very young, gently introduce the habit of visually scanning or counting objects from left to right. For example, you might line up a row of toys and hold his hand to count each one, beginning with the left side and moving toward the right. You can begin this even before the child knows the difference between left and right; the idea is to try to create a habit of always beginning from the left and moving to the right, in the hope that will make the transition to reading easier.

Learning Letters

Introduce your child to letters by teaching both the sound and the name of each letter. The letters do not need to be taught in order, but it is important that a young child associates a letter such as *K* with both its sound (kuh) and its name ("kay"). You may want to start by helping your child learn the letters in his own name, and then move on to names of other family members. Show your child how each letter relates to the sounds in the name, but do not try to drill or teach a very young child to apply that information in other contexts. For example, you might point to each letter in the name Kevin and say the sound; you might even show your child how that name contains the word "in" and later remind him of that pattern when showing him rhyming words like "bin" or "tin." With a very young child, keep these "lessons" casual, as things that you mention when the occasion arises. You want your child to start to understand the idea that letters represent sounds and that words are composed by combining the sounds in an orderly way; formal instruction can wait until your child starts school.

Draw your child's attention to different letters on signs and in print, such a words on the front of cereal boxes. Encourage him to make his own letters by molding them with clay or playdough, and supply toys such as magnetic letters that allow him to move and touch the letters.

Never push your young child to learn something he seems to have difficulty with. It is cute when a preschooler has learned to sing his ABCs, but if he doesn't have a clue as to what each letter looks like or that letters represent sounds, it is not going to help him read. Once frustration sets in, your child is not likely to learn from the experience.

Supporting the School-Age Reader

Your child with dyslexia probably has experienced great difficulty learning to read at school; even after your child has mastered the basics, he may read slowly and laboriously, with considerable effort. If your child is receiving intensive remedial instruction at school, you should focus efforts at home on making reading a fun and pleasurable activity—this will help build and sustain motivation and build a familiarity with literature that will support development of advanced comprehension skills.

Reading With Your Child

Continue to read aloud to your child at home. When reading for pleasure, allow your struggling reader to relax and listen attentively without being expected to read. You should still encourage your child to sit next to you, so he can see the pages of the book as you read. If you are helping your child with a book that must be read for school, encourage your child to participate by taking turns reading; you can ask your child to read a sentence or a paragraph, then read several paragraphs yourself, then let your child have another turn.

In books with a lot of dialogue, another technique for shared reading is to let your child take the role of one (or more) of the characters, reading the quoted words for that character. This is also a good opportunity to help your child focus on punctuation, such as quotation marks, commas, periods, exclamation points, and question marks. Many children with dyslexia do not understand what punctuation means, and they tend to ignore or disregard punctuation marks when reading because they are so focused on trying to decipher the letters and words. With oral reading, punctuation takes on added significance, as it provides information about when the reader should pause and the intonation that should be used.

When your child is reading aloud, do not interrupt to correct mistakes that do not change meaning, such as reading "mom" for "mother." Frequent interruptions will cause your child to lose confidence and make comprehension more difficult. If your child stumbles over a word, simply tell her what it is. Do not try to use teaching techniques such as having her sound out words at this time. Instead, enjoy the story together, discuss the plot, and praise your child for her efforts when she reads aloud and is able to figure out some words on her own.

Teaching Reading Skills

If you are working with your child to try to teach reading or supplement instruction at school, do the "lessons" at a separate time—and with different books—than reading for pleasure or to gain experience. Oral and shared reading should be used to build fluency and comprehension skills; that simply cannot be combined successfully with teaching the mechanics of reading and decoding.

ALERT!

If you are satisfied with the quality of instruction your child receives at school, do not try to supplement with lessons, drills, or practice basic skills at home unless your child's teacher asks for such support. Otherwise, you run the risk of overwhelming your child and confusing him with conflicting information.

If your child is in school but is not receiving specialized reading instruction or if you are not happy with the methods being used, you may choose to tutor your child on your own. Make sure that your child wants to learn from you; if your child feels overwhelmed and exhausted from his efforts each day at school, he may need your loving support and a chance to relax far more than he needs more lessons.

If you are teaching your child on your own, you will probably want to use some of the methods and techniques profiled in Chapters 6 and 7, using books or kits developed for home use. Try to choose a single method, starting with one that seems comfortable for you and easy to implement; mixing more than one approach at the beginning can simply cause greater confusion. If your child does not seem to be making progress after several weeks, or seems to reach a plateau or barrier after several months, you can then consider moving on to a different method.

If your child is in school and you are teaching at home using different techniques, explain to your child that there is more than one way to figure out words. Point out that you are going to teach or practice a different strategy than the one his teacher uses.

Explain that he should use the time with you to practice the new strategy, but when he reads on his own he should use whichever is easiest for him.

If your child has difficulty with sounding out by sequentially blending separate word sounds, such as putting the sounds of /b/, /a/, and /t/ together to make "bat," you might try an alternate approach of teaching—onset and rimes. This involves focusing attention on the beginning sound (onset) of a word or syllable, and then teaching the remaining single-syllable sound combination (rime) as a whole. For example, in the word "bat" the onset is /b/, while the rime is "at." Knowing the "at" rime will make it easier for your child to learn cat, hat, rat, and so on.

 FACT

> Your child may find it helpful to hold an index card or ruler under each line of text as he reads. This will help him stay focused on the text. It is also possible to purchase a reading guide with a colored filter in the center, which is designed so that your child can move it down the page as he reads.

Observe your child to see what sort of words give him the most trouble, and to see what sort of strategies he typically uses for decoding. Use common sense so that you can make practical suggestions, geared to the types of problems he is having and the type of words he is trying to read. Keep in mind that once your child is able to read at first- or second-grade level, he will encounter more words that are phonetically irregular, and will need to learn other skills beyond simply phonetic decoding to progress. You may be able to help him improve reading skills by learning to look for familiar letter patterns, to break words down into syllables or word segments, or to recognize common roots and affixes. Teach him to look at the whole word before starting to decode; he may recognize a familiar pattern or segment toward the end or the word that will make word recognition easier.

Games and Software to Build Reading Skills

Your child may be able to learn from educational games, toys, and software geared to building basic reading skills. Skill-building software such as the "Reader Rabbit" series is not designed to help with dyslexia, but there is no harm in your child using the software, as long as your child seems to enjoy working with it. The same is true for any game, whether it is a game specifically designed to teach reading skills, such as The Phonics Game, or a game that incorporates word play, such as Boggle or Scrabble. Many children with dyslexia enjoy doing puzzles and may be able to gain reading and decoding practice with games.

However, it is a mistake to force your child to play or work with a game that he finds frustrating. The value of presenting information in the form of a game is that your child is more receptive to learning when he is relaxed and having fun, and he may be more motivated if he stands a chance of winning the game or improving his score. But this purpose is defeated if the game makes your child feel discouraged or inadequate. You may be able to make the game more palatable by changing the rules or the way that you use the game; but if your child still balks, put the game away.

Chapter 15

Helping with Homework

I N ADDITION TO PROBLEMS WITH READING, your child is likely to have difficulty in a number of school subjects. Some of the problems will be directly related to the reading difficulty; he may have difficulty keeping up with textbook reading or with completing writing assignments in any subject. Most likely you will find that daily homework assignments are particularly frustrating. This chapter explores some of the strategies and techniques you can use to help manage the load and steer your child toward success.

Taming the Homework Dragon

Homework can often become a family battleground, with your child's efforts to complete even routine assignments regularly leading to hours of frustration that invariably end in tears or tantrums. When you try to help your child, you may find that you simply end up arguing, resorting to threats and punishment out of your own frustration. Home life is disrupted as your child's homework demands keep him up well past his expected bedtime, and take away time that you can relax with your spouse and your other children.

There is only one solution: Don't let homework manage you. You need to set limits and stick to them, both with your child and with the teacher. The purpose of homework is to help your child learn; if it is not fulfilling that purpose, then it simply is not worth the stress that it can cause.

Setting Limits on Study Time

Ask your child's teacher how long she expects her students to spend on homework each night. One good rule of thumb is ten minutes for every grade in school—so a fourth grader may have forty minutes of homework, a sixth grader an hour. Your own child's teacher may expect something more or less. If the teacher gives you a time range that you feel is reasonable—tell her how much time your child is actually spending. The teacher may be stunned to learn that a routine assignment that she expected would take twenty minutes actually takes three hours to complete at your home.

Ask for Modifications

Explain what aspects of the assignments cause difficulty for your child, and ask if the assignments can be modified to better meet your child's abilities and eliminate sticking points. For example, some teachers may insist that children copy out the questions in a book as well as writing the answers. A modification to allow your child to provide answers only may immediately cut homework time in half.

 ESSENTIAL

A teacher may object to revising homework assignments on the grounds that it is not fair to other students. Remind the teacher that your child has a disability that makes it harder for him to do the same work as the other children. Fair doesn't mean giving every child the same thing, but giving every child what he needs. To be fair, you have to treat a child with learning differences differently.

An easy timesaver is simply to reduce the number or length of assignments. If there are thirty multiplication problems on the page, perhaps your child can do ten. If the teacher wants a five-paragraph essay, perhaps your child can write two paragraphs.

Set a Time Limit

Whatever modifications you can agree on, also include a time limit. Tell the teacher that you will monitor your child to make sure he puts in effort on homework, and if he is unable to complete the assignment, you will send a note indicating how much time was spent. Ask the teacher to accept partially completed homework if a minimum agreed time has been spent, to give your child credit for doing his homework, and to at least give your child a passing grade.

At home, make sure that your child has a place to do his homework that is free of distractions and where all materials he needs (pens, pencils, paper) are at hand. This should also be a place where you can observe and monitor your child to make sure he is focused on homework. If he is working with a computer, make sure you can see the screen; otherwise, you may find that your son has achieved record high scores with *Tetris* but failed to even open the word processing program.

Reach an agreement with your child about the total time to be spent on homework, including the time he will start and the time he must finish. Use a kitchen timer to keep track of how long your child has been working. If your child has a hard time sustaining attention or sitting still, break up the session with opportunities to relax, stretch, and move around; stop and restart the timer as needed to keep track of actual time worked.

When your child has worked for the requisite time, tell him that his time is up and you are ready to write the note to the teacher. If your child wants to continue working and he seems to be working at a good pace without frustration, allow him to do so— but remind him that he is allowed to quit at any time. However, do not allow your young child to work beyond the hour that is your family deadline for completing homework, usually the time when your child must start getting ready for bed. Give your child a warning about 10 minutes before that time, and suggest that he set his alarm early to complete work in the morning if he protests. Your child's bedtime should be age-appropriate, but it should also be firm.

 **FACT**

Sleep is essential to learning. During sleep, information and experiences learned during the day become integrated into long-term memory. Thus, it is counterproductive for a child to forego sleep in order to study; he may finish the assignment, but he will weaken his ability to remember and understand the content. Rest is particularly important to children with dyslexia, as their performance deteriorates markedly under conditions of stress or fatigue.

There is one exception to the bedtime rule: If your child ever becomes actively engaged in a task that has always been difficult for him, don't fight success. There may come a time when something seems to click for your child, and for the first time in his life he becomes absorbed in reading a book or excited about a poem or a story he is writing. If and when this happens, rejoice. Thomas Edison said, "Genius is one percent inspiration and ninety-nine percent perspiration"—don't get in the way of the inspiration when you see it. You can reinstate the rules later on.

Setting Priorities for Schoolwork

Help your child learn to set priorities for his schoolwork. Some of your child's homework is probably easy for her; some is quite difficult. Some requires her to do things that she doesn't enjoy, but some tasks might be fun. Some of the homework is important to help your child master a particular skill or learn required material; some is mere busywork, assigned mostly for the sake of having the child do something.

Your job is to help your child learn to sort her work so that homework can be completed in the most efficient manner possible. When your child is very young, this may means that you make the decisions for her; as she grows older, she will better be able to make these choices on her own.

Encourage your child to complete all assignments that are easy or fun whether or not they seem useful. Typically, an art project might fit this category. If the project is likely to absorb your child's interest for a long time, have him begin work on it after the more difficult work is completed.

 **FACT**

One bright third grader with dyslexia asked his teacher to allow him to write one sentence containing all twelve weekly spelling words, rather than a separate sentence for each word. The boy enjoyed the challenge of trying to pack all the words in the list into one or two very silly sentences, and the teacher looked forward to reading the very creative and often amusing results. What had once been frustrating was turned into a fun and challenging game.

Difficult work should be attempted only if it is educationally useful to your child. That is, if the assignment seems to be busy work with no apparent purpose, do not force your child to complete it; instead, ask the teacher the purpose of the assignment. Understanding the purpose will provide a guide for development of appropriate modifications. If the assignment seems to be useful for other children but doesn't help your child—look for an alternative that will achieve the same goal. For example, a teacher may ask that a child write a separate sentence for each word on a spelling list, with the idea that this will help children know the meaning of the words and give them writing practice. For your child, sentence-writing may be so overwhelming that there is no time left to study and learn the spelling words; your child might do better to focus on studying and writing the individual spelling words, and dictating sentences or writing short definitions instead.

You and your child might also find the task of managing homework easier if the teacher provides a weekly assignments sheet listing all homework to be completed by the end of the week, rather than ask for separate assignments each day. This will help you plan for assignments that are likely to be more time consuming by spreading the work out over several days.

Working Effectively with Your Child

Learn to work effectively with your child when helping with homework. Offer help, but don't take over, and by all means do not do the homework for your child. To work effectively, it is important that you are able to communicate well with your child, and that you are able to supply useful strategies to help him overcome barriers.

The first step of good communication is to be able to listen well—do not argue or chastise your child when he says that a task is "too hard" or that he can't understand what the teacher wants. Instead, ask questions to try to find out what is giving him trouble. Keep in mind that children with dyslexia often have difficulty making sense of ordinary language, and your child may need to have an instruction or concept explained or illustrated several different ways before he can understand it.

When helping your child, keep the goals of the homework assignment in mind. If your struggling reader is asked to read and answer questions about a section in his history book, the goal is to learn about history, not reading and writing. In that case, it is fine for you to help by reading the chapter and the questions to your son, even letting him dictate answers to you if he also has problems with writing.

However, if your child's resource teacher wants him to build fluency by reading a story at home, he needs to do the reading on his own. You can help by sitting next to him as he reads, helping him recognize words that are difficult for him and listening to him practice reading aloud. When the goal is reading practice, then it is more important that your child work for an appropriate amount of time than to finish the assignment; you can send a note to the teacher letting her know how far your son was able to progress.

It may be useful to have your child work with a sibling or friend for some of her homework. If she is working with another child, observe from a distance to ensure that the children seem to be getting along well and are offering help and suggestions without taking over and doing the work themselves. Your child may feel more highly motivated and be more ready to accept constructive criticism from a peer. In some cases, a younger sibling who is reading at close to your child's level may be a good study partner.

You may want to hire an older child or teenager to help your child. You shouldn't expect a teenager to have the same skills as an adult teacher or use this as a substitute for getting quality tutoring for your child; rather, look simply for someone who can establish a good rapport with your child and can work cooperatively with him to help complete assignments.

Group Projects

From time to time, your child may be assigned to work with other children to complete a group project. While it is good for children to learn to work cooperatively, it is often the case that one or two children in a group end up doing most of the work and feel frustrated and resentful of those who cannot contribute much to the effort. Of course, your child with dyslexia is likely to be the one who bears the brunt of that resentment.

The group project is a good occasion to help your own child recognize her particular strengths and talents and to help the other children develop a greater appreciation of those abilities. Encourage the children to assign roles and responsibilities that will build on each of their talents. For example, one group of sixth graders were assigned to prepare a class presentation on African history. Two highly verbal girls in the group immediately divided up topics and got busy researching and writing their own sections. They quickly became frustrated with the third member of their team, a boy with dyslexia who seemed to take little interest in the project, and shared their anger with a parent. The mom asked what kind of things the boy was interested in, and was told that he liked music and art. The mom then asked, "Did the people in Africa have music? What kind of instruments did they use? What kind of artwork did they create?" The group quickly recognized that music and art were indeed important aspects of understanding African history, and the boy was assigned to find books with African artwork at the library and to create music for their class presentation. He quickly became the most enthusiastic member of their team and their colorful class presentation, presented to the background beat of an African drum, was a huge success.

 ESSENTIAL

If your child is tense and frustrated while doing his homework, take a break. You may have to structure homework sessions to include frequent, short breaks for your child. Have him do something physical, like stretching or bouncing a ball, to relieve pent-up energy.

These same principles can be used in almost every context. It will help your child for you to find ways to express his talents, and it will help his peers to realize that there is more to learning than simply reading and writing about topics. Of course the book learning is important, too, but the group project should be an occasion for exploring other ways for your child to contribute.

Using Technology

Computers are your child's best friend. The sooner your child learns to use a word processing program, the better off he will be. The word processing program will eliminate a good deal of the frustration that makes writing difficult for individuals with dyslexia. It will eliminate the mechanical barriers your child faces—poor penmanship, bad spelling—enabling him to showcase his ideas through his writing. Although your child may encounter resistance to producing typewritten assignments in elementary years, by the time he reaches high school his teachers will expect all significant written work to be typed; at the college level, he is likely to bypass the printer altogether and frequently submit work via disk, CD, or e-mail.

Word Processing Programs

There are many software programs available to help a young child learn keyboarding skills. While typing is generally a slow process for very young children, it may still be more efficient for your child with dyslexia to use a hunt-and-peck approach than to rely on handwriting, especially if he has difficulty writing legibly. Generally, typing speed will improve when the child is about age ten to twelve. Most children want to be able to use computers to access the Internet and play computer games, so your child is likely to be quite willing to work at improving typing skills.

 ALERT!

Help your child set automatic save options to preserve a copy of his work at frequent intervals. You should also set the program to automatically preserve a backup copy of a document each time it is saved. There is nothing more frustrating to a budding writer than losing the product of several hours' work due to a computer malfunction or keyboarding error.

There is also a product called the AlphaSmart Keyboard specifically developed for students with learning disabilities; it allows students to enter and edit text, and the text can later be transmitted to a computer for adjusting layout and printing. The product costs about $200 and is popular in many schools; it is a good choice for younger children and in classroom settings.

By the time your child is about age ten, he should be introduced to a regular computer word processing program. In addition to learning to input text, your child should learn how to use specific features of the program, including use of the spell checker and grammar checker, and use of features like "autocorrect" and automatic text completion options that can simplify text entry and help avoid common spelling and typographical errors.

Using a word processing program also enables your child to work with his teacher to improve the quality of his writing through revisions and redrafts. Because the student is spared the laborious process of writing out a second draft by hand, the teacher is free to offer detailed comments and suggestions. Your child will become more confident about writing when he realizes that his first draft does not have to be perfect.

Another advantage to using the computer is that the child can set display options to make it easier to read material—for example, by choosing to view a magnified version of the text—and can also choose a preferred font. Many children with dyslexia are easily confused by different font sets, and so often develop a strong preference for those which seem to be more readable. The Comic Sans font, which comes with Windows systems, is a popular choice partly because it more closely resembles penmanship generally taught in school.

Special Software for Dyslexia

You may also be interested in specialized software designed to help individuals with dyslexia. The TextHelp company makes software products called Read & Write and Wordsmith that have enhanced features including a phonetic spell checker, homophone support, word prediction, dictionary, pronunciation tutor, and text-to-speech features. These features are more helpful to many children than a standard spell checker, as it will help them to more accurately identify words. Text-to-speech features allow the computer to be set to read aloud words as they are typed in or to read aloud any text in compatible file formats.

The text-to-speech function is also available through many other inexpensive software formats, including many that are offered for free. A program that also enables speech for Web site content can be very helpful, especially if your child is a slow reader, when he needs to do Internet research to prepare school papers and projects.

For an older child (about age twelve and older), you may consider getting speech-recognition or dictation software; this will allow your child to use a microphone to dictate into the computer. Two popular packages are Dragon NaturallySpeaking and IBM ViaVoice. The drawback with these dictation programs is that the software must be trained to recognize the voice and speech patterns of the user; generally this is done by reading specific passages into the computer. The passages may be difficult for a younger child to read; even an older child may have some difficulty, but the older child is likely to have more patience for the process. Also, although dictating seems like an easy way to get words into print, the user must be able to read well enough to catch and correct some of the more egregious mistakes this software is likely to produce. Although accuracy of the software improves with each new version, it still transcribes many words erroneously, especially proper names.

 FACT

> Use of a computer spell checker will help many children with dyslexia improve their spelling skills. The computer can be set to automatically highlight spelling mistakes, which not only focuses the child's attention on the error, but also requires interactive participation to repair it by choosing the correct alternative from a drop-down list.

Hand-Held Devices

Your child may also benefit from hand-held dictionaries or spell checkers. A simple and inexpensive product (approximately $25) is the Franklin Spelling Ace, which enables the student to type in a phonetic or guessed spelling in order to find the correct spelling. A child with reading difficulties might prefer a slightly more expensive option with speech capabilities, the Franklin Speaking Homework Wiz (about $50).

As your child encounters more difficult reading tasks, you might consider the WizCom Reading Pen, which is a handheld device with a small electronic scanner that can scan a word or line of text and read it aloud to the student; it also has a built in dictionary with definitions of all words. Accuracy is poor for scans of full lines of text, so the tool is not helpful for a child with no reading skills. However, for individual words accuracy is quite high, and the product's built-in dictionary contains many technical terms that a high school student is likely to encounter in textbook reading. Thus, the Reading Pen can be extremely useful to a student who has difficulty deciphering new and unfamiliar words.

Using Study Guides

As your child grows older, he may also find it helpful to use commercial outlines and study guides. One of the most popular products is Spark Notes, which produces inexpensive study guides in just about every academic subject your child is likely to encounter, and also makes the contents of all its material available free of charge online. The site also has the entire text of many classic literary works available online, as well as supportive study material; with the aid of speech-to-text software this makes a wide array of difficult material very accessible to your struggling reader. Some materials are also now available in audio format.

Is It Cheating?

One drawback of modern technology and the wide array of support materials available to your child is that it makes cheating very easy. There is no way for a teacher to know who actually composed written work presented in printed form, and as your child's sophistication with computers grows, he will soon discover the ease with which he can cut and paste text from Internet resources and reference software.

Your child should not be deprived of access to resources and technology that will enable him to learn merely because of the risk that he may misuse them. Rather, it is important that you discuss with him your own expectations about intellectual honesty, as well as legal and ethical concerns. Many children simply do not know or understand that it is wrong to copy or paraphrase material from Web sites; others simply are overwhelmed with their workload and feel they have no choice but to take shortcuts. A child with a learning disability is far more likely to be tempted to copy others' work.

You can help by continuing to supervise your child's work and being an active participant in the writing process. Offer to proofread your child's written work, both as a way of helping your child and so that you are aware of what his original work looks like and have an opportunity to see work that he is turning in.

 ESSENTIAL

If it appears that your child has copied passages of his work from the Internet, take the time to discuss with him the importance of putting information into his own words. Most children with dyslexia are highly creative thinkers; compliment your child whenever possible on his originality of thought and encourage him to voice his own opinions in his writing.

Keep in mind that until the time he overcomes all aspects of his reading disability, your child is at a disadvantage in comparison to his peers for reading and writing assignments. Many children with dyslexia do overcome most of their learning problems by the time they reach high school, but many others do not. Your child is as intelligent as his classmates and should be entitled to the same quality of education. For him, books on tape, videos, and study guides are necessary tools that will afford him access to the same quality of learning as children who are stronger readers. If your seventh grader receives tutoring because he reads at a third-grade level, he cannot reasonably be expected to read *Huckleberry Finn* on his own. His mind is ready to appreciate the rich vocabulary and complex themes presented in the book, and he will certainly learn far more by listening to an audio book and watching a movie than by trying to struggle through reading the book on his own. This alternative is far preferable to reading an abridged, limited vocabulary version of the book or being denied the educational benefit of advanced literature while consigned to reading material geared to third graders. No teacher would deny a blind student the opportunity to rely on recorded books; if your child does not have the ability to read at a level equivalent to his intellectual ability to understand, he should be entitled to use whatever forms of educational aids are available.

As a parent, it is important for you to help your child learn to strike an appropriate balance between reading on his own and using technology and available media to supplement his learning. Make clear to your child that you expect him to be honest about letting you and his teachers know when he has relied on supportive material. Keep in mind that reliance on such support will help your child develop a more advanced vocabulary and thinking skills that will, in turn, allow him to develop into a better reader. Scientific research shows that individuals with dyslexia rely heavily on the thinking and problem-solving frontal areas of their brains for reading; these areas will be developed as your child is exposed to advanced literature and concepts through other means.

CHAPTER 16

Strategies for Spelling, Writing, and Math

YOUR CHILD WILL PROBABLY have specific difficulties with other academic subjects. While he may receive specialized tutoring and support for reading at school, he probably will not have such support with other subjects. You will want to help him, but as with reading, his dyslexia means that he will have difficulty learning with conventional strategies. This chapter will help provide ideas and specific strategies for helping with the most common areas of difficulty—spelling, writing, and math.

Building Visual Memory for Spelling

Difficulty with spelling is the most common and persistent difficulty that accompanies dyslexia. Even after your child becomes a capable reader, his writing is likely to be riddled with spelling errors. One reason is the extreme variability of English spelling; almost every "rule" that can be taught has numerous exceptions, and many words simply are not spelled the way they sound.

Good spellers generally have strong visual memories for what words look like in print. Try to avoid study or practice techniques that expose your child to incorrectly spelled versions of the word. Many children with dyslexia have strong visual memories, but they will remember erroneous spellings as easily as correct ones, and they will have no way to remember which is right. Teachers might try to make spelling homework fun by offering a practice quiz where your child must select the correct word from a list of incorrect spellings or find the word in a puzzle where the letters are scrambled. Your child may enjoy some of these games, but they are counterproductive for learning correct spelling.

 ESSENTIAL

When practicing spelling words at home, observe your child to see whether she does better when asked to orally spell the words as opposed to writing them. This will give you a clue as to how to best reach your child. If your child does better with oral spelling, encourage her to say the letters out loud as she practices writing her spelling words.

One technique that sometimes works for children with dyslexia is to learn how to spell a word backward as well as forward. Encourage your child to try to visualize the word in his mind; with a clear mental picture, the word can be spelled backwards by "seeing" the letters in order and calling off the letters from right to left.

Word Families and Patterns

Good spellers also recognize familiar spelling patterns and understand morphological word structure including common prefixes, roots, and suffixes. It will be easier for your child to learn when words are taught in groups that share a common pattern or structure. This is better than learning "rules" in isolation, especially rules that have many exceptions. A popular program for home use that builds on common word elements is AVKO Sequential Spelling, which was developed specifically for children with dyslexia. Make sure that your child's word list for each study session includes only words reflecting the pattern being studied. Work with your child's teacher to modify school spelling lists so as to avoid confusion, and limit the number of words being studied.

Do not try to teach your child homophones, such as "their" and "there," in the same session. Most people with dyslexia find homophones extremely confusing, and they will not be able to simply memorize the difference. It is better if the words are taught separately with words sharing a similar pattern; for example, "there" can be taught along with "here" and "where." Make sure your child learns word meanings along with spelling; it will aid in memory to associate meanings with spelling patterns, as opposed to individual words. That is, it may be easier to remember that the "ere" sequence is associated with words signifying place ("here, there, everywhere").

Have your child look up words with irregular patterns in the dictionary to learn about the word derivations and etymology. She will soon discover other keys to spelling—for example, that the word "their" comes from the Old Norse *theirra*. Knowing that some words with similar sounds come from different languages will help your child understand why they are spelled so differently.

Tips for the Reluctant Writer

The best way to help your child become a better writer is to separate the mechanics of writing (spelling, handwriting, punctuation, grammar) from the creative aspects. Your child's strength is in his vivid imagination, a valuable asset in a writer. Help your child learn that writing is a two-stage process; the first stage is getting the ideas on paper; correcting or editing work is the second step.

 **FACT**

Your child may enjoy reading books written by children's authors who also have dyslexia, such as Patricia Polacco's many richly illustrated storybooks, including *Thank You Mr. Falker*, where she describes her own early struggles with reading; or Jeanne Bettencourt's novel for young readers about a boy with dyslexia, *My Name Is Brain Brian*.

For writing the first draft of an essay or story, follow this rule: there will be no corrections or criticism for spelling or grammar. Your child should be encouraged to write things down in whatever form or order she is comfortable with. Once the ideas are in written form, you can guide your child to developing a more polished version. When your child is very young, you will give a lot of help; as she grows older, she will learn to do more for herself. Remind your child that even professional writers rely on editors to proofread and correct their work.

Mind Mapping

Once good technique for getting ideas to flow is mind mapping. To do this, your child starts with a main subject, and writes down a few words or draws a picture representing the idea in the middle of a blank sheet of paper. He should then draw lines or branches radiating out from the center for each main idea he has about the subject; with each line he should write a few words or draw another picture. He can add details to each idea by again writing a few words, connecting them via a line or branch to the idea they relate to.

Once the ideas are written down in a mind map format, you can help your child develop them into written sentences, using the map as a guideline for developing the structure of his paragraph or essay.

Experiment with Different Formats

If your child seems to balk at writing anything in narrative format, have him try writing poetry or verse. Introduce your child to the concept of free verse—poetry that does not have to have a particular rhythm or cadence, and does not have to rhyme. One of the advantages of writing poetry is that it frees the child from writing conventions, such as the need to use complete sentences. It also allows your child to experiment with the sounds of words and to use novel words that are evocative of a particular mood or feeling.

Your child might enjoy writing haiku, in part because it is short. Haiku traditionally has three lines consisting of seventeen syllables in total, usually arranged in lines of five, seven, and five syllables. Although the form is very brief, writing haiku will help your child develop sensitivity to the phonetic structure of word segments.

You might also encourage your child to write a play; it is sometimes easier for the budding writer to focus only on the dialogue among the characters. Your child might enjoy presenting her play as a puppet show or using a video camera to make her own movie using her own written screenplay.

Use Artwork as Inspiration

Your child may do better with writing if you encourage him to draw a picture of his ideas or a story he wants to write, and then use words to describe what is going on in the picture. He might want to write in comic-book or storyboard format, with a series of pictures and a short sentence describing each one. Alternatively, your child might draw a larger, more complex picture and then write several sentences or paragraphs describing what is going on in the picture. You might also want to encourage your child to write a story, a set of impressions, or a poem about an illustration or artwork in a book.

 FACT

You will find an intriguing set of pictures to use as writing prompts in *The Mysteries of Harris Burdick*, by Chris Van Allsberg. The book's premise is that the pictures were drawn by a man who disappeared before he could explain what the pictures were about, leaving it up to the reader's imagination to find the story behind each.

Understanding Math Concepts

Most children with dyslexia are ready to understand math concepts, but they often struggle with pencil-and-paper math as it is taught in school. The problem generally stems from difficulty understanding and manipulating math symbols, including numerals as well as symbols for operations, and with difficulty understanding and applying words commonly used to express mathematical concepts. Thus, the language-based disability that is part of dyslexia becomes a liability for learning arithmetic.

Modeling Math Concepts

When your child asks for help with arithmetic, start by finding out whether he understands the concepts underlying the problems he is working on. A child with dyslexia often has unexpected gaps in learning, and so sometimes even a very simple concept may be at the heart of a misunderstanding. Use three-dimensional objects to model mathematical concepts. You might use beans, coins, or small blocks to model functions such as addition, subtraction, and multiplication; you might demonstrate the concept of fractions by measuring liquid in a cup or by cutting a slice of bread into halves or quarters. Place value can be demonstrated with pennies and dimes. If your child understands the relative value of coins, they can also be used to model fractions or equivalencies.

Many arithmetic or algebraic concepts can also be modeled using geometrical shapes, and a set of pattern blocks can be useful to help your child visualize numerical relationships, such as understanding multiplication, division, and fractions. For example, your child can discover that a rectangle constructed of square blocks that is 3 blocks high and 4 blocks wide will have 12 blocks in all—the same as the problem 3 x 4 = 12.

Explain Words and Symbols

Make sure that your child understands all the symbols used in arithmetic problems, and also understands numerals and what they mean. While your child may understand isolated numerals, he may be confused by two-digit numbers, the meaning of 0 (zero), negative numbers, decimals, or commas used in numbers with four or more figures.

Be sure that your child understands all the words used in describing a problem. Your child may be confused by specific terminology—words such as "sum" or "reciprocal," and he may be equally confused by words that are used outside of mathematics, such as "positive" or "even," as well as words signifying relationships such as "from" or "than."

ALERT!

Try to avoid situations where your child must copy problems from a book, as children with dyslexia commonly make transposition errors. If your child must copy, encourage her to vocalize the numbers as she writes them—she is less likely to transpose 346 if she says "three, four, six" or "three hundred forty-six" as she writes the numbers. Your child may prefer to have you dictate the problems to her to write down, rather than trying to copy them on her own.

When your child writes out a mathematical problem, use paper with a grid or graph paper to help her keep the numbers lined up properly. If your child is working from a printed sheet of problems, have her circle operational signs such as (+) or (–) in different colors, so that she understands what is expected with each problem. Check to make sure she has copied correctly before she begins to work the problems.

Use Multiple Approaches

Most mathematical problems can be solved in more than one way; the more complex the math, the more likely it is that there are multiple strategies that can be applied. Often, the conventional algorithms taught in school cause unnecessary confusion. For example, your child may be stymied by the concept of "borrowing" or "regrouping" to subtract 6 from 12 on paper, but might be able to solve the same problem quickly in his head, simply by recognizing that 6 is half of 12. Many very complex arithmetic problems can be solved more efficiently by factoring or manipulating the numbers.

Encourage your child to use his knowledge of number concepts to find different approaches for calculation. Although these skills may lead your child to deviate from the approaches taught in the early years, they are the foundations of understanding algebra and higher mathematical concepts. In the long run, your child will do better in math if he is able to turn a problem on its head or restructure the problem to make it easier, such as restating the problem 15 x 9 as [(15 x 10) – 15] because it is easier to subtract 15 from 150 than to do double-digit multiplication.

Handling Word Problems

Word or story problems are very difficult for children with dyslexia, even when they have a strong understanding of math concepts. To start with, the problem requires reading, which is an effort for your child. Word problems also require highly accurate reading; a missed or misunderstood word can change the entire meaning of the problem. Many of the words used in story problems are also confusing; your child may understand how to "subtract" but be confused by the use of words like "less" or "from" to describe the same concept. Your child may also be confused by the use of pronouns in a story problem—the question "How many of them did he have left?" may leave your child scratching his head wondering what "them" refers to and who "he" is. Finally, your child may be confused by extraneous information in the problem used to describe the setting—the problem may be asking for a calculation of the amount of change to be given for buying movie tickets, but your child is trying to guess from the illustration in the book what movie was playing.

Help your child visualize the problem by imagining or acting out the scenario depicted. Explain that an arithmetic problem is a puzzle that always requires her to figure out a piece of missing information. Have your child read through the problem—or read it to her—and then ask her if she knows what information the problem calls for her to figure out. (For example, the number of cookies that each child will get.) Then, ask your child what information she will need to figure out the answer; guide her, as needed, to look for the specific information in the problem (the total number of cookies and the total number of children). Allow your child to explore the possible ways that she can figure out the answer; there may be more than one acceptable strategy.

Specialized Therapies for Math

Two providers of dyslexia treatment services profiled in Chapter 7 have also developed specialized programs for helping with math. Both programs begin by focusing on very basic math concepts, and children work with them to develop more advanced proficiency. The goal of each program is to ensure that your child has an intuitive or image-based understanding of the concepts underlying arithmetic concepts and to help your child relate the concepts to the words and symbols used to represent them.

 **FACT**

> The Davis Math Mastery program takes four or five full days of one-on-one work with a trained facilitator to complete. Like the corresponding dyslexia program, your child will need to do follow-up work at home, continuing to use clay to model words that represent math concepts or cause confusion when used in word problems. The specific techniques used are also explained in the book *The Gift of Learning* by Ron Davis.

The *Davis Math Mastery* program applies clay modeling techniques to help your child master foundation concepts underlying mathematical relationships such as change, cause-effect, before/after, consequence, time, sequence, and order/disorder. Clay modeling is also used to master the meanings of words commonly used in math story problems that are somewhat different than everyday use. For example, the word "by" is generally used to mean "close to." But in word problems, it sometimes used to mean two separate things: for multiplication, to mean "using as a multiplier," and for division the meaning would be "into groups of."

A Davis facilitator then guides your child through a series of twelve participatory mathematics exercises to move rapidly from counting, to multiplication, to understanding fractions, to developing proficiency with pencil-and-paper math. The exercises can be done quickly because the focus is on helping your child understand the concepts underlying each mathematical function; for example, using exercises counting forward and backwards in multiples to lead into the concept of multiplication.

The *Lindamood-Bell On Cloud Nine Math Program* is geared to developing the ability to connect imagery to language to express mathematical concepts. The program uses manipulatives to develop concepts for reasoning and problem solving with numbers. Beginning with the most basic concepts of counting, adding, and subtracting, the steps progress to word problems, multiplication, division, fractions, and decimals. A kit is available for home use.

The Paradox of the Math Whiz

Some children with dyslexia have very strong mathematical skills, and they are often able to understand very advanced mathematical concepts and calculations. Often the knack for math was demonstrated very early, perhaps when the child was able to understand and apply concepts of multiplication or fractions as a preschooler. Yet these budding math geniuses often encounter problems at school. Typically, they have difficulty learning their multiplication tables; they have problems with paper-and-pencil math, such as with the concept of "borrowing" in multidigit subtraction or with doing long division; and they often are able to correctly give the answer to a complex problem but are at a loss to explain how they arrived at it.

If your child follows this pattern, he may experience difficulties in school, particularly during the elementary and middle school years, because of his inability to satisfy the teacher's expectations for written math. Your child may write the correct answer to problems on a math worksheet or exam, but be denied credit because he failed to write out the steps for solving the problem, or because he wrote the steps incorrectly. You may observe him following a process of writing the answer to a problem first, then working backwards to write the steps. He may be able to understand advanced concepts in algebra or trigonometry, but prone to make frequent errors in calculation. Don't worry, he's in good company—Albert Einstein had the same problems.

 FACT

> You may be surprised to find that your child with strong math skills is not interested in working with math manipulatives. This is because, unlike the math-challenged child, your son already understands the concepts and has strong internal visual imagery. He does not need help with concepts, but rather with learning to associate his intuitive answer with the words used to describe the concepts.

The reason for this disparity in skill level is that there are two separate modes of thought used for math problems. Researchers have found that when students memorize their multiplication tables or do precise mathematical calculations, they rely in part on language processes of their brain—thus, in one study, if bilingual students were taught math procedures in one language, they had difficulty doing the same procedures when the problem was presented in the other language, despite their fluency in both. However, another part of the brain governs understanding of mathematical and spatial relationships—for example, recognizing that the number 56 is larger than 12. In the language experiment, the bilingual students could perform equally well on those sorts of math generalization tasks in either language; they were relying on their inherent sense of concepts of quantity or size, or their ability to visualize the problem, rather than on language.

The problem for your math whiz child, then, is actually the same as the problem experienced by the child with dyslexia who struggles: both have difficulty using and applying words and symbols to mathematical concepts. Thus, you can help your math-capable child in the same way you would help the math-challenged child, except that in most cases you don't need to teach the underlying concepts.

Another reason that your child may struggle with paper-and-pencil arithmetic is that she instinctively uses different strategies for solving most math problems. Students with strong spatial reasoning skills understand that numbers can be manipulated in a number of ways, and they will tend to adopt different approaches to more efficiently resolve different problems. They are often very good with mental math, sometimes amazing others with how quickly they can answer a difficult problem, such as multiplying 19 x 21—the math whiz understands immediately that this problem is the same as (20 x 20) – 1.

The language-based math processes that cause so much difficulty are generally functions of basic arithmetic; in more advanced mathematics, understanding of basic numerical and spatial relationships takes precedence. If your child is not discouraged by early experiences with grade-school math, he is likely to do very well in high school and college.

CHAPTER 17

Home and Family Issues

YOUR CHILD'S DYSLEXIA is more than just a school problem; it affects the way your child feels about himself, and it impacts your home and family life in many ways. You may find that a good deal of your life is spent worrying about trying to help your child and that you are uncertain as to how to treat him. If he seems overwhelmed at school and emotionally fragile, you may be reluctant to criticize him or enforce household rules. However, even though your child has a learning barrier, it is important for you to understand that he is a normal child, with normal wants and needs, who simply has a different way of thinking and learning.

Effective Communication

One of the most frustrating aspects of living with a person with dyslexia is difficulty with communication. It will often seem as if your child is deliberately ignoring you or purposefully mocking or disobeying you when he does exactly the opposite of what you say or ask. But these problems arise directly from your child's language processing difficulties—he really does miss half of what you say, as his mind cannot keep pace with the flow of verbal information. He compensates by filling in the gaps with what he thinks you probably meant to say.

You can effectively address or eliminate most of these problems at home by changing your own communication style. You cannot change your child, but you can change the way that you talk to him. Here are some suggestions:

Make sure you have your child's attention. Say her name and make physical contact, such as gently putting your hand on her shoulder. Try to establish eye contact; at least make sure your child is able to see your face. Announce that you have something to say, using a neutral tone of voice, so your child doesn't think you are angry. If you have a series of instructions or directions to give, say at the outset how many items you will be talking about: "There are three things I want you to do. The first is . . ." This will prepare your child mentally to listen for three different things.

Eliminate distractions. Make sure your child is looking at you and not at the TV or computer screen. Wait for a break in the action if your child is watching TV, and ask to mute, pause, or turn off the TV or video game if possible. Do not allow your other children to interrupt; if they do, take a deep breath and start over from the beginning.

Speak clearly. Speak slowly; use words that clearly describe what you want and be concise. Try to use "picture words"— words that will help your child visualize what you are talking about. Give accurate and specific directions, and call items by their names—that is, say "please go out to the car, open the trunk, and bring in the bag of groceries," not "go bring in the stuff from the store." If you need to give a complex set of directions, begin by stating the purpose of the instructions: "I want you to start cooking our dinner while I am gone, so here's what you have to do . . ." will give a context for understanding why you are talking about a chicken, a baking pan, and preheating an oven.

Verify that your child has gotten the message. If you have given a set of instructions, ask your child if he understands. If "no," ask what he is confused about and answer his questions. If "yes," ask your child to tell you what it is that you want him to do. Do not be patronizing in tone; at first you can simply explain that you trying to improve the way you explain things, and that you want his help in letting you know if you are being clear. Later, verbal confirmation will simply become a habit. Use the same pattern of communication when your child wants something from you; instead of simply saying "hmmn" or "OK," verify that you understand the message: "You need me to give your friends a ride home from soccer practice at 6 P.M. today. I'll be there."

If you want something done immediately, say so. Don't assume that your child understands something that you haven't explicitly said.

ESSENTIAL

Treat your child with courtesy and respect. Say "please" when you want your child to do something, and "thank you" when she completes the job. If she tries to do what you asked but makes a mistake or forgets a step, show appreciation for her efforts and gently remind her of the part that she missed. Your courtesy will set a good example and will help prevent her from habitually tuning you out.

Be careful that you don't set up situations that are bound to fail. If you know from experience that your son will lose track of time and forget to do a task, set an alarm or find some other way to remind him. If your child is a daydreamer and a dawdler, don't expect his habits to change—instead, plan on giving him frequent reminders or supervising the task.

Chores and Family Responsibilities

Your child's dyslexia does not affect his abilities to participate in household activities, including taking on age-appropriate responsibilities like regular chores. A child with dyslexia can care for a pet as well as anyone else; he can wash dishes, use a mop, handle a vacuum cleaner, take out the trash, or wash the family car. If your child is particularly disorganized or clumsy, there may be some tasks that you may find that you prefer he not do—but there are plenty of areas that can be his own responsibility.

Many parents are tempted to want to protect a child who has a disability, but your child will be better off if he has regular responsibilities. The more he is struggling in school, the more important it is that you show him that he is a valued member of the household. Of course you do not want to overwhelm him with chores— but responsibilities like feeding a pet or setting the table for dinner are not time-consuming. If you notice that there is a task that your son does particularly well or seems to enjoy, praise and encourage him. For example, if your child likes to cook, encourage him to help with preparation of family meals; as he grows older, he can take pride in his culinary talents.

Behavior and Discipline

Just as you should not excuse your child from regular chores, you should have reasonable behavioral expectations. If your child misbehaves deliberately, then the consequences should be the same as for any of his siblings. However, you should be aware that not all misbehavior is deliberate. For example, if your child has problems with focusing or sustaining attention, then it is natural for him to lose track of time or forget to do his chores. Help him devise better ways of remembering, such as using a chart to keep track of tasks, rather than repeatedly chastising him for forgetting.

Be careful not to punish your child for his disability. Don't withhold privileges or punish him for academic problems, such as poor grades or forgetting to complete his homework, or for predictable areas of difficulty, such as a messy room or a tendency to lose track of possessions. Over time, you can help your child build skills and become more responsible, but you need to offer guidance and support. You will do better to break down tasks into manageable segments, offer praise when your child does well, and use small incentives to encourage him to succeed in areas that are in his grasp. Keep in mind that children with dyslexia tend to be very inconsistent in performance. Your goal is to help motivate your child to improve. Fear of punishment in a situation where he cannot be sure of his own abilities is demoralizing and can lead to a tendency to give up without trying.

 ESSENTIAL

> Keep your emotions under control. It is natural to feel frustrated at times with your child, but it is risky to lose your temper, as it is too easy to say something hurtful that you will regret. If you need to, take a timeout for yourself before trying to correct or discipline your child.

Keep in mind that your child's communication and attention focusing difficulties may lead to confusion on his part. Children with dyslexia tend to be highly imaginative, and they have an inconsistent sense of time; they may confabulate to make up for gaps in understanding. This can lead to disputes over what someone said or did that seem like your child is lying—when in fact the truth is that your child actually believes that he is reporting events accurately. Keep calm and gently question and guide your child to help him sort out remembered from imagined facts; use questions like, "Is it possible that the teacher did say that, but you just didn't hear?"

Do be aware that frustration at school can lead to serious misbehavior. Having empathy for your child does not mean that you should tolerate acts of violence, destruction, or hostility. It is understandable why a child who is hurting inside may vent his rage by smashing a vase, but it is not excusable. But harsh punishment will also be ineffective if the reason your child's misbehavior arises because he feels demeaned and humiliated every day at school, or he is angry because other children make fun of his difficulties—it will only increase the level of your child's anger. You will need to help your child develop better coping strategies and be very consistent with imposing reasonable consequences that your child can directly relate to his behavior. For example, if he breaks something, working to pay the cost of replacement may be a more effective lesson than being grounded or losing privileges. You may need outside help such as family counseling to help understand and address the problems.

Sibling Rivalry

Conflicts among siblings usually stem from feelings of jealousy or resentment. Your child with dyslexia will feel frustrated if siblings close in age or younger than him are allowed extra privileges that are denied to him because of his learning problems—this may occur because of the need for your child to spend time outside of school receiving special tutoring, while siblings have more free time to participate in sports or social activities.

Conversely, your child's siblings may feel that she has monopolized all of the family attention and resources—for example, a sibling may resent being denied the opportunity to go to summer camp because you don't have the money after paying for intensive tutoring at a summer program for dyslexia. Or a sibling may feel frustrated that her good grades and accomplishments are not honored by the family when you are simply bending over backward trying to make sure that the child with dyslexia doesn't feel humiliated or inadequate in a house full of honor-roll students.

Maintain Balance

It is important for you to try to maintain balance. Your children do not have equal abilities, but each child deserves recognition and encouragement for her abilities, and support and understanding for areas of weakness. At the same time, you need to guide your children toward having respect for each other's differences. Start by making sure that your child's siblings understand what dyslexia is—and at the same time they need to know that their sibling is not fragile or inept.

 ESSENTIAL

A healthy sense of humor will help everyone get along. No one likes being the butt of a joke, but everyone gains from learning to laugh at his own mistakes. You can help set the tone in your family by maintaining a lighthearted attitude.

It is important as well that you avoid being overprotective of your child with dyslexia; you may wince when you hear a sibling crack a joke about his brother's spelling errors, but you can cause more strife if you overreact by yelling or punishing the offending sibling. A gentle reminder that the comment was hurtful is more appropriate. Keep in mind that healthy siblings do tend to tease and criticize one another; observe your child's reactions before lashing out in anger. You may discover that your child with dyslexia is quite capable of standing up for himself—you may even discover that the one with dyslexia is the instigator of many sibling battles.

Try to keep the family focus on more than academics. This means that you will give your child with dyslexia recognition for accomplishments outside of school, and that you do not allow your efforts to address his school problems to prevent you from acknowledging the importance of your other children's extracurricular activities. Encourage family hobbies that everyone can participate in and enjoy.

Foster Strong Sibling Relationships

Look for ways to spend time individually with each sibling, and allow each child free rein to vent their feelings of frustration or anxiety. You may be surprised to learn that an older child is as worried about your child's dyslexia as you are. Help your older child understand ways that he can help; if he learns more about his younger sibling's learning style, he may be better equipped to offer help with homework.

Younger siblings rarely perceive the child with dyslexia as being disabled. They are more likely to simply accept their older sibling at face value, and to be fully aware of his many strengths—after all, their older sibling has always been bigger and stronger and quite capable in many ways. However, the younger child is also less apt to understand why so much attention is being focused on the sibling with dyslexia.

At some point, a younger sibling is likely develop better reading and writing skills than the child with dyslexia. This can be a source of confusion and resentment; the older child may feel embarrassed, and the younger child may not understand why her older brother needs extra help with skills she has easily mastered. At this time, it is important that you answer the younger child's questions about dyslexia. Be sure to explain that it is a learning difference and not an illness—many children mistakenly believe that their sibling has some sort of disease.

Siblings can also be a great source of support for one another. Rather than feeling resentful, a child with dyslexia may feel a sense of pride when her younger brother starts reading. While understanding her own limitations, she may feel relieved that her sibling doesn't face the same barriers, and the younger child may be eager to help the older one.

Sports and Other Activities

You should encourage any interest your child has in sports or athletic activities. If your child is good at team sports such as basketball or soccer, his abilities will help build his self-esteem and allow him to earn the respect of his peers. Moreover, exercise and physical fitness will improve your child's energy levels at school, and make him better able to cope with academic demands and stresses.

Try to steer your child toward activities where he can feel successful. Unless she seems to have a very strong talent or dedication to a particular sport, look for team sports where the emphasis is on having fun and developing good sportsmanship, rather than being highly competitive. Attend practices at first, and observe the coach; look for an individual who gives his players praise and encouragement. Unlike school, your child does not have to participate in any sport, so there is no point in exposing her to the additional stress of a verbally abusive coach or the scorn of other players bent on winning every game.

If your child has problems with coordination that make it difficult for him to keep up on the playing field, look for noncompetitive activities where he can begin by taking lessons, such as gymnastics, martial arts, dance, or swimming. You should be able to find a class that takes children of varied ages; if your child sees that he is not the oldest "beginner" he will not feel embarrassed. These types of activities can help your child develop improved balance and coordination skills, which may help address some aspects of his dyslexia as well as build confidence and improved self-esteem.

 ESSENTIAL

Athletics and fitness are an important part of your child's life; your child should not miss out on these activities because of after-school tutoring or the need to spend extra time on homework. Your child's academic needs may mean that you have to limit the hours and days spent on sports, but make sure to reserve time for both.

You should also encourage your child's interest or aptitude in other areas, such as learning to play a musical instrument. Again, these activities are an important part of your child's emotional life and development, and they may have positive affects on her school work as well. Practicing an instrument or singing in a choir, for example, may help boost your child's listening skills. Of course you shouldn't expect karate classes or violin lessons to substitute for specialized therapy for dyslexia; just keep in mind that while these activities are primarily for your child's enrichment, they may have added side-benefits when it comes to school.

Keep in mind that your child's aptitudes or outside interests may also be the key to his future career. Of course you want your child to learn to read, to do well in school, to go on to college— but the world is full of actors, dancers, singers, musicians, and athletes whose talent is far more important to their success than their education. For a child who struggles in school, exploration of arts and athletics is particularly important, and it may help build motivation to succeed in academics as well.

Rest and Relaxation

It is vitally important that your child also have time in his life for rest and relaxation. The tension, effort, and stress that he experiences at school make it especially important for him to have time to simply let go, and not have to worry about academics and schoolwork. If he is outgoing and sociable, he will want to have time to hang out with his friends. Introverted children have a strong need for time alone, sometimes seemingly doing nothing; for them, this is important time to recharge. Most children need a little bit of both—time with friends and time alone.

 ESSENTIAL

> You can help your child sustain energy to focus on schoolwork by feeding nutritious, high-protein snacks. Sliced cheese, peanut butter on whole grain bread, or a smoothie made with yogurt and fresh fruit are all good ideas for wholesome snacks that will help boost and maintain energy levels.

Individuals with dyslexia generally do not perform well under stress. In fact, many children will have periods in which they seem to do quite well, alternating with periods when their reading and writing regresses. When their skill level seems to inexplicably deteriorate, it is often related to stress or fatigue.

The irony is that your child needs to work harder than his peers to complete the same tasks, yet he is particularly prone to mistakes and confusion when his energy levels are low. So staying up late to study is often the worst thing that your child can do. Thus, as a parent, you need to make sure that your child has time to rest and relax. Each child has a different pattern; you need to observe your child to get a sense of his energy cycles. For some kids, it is important to do homework right away after they get home from school, as they tend to be too tired to do it later on. Other kids really need to take a break to recoup their energy after a trying day at school. Some children will fade early in the evening, and need an early bedtime. Other children are night owls who seem to get a burst of energy as the evening wears on, and may do better with a short nap in the afternoon after school, postponing homework until after dinner.

Your child may also benefit from learning some techniques for stress relief. Yoga, stretching, tossing a light Koosh ball or Nerf ball, or deep breathing are all good ways to help let go of tension and anxiety. Help your child learn what works best for her, and develop habits of self-awareness and self-monitoring. Learn these techniques for yourself, too—you will be a better and more nurturing parent if you also make sure to take time for rest and relaxation for yourself.

CHAPTER 18

The Teen Years

A S YOUR CHILD REACHES ADOLESCENCE, you will face new challenges. Some will be the normal issues parents of teens face—your child with dyslexia will experience the same emotional and physical changes as any other teenager. However, the teenage years are also a time when children begin to think about their future, and your child's school struggles can translate into a negative self-image, which in turn may lead your teenager to become depressed or engage in risky activity. As a parent, it is important for you to recognize and acknowledge your teenager's needs, and at the same time help him become more self-reliant and independent.

Fostering Independence

During the elementary school years, you may find that you need to constantly monitor your child at home and intervene at school to help your child along. At home you may be in the habit of doing many things for your child, such as reading aloud to him or writing things down for him; you know that your child needs extra help, and you are happy to give it. There is a tendency for parents of children with learning disabilities to become overprotective; partly it simply becomes habit for you to anticipate your child's needs and try to help him, and partly you have become conditioned over time to expect problems unless you take action to prevent them.

As your child moves into adolescence, it is critical that you begin to let go and begin to transfer responsibility to your child. That means that over time, you have to guide and encourage your child to take responsibility for keeping track of his own books and supplies, remembering to do his own homework, advocating for himself with teachers, and making his own academic choices.

 ALERT!

Beware of assuming too much responsibility for your child with dyslexia. This can lead to a cycle of dependence that lasts into adulthood. Your child must be given the opportunity to take risks and learn from mistakes or he will not develop the self-determination that is critical to independent adulthood.

Your child may or may not become a good reader, and he may or may not achieve academic success; but he certainly will grow to adulthood and some day need to be able to take care of himself and hold down a job. Your child with dyslexia has the potential to develop all of the skills he needs for these life responsibilities, and like all children he needs to your support and guidance to make this transition to adulthood. The more difficulty your child has with academics, the more important it is that you equip him with the social and emotional skills he will need to become a productive member of society. For many young people, college is a four-year-cushion between high school and the responsibilities of adult life. If your teen does not enjoy or do well in school, then he will not have that extra time—he will need to be prepared to enter the work world in his late teens. His educational limitations do not need to stand in the way of gainful employment; there are dozens of vocational skills that a young person can learn that will lead to employment in environments where high-level reading and writing skills are not necessary, and many young people do well in positions in retail business and sales. What your child does need is emotional resiliency and values like a strong work ethic, persistency, and reliability.

Taking on New Challenges

One of the most difficult—and necessary—parts of parenting a teenager is that you must be prepared to allow your child to risk making mistakes and failure. Of course you will still provide support and assistance, and you will try to exercise good judgment as to how much responsibility to take on; but you have to avoid the tendency to continue to do work for your child or intervene constantly on his behalf. At age eight, it is unfair to a child with dyslexia to expect him to "tough it out" and simply "work harder"—but at age fourteen it is important that the child begin to develop some of the work habits he will need to succeed in life.

Adolescence is a time of extraordinary mental and intellectual growth for your child. With dyslexia, there is often a pattern of "late blooming"—it is very typical for a child who has struggled tremendously in the early years to suddenly develop new competencies during the teenage years; a child whose parents were told that he would never be "college material" may end up excelling in high school and later go on to earn a Ph.D.

As a parent, you love your child and want the best for her, but there is a natural tendency to see your child in the light of your previous experience. If she has always needed extra help to keep up in school, it is hard for you to believe that she is going to suddenly change and become an honors student. Your daughter may want to enroll in an honors or college preparatory class at school such that you feel, in your heart, is too difficult for her; you don't want to see her hurt, so it is natural for you to try to steer her to something more suited to her abilities. But that is a mistake; you may find to your surprise that the more challenging the course, the better your child does. You can't know that this will be the case, of course—but you can never find out unless you allow your child to try. The fact that your child wants to meet a challenge is usually a good indication that she will be successful. Individuals with dyslexia seem to be blessed with an extra dose of persistence and perseverance, perhaps because their early struggles have conditioned them to expect to work hard to succeed.

 ALERT!

Do not push your child to take on challenges that he does not want. The key to your teen's success in meeting new challenges is his own internal motivation. A student with dyslexia with a passionate interest will overcome many odds in pursuit of that passion; parental prodding cannot substitute for that inner drive. Just as you should support your child if he feels ready to work to a higher standard than he has in the past, you must also respect your child if he prefers to choose an easier path.

Accept Your Child

If you have been working on getting help for your child for many years, by the time your child is a teenager you may have become something on an expert on the subjects of what your child needs and what program he should have to get it. You are accustomed to advocating and planning for your child, and you have come to see his dyslexia as your responsibility

When your child is in his early teens, it is time to reassess and allow the dyslexia to become his responsibility. That doesn't mean that you stop caring, but it does mean that you allow your child a much greater role in planning for himself, including giving him the right to choose what sort of special educational intervention he wishes to have or to discontinue specialized therapy or tutoring. You don't want to give up on your child, but acceptance of limitations is not always the same as giving up. It is very rare that a teenager with dyslexia has no ability whatsoever to read; what is more common is that the teen reads at an elementary school level and that reading is difficult. Most teens in that position would like to read better, but teens also want to explore other interests. Your teen may simply decide he would rather devote his energies to something he is good at than on continuing to improve reading skills that he now feels are adequate for his needs. He may have talents in other areas, such as art, music, or athletics, where he would rather focus his energies, and he may be comfortable with the compensation strategies he has developed for areas of weakness.

It is important for your teen's self-esteem, and for family harmony, that you show her that you respect and accept her the way she is. A young child will simply accept the idea that her parents know what is best, and go along happily. Around the time of puberty, your teen may begin to see parental urging in a different light. Though your love and concern has not changed, your teen may see your well-intentioned advice as an indication that you do not have faith in her, or that you do not think she is good enough to meet your standards. During early adolescence, your teenager is essentially reshaping her own self-image and is very vulnerable to perceived negative messages. Thus it is crucial to her self-esteem that your role shift from manager to advisor, and that you allow her to exercise an increasing amount of control over her own life. Of course you are still a parent and should intervene when clearly necessary, but you need to also accept that your teen may make some decisions that do not fit with your hopes and aspirations for her future. If you secretly dream that your child will become a doctor, and instead your teen announces that she has decided medical school is too difficult and she has decided to train to be a paramedic instead, you need to be ready to accept that your teen's plans may be far more practical.

Extracurricular Activities

You should encourage your teen to participate in any sports or extracurricular activities that he is interested in, including church youth groups, recreational clubs, hobbies, volunteer work, working for a political campaign or cause, theater, musical performance, or scouting. If your teen doesn't seem interested in much of anything, try to nudge him toward any activity that you think might pique his interest.

 ESSENTIAL

It is important for your teen's self-esteem for him to have social opportunities with other young people; if school is a struggle for him, nonacademic pursuits provide an opportunity for him to demonstrate competence or even to excel.

When your teenager is struggling to keep up in school, you may feel that he needs more time to study. If you see that his outside activities are taking up a large amount of his time and energy, you may wish to see him drop some activities or cut back on his participation. It is important for you to help your teen to find balance in his life, but it is vital that your teen is able to participate in activities where he has a sense of fulfillment and self-worth. If your teen is struggling to keep up in school, the message he is getting with his grade reports is that he must not be very smart; and over time he is likely to get discouraged. Teens who are under stress or have a poor self-image are at risk for depression, which can lead to alcohol and drug abuse, risk-taking behavior, sexual promiscuity, eating disorders, and suicidal thoughts or attempts. Thus, it is important for your teen to have the opportunity to participate in activities that keep him active and engaged.

Your teen's activities can also be a powerful motivating force that will lead to her putting more effort into her schoolwork. If participation in a school sport or club requires that your teen maintain a minimum grade point average, she will have a motivation to work harder even if she has decided that she doesn't plan on attending college. If the sport or activity is something that she could continue in college, then participation may itself be an incentive to aspire to a college education. Activities outside of school may bring your teen in contact with peers or adults who become her mentors or role models.

If your teen discovers an endeavor that he feels passionately about, or if he seems particularly talented in a sport or visual or performing arts, do everything you can to support and encourage this activity. You will still want to help your teen maintain balance in his life; if the outside endeavor becomes all-consuming or stressful, it may be time to place some limits. However, your teen's passion will be the fuel that will inspire him to succeed in life, and it may also plant the seeds of a future career.

Getting a Job

Your teen may want to get an after-school or summer job. Although you may rightfully be worried about whether the job will cut into time needed for study during the school year, employment offers many benefits for a teen with dyslexia. Talk to your teen about how many hours of working are reasonable. You may find that your child actually becomes more disciplined about studying once he is working; his commitment to his employer will help motivate him to better manage his time.

 ALERT!

If your teen is required to fill out a written application for a job, suggest that he bring it home to fill out. Have him fill it out in pencil first, or make a photocopy for him to work with. Misspelled words, illegible handwriting, and questions left unanswered give a bad impression. You can help by proofreading and reviewing the application for your teen.

If your child struggles in school, the job can offer a welcome respite and an environment in which he feels more confident of his abilities. Your daughter will learn new skills through on-the-job training, where she will usually learn through observing others do a task, and then doing it on her own while being supervised. This learning-by-doing is ideal for her learning style, so in the workplace your teen may turn out to be a quick learner who earns praise from her employers. Her social skills play a greater part in success here as well; a winning smile or an eager attitude is a great asset.

Of course, dyslexia can also create problems in the workplace, especially if your child takes on a job for which he is not well suited. His career in a fast-food restaurant may be cut short by a habit of repeatedly mixing up orders or incorrectly counting out change. It is important for you to help direct your child to seek jobs in areas where he has stronger interests or abilities.

Community service or volunteer work is another great way for a teen with dyslexia to build a sense of confidence and self-esteem. Helping others simply feels good, and your child will quickly see that his efforts are needed and appreciated. Volunteer work also often involves hands-on activities which your teen is well able to handle, whether it is preparing meals at a homeless shelter or wielding a hammer for Habitat for Humanity. Volunteering can also help your child meet people or gain skills that will later lead to a paying job.

Keep in mind that your teen's experience in school has been that she is expected to be able to succeed in a wide range of academic subjects, whether she is interested in them or not, and she has generally been graded and measured by comparison to same-age peers. Her sense of her place in the world may be profoundly influenced by the grades she has received in school; she may have gotten the message that she is a C student and therefore cannot expect much out of life.

Through work, she will discover a different reality. Individuals of varied ages and abilities work together, and few employers expect anyone to be a jack-of-all-trades. Rather, in the workplace individuals have the opportunity to specialize based on their interests and inclinations, and nonacademic skills are often very highly valued. Through work, your teen may discover what she is "good with," and she will also likely receive positive feedback from her employer, coworkers, and customers for a job well done.

Getting a Driver's License

Learning to drive can present extra challenges to some, but not all, teens with dyslexia. Usually, by the time your child has reached high school, his reading skills will be adequate for purposes of taking driver's ed and passing a typical written test to get a permit. If your teen has problems, it is more likely to be with controlling the vehicle or passing the behind-the-wheel test. One problem your child may face is simply the process of motor and perceptual coordination; driving essentially involves a heightened level of awareness and the need to perform several visual and motor tasks at once. For most people, this quickly becomes second nature with practice. For some individuals with dyslexia, it is difficult to reach this point of automatic response for the same reason that other skills involving motor coordination and balance may be difficult to master. If your child had a hard time learning to tie his shoes or ride a bicycle, he may experience the same sort of difficulties with driving. Your teenager can eventually learn to drive comfortably, but it may take longer than average to get to that point. If your child has difficulties learning to drive, you may find it worthwhile to pay for extra lessons from a professional driving school.

 **FACT**

Some teens don't want to drive. They may be reluctant to take driving lessons, or avoid driving even after they have their licenses. For some teens, the experience of being behind the wheel is simply frightening; they are unsure of themselves and have difficulty coping with the demands that driving makes on their ability to focus attention and respond quickly. Unless it is absolutely necessary for your teen to drive for family reasons, do not put pressure on him. Many teens simply are not ready to handle the responsibility.

Another common problem is communication between parent and teen—you tell your son to watch out for oncoming traffic on the left, and he looks over to the right. If your teen has difficulty with remembering left from right, you need to simply avoid using those words in giving instructions—say "driver's side" and "passenger's side" instead. Your teen may also have a slow response time to verbal commands, again a function of his language processing issues; be sure that you give directions while he is driving well in advance. Your teen may also find it very difficult to use the rearview mirror, which can intensify the directional confusion that is part of dyslexia. These issues can also cause problems when your teen takes the behind-the-wheel test.

 **FACT**

Some people with dyslexia are excellent drivers. Championship race car driver Jackie Stewart and Indy 500 racer Stan Wattles both have dyslexia. After retiring from racing, Stewart became president of the Scottish Dyslexia Trust and vice-president of the British Dyslexia Association; Wattles donates a portion of his earnings from each race to a foundation he created to help children with learning disabilities.

If your child is a very slow reader, this could also create problems. Your teen will recognize most traffic signs by their shape and color, and will have no difficulty understanding signs with pictures and symbols like arrows. But she may not read quickly enough to recognize the name of a street or freeway exit before she has passed the sign; if giving directions, you should try to give other visual clues besides the name of the street.

Finally, some—but not all—individuals with dyslexia have a terrible sense of direction and easily get lost or disoriented while driving. Over time, your teen will develop coping strategies, but there may be some interesting adventures along the way.

You should not assume in advance that your teen will have problems learning to drive. Although the problems mentioned earlier affect some individuals, many teens with dyslexia have no problem at all learning to drive and in fact they can be extremely skilled drivers. For some, the strong spatial-reasoning skills that accompany dyslexia give rise to a greater sense of awareness of the vehicle's position in relation to other cars, as well as stronger peripheral vision. Getting a license is also a great ego-booster for a teenager. If your teen is one of the first of his peers to get a license, which might happen if your teen was ever held back a year in school, the license is an important status symbol. Because driving is so important in the lives of many teenagers, getting a license can feel like a great accomplishment. Additionally, the license allows your teen more independence, and may give him the means or the motivation to take on an after-school job or volunteer activities, which can also lead to greater self-confidence.

CHAPTER 19

Making Choices in High School

H IGH SCHOOL IS A TIME for tremendous physical, intellectual, and emotional growth and exploration. Your teenager will find his school life now includes an expanded array of social, athletic, and extracurricular activities, as well as an enticing choice of elective courses. He experiences a changing relationship with teachers, and is likely to find some who are able to challenge and motivate him, as well as to experience problems with others. The choices he makes now have direct and lasting impact on his adult life. He may find that with his greater maturity and ability to shape his own education, his academic life becomes easier. While he once may have struggled with basic arithmetic and reading his science text, he may find he has a knack for understanding concepts introduced in algebra and geometry, and is at home in the hands-on environment of the chemistry lab. On the other hand, your may be the parent of a teen who was previously able to cope well despite his dyslexia, but now suddenly finds himself overwhelmed by increased demands for reading and writing and meeting multiple deadlines for his different classes. This chapter covers some of the issues your teen may face, and options that may affect the choices he makes.

Choosing a High School

If you live in a larger community or urban area, your teen may have the choice of several different high school programs. The choice of high school can be an important turning point in your teen's life, because he may be able to choose a school that more closely meets his individual needs or learning style, or focuses on a program geared to his interests.

Specialty Schools

Many communities have magnet schools or specialized schools, such as schools with a focus on the visual or performing arts, an emphasis on science and technology, or a strong college preparatory curriculum. If your child has a strong interest and aptitude, the magnet school may provide a more stimulating environment. Because of the high coincidence of dyslexia with creativity, schools with a focus on arts often have a large population of kids with learning styles similar to your teen's, even if they are not formally diagnosed with dyslexia. Attending a school where the students share a common interest may help keep your teen motivated and foster stronger friendships with his peers. Many magnet schools have special audition or testing requirements to gain entry; be sure to inquire about these procedures at least a year before your child is scheduled to start high school.

 ALERT!

Even though your child may have had academic difficulties in the past, do not allow a school counselor to dissuade your child from following a college preparatory track if she thinks she may want to attend college. Your child's motivation is the key to her success; she should use her high school education to lay the groundwork for her future educational or career objectives.

If your teen continues to struggle with academics or seems to lack motivation to complete a college preparatory curriculum, he may want to choose a vocational high school. These high schools will provide training geared to giving your child marketable skills, as well as including a basic academic curriculum. Many students at vocational high schools do go on to college. Usually the classes given in the student's chosen area of concentration are hands-on and very practically oriented. Many students with dyslexia begin to feel comfortable with school for the first time when they are able to begin to learn and apply skills in areas of interest.

There are a wide array of skills and programs taught at vocational high schools in various parts of the country. Some examples are electronics, graphic design, television production, carpentry, cosmetology, culinary arts, horticulture, information technology, automotive, child care, architectural drafting, data processing, telecommunications, and marketing. Attending a vocational high school can be a rewarding experience for a student who is uncertain about her academic interests and abilities. The teen can experience increased self-confidence through gaining technical job skills, and this can be a valuable boost for a student whose difficulties with reading or writing might otherwise make it difficult to gain employment.

Most school districts also have alternative or continuation high schools. These are schools that usually serve students who have become disenchanted with the regular high school environment. The schools provide a focus on building student self-esteem and helping to get disaffected high schoolers back on track. Generally faculty-student ratio is quite low and the schools are very small compared to regular high schools. Many of the students have had disciplinary problems at other high schools, but students may choose to attend an alternative high school for many reasons. The goal of these schools is to provide students who are not able to function well in the traditional high school environment with the counseling and teaching needed to earn a high school diploma. If your teenager is in danger of failing or considering dropping out of high school, the alternative high school environment may be the place where he is able to regroup and salvage his education.

School Size and Scheduling

Even if the school does not have a special academic or educational program, your teen may be faced with some choices related to the way courses are scheduled or the size of the school. Traditionally, high school students will take six or seven classes daily, moving from one period of approximately forty-five minutes to another with very short breaks in between. Many high schools have shifted to block scheduling, which allows the student to take the same number of courses overall, but class periods are longer and there are fewer classes each day; usually there are also longer break periods between each class.

The advantage of the block schedule is that the student has fewer classes to worry about each day—usually only three or four— and longer class periods allow teachers to explore subjects in greater depth and give more attention to their students. Many students with dyslexia have a very difficult time handling transitions, and with organizing and keeping track of assignments for their classes. For these students, the traditional high school day may simply be overwhelming, and the more leisurely pace of the block schedule may be helpful. The drawback with block scheduling is that more material must be covered in each class; in a difficult subject, such as mathematics or chemistry, a student may find that the teacher is simply covering too much ground in a single class session. A student with difficulty focusing attention for sustained periods may simply not have the stamina for a class that lasts ninety minutes or more.

More school districts are moving toward "small schools" or "learning communities," often housing several small high schools with a few hundred students each, within a single campus once occupied by a larger, traditional high school. The concept of a small school is simply to provide a more supportive environment for students in a context where the faculty has a better opportunity to know the students, and students have a greater sense of responsibility because they get to know one another and their teachers quite well. Discipline problems tend to be reduced, because the small school setting simply allows teachers to keep a closer watch on their students. The small school movement may also lead to a greater number of options, as schools can develop very specialized areas of focus. The disadvantage is that the smaller schools have more limited resources, and within each school there will be fewer choices for classes and electives than is typical at a larger high school.

The High School Guidance Counselor

High school also introduces a new person in your teenager's life, the high school guidance counselor. Your child's counselor will be working with him to help shape educational choices, including choice of classes and planning for the future. If your child has an IEP, he will now also regularly be included in the IEP planning process, and IEP meetings will include transitional planning for life after high school.

Although the counselor is important in your child's life, the counselor may not understand the unique issues that are part of dyslexia. It is possible that the counselor may guide your child toward choices that may limit future options. You need to keep informed of your child's options on your own. Talk to your child regularly about his plans and aspirations and about the classes he is taking at school. Find out what types of courses colleges typically require of high school students, including colleges offering specialized majors or courses of study that your teenager may be interested in pursuing. The counselor may advise course selections that seem appropriate based on your child's past performance and history of academic difficulties, but may not meet minimum requisites for admission to your state university or to more selective colleges. While you should not push your child toward unrealistic goals, you also need to keep in mind that his early struggles with reading and writing may mask his true intellectual capacity.

Your teen's unique combination of strengths and weaknesses may also indicate that he should forge a specially tailored path through high school. For example, while the counselor may be used to directing college-bound students toward a uniform schedule of challenging courses, your son may need to strike a balance between English and history classes geared to the ordinary student, with a focus on advanced math and science courses.

 ESSENTIAL

The academic performance of students with dyslexia often follows a paradoxical pattern. Often, students who have difficulty earning strong grades for easy courses do very well in more challenging courses. You should let your child's interest and motivation be the guide to choosing his path through high school; support and encourage your teenager if he wishes to select a demanding academic schedule. It is generally easy for a child to drop a difficult course in favor of an easier one if he cannot keep up.

If your teen is planning on attending college, she may also wish to take honors or Advanced Placement (AP) classes. These classes may have "weighted" grades, meaning that the grades earned are given added points for calculating your child's grade point average; for example, a "B" in AP English may be the equivalent of an "A" in the regular English class. The AP courses are also geared to helping students prepare for an exam that can qualify them to receive college credit for the courses. Your child's counselor may not be aware of her interest in AP courses; encourage your teen to ask early about the process for obtaining entry into these courses, which usually are available in junior and senior years. In some schools the courses are open to all students, whereas in others they may require a teacher recommendation or an application process to win entrance. If your child is "tracked" into remedial level classes when he enters high school, it could be difficult to gain entry into more advanced courses later on.

Electives and Extracurricular Activities

Your teenager will find that high school is an exciting time to pursue new interests and develop talents. Your child's choice of electives will likely include art, band, or drama. Activities outside class such as debate or mock trial may provide an opportunity to improve verbal skills. Your teen may choose to participate in activities like student government or production of the school yearbook.

High school athletics can be very important; in addition to the health benefits of active participation in sports, your teenager may now find that prowess in sports opens important doors to college admissions. Even if your teen does not play a sport well enough to attract the attention of college recruiters, however, she will likely benefit from the experience of participating on a competitive team.

Foreign Language Learning

Many high schools require students to study at least two years of a foreign language, and colleges may prefer students who have three or four years of language study. Students with dyslexia often encounter difficulties when studying a foreign language. For this reason, many students seek an exemption from foreign language requirements.

 ESSENTIAL

Many colleges require their applicants to have taken at least two years of foreign language study in high school. Although it possible that a college would waive the entrance requirement in cases of dyslexia, there is no law requiring that they do so—Section 504 has not been held to require colleges to grant exemptions from foreign language study in such cases. Thus, if your child plans on attending college, it makes sense to at least attempt studying a language.

However, it is a mistake to assume that because your child has dyslexia, he will not be able to do well in a foreign language class. There are many ways in which your child can benefit from study of a foreign language, and your child may do well in an immersion-style classroom, where the emphasis is on developing oral communication skills. Many students find that their reading and spelling in English improves after studying a foreign language such as French or Spanish, as they become more aware of the roots and structure of English words and grammar. Students with dyslexia also sometimes find it easier to read material in a foreign language that is phonetically consistent, such as Spanish. Some students with dyslexia enjoy foreign language study and even go on to major in a foreign language in college.

Choosing a Language

In theory, it is best if your child chooses to study the language which seems easiest, but there are also other factors to consider. If your child has a choice of languages, try to find out something about each of the teachers and the methods they use. Your child may do better in a class where the emphasis is on learning oral conversational skills, and students are taught in an interactive setting, with games and songs used to keep kids motivated. If the teacher expects the students to memorize a lot of material and learn primarily through reading, or places great emphasis on writing and learning correct grammar, your child may encounter significant barriers.

 FACT

If your child is interested in learning a foreign language, you should certainly encourage her. However, some languages, such as Spanish, Italian, and Latin, may be easier to learn than others because of the simpler rules of spelling.

If possible, encourage your child to arrange to sit in as a visitor to a class with each teacher in advance; this will help your child get a sense of where she might do best. Some students are overwhelmed simply because the teacher talks too fast for them to catch what is being said; your child will probably prefer a teacher who has a relaxed style and is careful to speak slowly and clearly enunciate words, with many opportunities for repetition and practice.

Some factors to consider with each language are:

- Your child's level of motivation to learn the particular language
- Whether your child already has some familiarity with or exposure to the language
- Whether the language uses the Roman alphabet or a different alphabet
- Whether the language is written in a phonetically consistent manner
- The relative ease or difficulty of pronunciation of words in each language
- The relative complexity of the grammatical system
- Your child's preferred mode of learning and his individual pattern of strengths and weaknesses

Some students who anticipate difficulty with learning to speak a language prefer Latin. Most study of Latin will involve written texts, and the study of Latin generally is extremely helpful to a student in learning English morphology, which in turn may increase reading comprehension and fluency in general. American Sign Language is another very popular alternative for students with dyslexia, who generally find it easy and fun to learn a language made up of gestures rather than words.

If your teenager's high school does not offer a particular language, he may be able to satisfy the language requirement by taking a course elsewhere, such as a local community college or a correspondence course via the Internet.

Language Approaches that Work

Despite concerns that foreign language instruction will be a barrier for learners with dyslexia, there are many students who have successfully gained fluency in multiple languages. Individuals with dyslexia are usually able to acquire basic conversational abilities in a new language within a reasonable time after moving to countries where the language is spoken. The problems experienced with classroom learning often simply reflects the failure of traditional approaches to teaching foreign languages, which often rely heavily on rote memorization or listening and repetition of short phrases.

 FACT

> One intriguing study showed that English-speaking children with dyslexia were able to rapidly learn and remember words they were taught using Japanese Kanji, a pictographic alphabet. (In the study, the symbols were used to represent English words). When learning Japanese, students usually are taught the phonetic Kana system first, but students with dyslexia often find that system is also easy because of its phonetic consistency.

The degree of difficulty with learning to read and write in the new language seems to be determined mostly by the level of complexity of the written system. Students with dyslexia do not seem to report particular difficulty with learning a new alphabet, if it represents a phonetically consistent system. On the other hand, numerous studies show that English is a particularly difficult language for people with dyslexia; so your child may be pleasantly surprised to discover the logic inherent in a different language.

Total Physical Response Method

Total Physical Response (TPR) is a method for foreign language learning that attempts to replicate the natural way that small children learn to speak and understand language. It incorporates physical movement and gestures in an immersion environment; the teacher speaks only the language being taught, while using gestures to help convey meaning. In the beginning, the teacher gives commands that require some sort of movement from the students. For example, a Spanish teacher might say *levantate,* motioning for her students to stand up; after the students correctly stand up, she might say *sientate,* gesturing for the students to sit down. After a few tries, the teacher simply gives the commands without the gestures—by then, the students have all easily learned the new words. The TPR method moves from simple commands to more complex interactive activities, such as acting out skits and playing games, but always there is some sort of movement or response from the student.

With TPR, students are not required to speak the language until they do so spontaneously; usually this happens after several weeks or a few months in the classroom. Written forms of the language are not introduced until students have developed a good oral understanding. This method was originally developed by a university professor, James Asher, who was interested in studying brain-based processes of learning; thus it is has been extensively researched. Dr. Asher believes that all learning is enhanced by methods that integrate left and right brain hemispheric processing. He has not considered or researched the application of his approach to dyslexia, but his approach is based on similar concepts that were at the heart of Samuel Orton's reasoning in favor of developing multisensory methods to teach reading and writing. In any case, the emphasis is on learning simple words and phrases before gradually moving on to more complex sentence structures. With reading and writing deferred until after the student has achieved a working knowledge of the language, the TPR classroom is a positive environment for a student with dyslexia. This method is widely known among foreign language teachers; many incorporate some TPR ideas even if they do not rely solely on the method.

Language Immersion Opportunities

One good way for a teenager to gain proficiency in a foreign language is to participate in a summer language camp, or summer foreign exchange program. Language camps or villages provide an immersion experience where there is intense instruction as well as around-the-clock exposure to the language. With a summer foreign exchange program, your teen will usually live in the home of a host family, with planned activities which may include attending language classes, sightseeing, or participating in volunteer work. Most summer exchanges are from 4 to 6 weeks. These programs are a good way for your teen to get added experience in a language, particularly if he has a strong motivation to learn; they also provide a wonderful cross-cultural experience and opportunity to travel.

Your teen will almost certainly become fluent in a foreign language if she chooses to participate in a longer foreign exchange program, for a semester or a school year. In these programs, students attend a high school in their host country, living with and sharing activities with a host family. Some of the more well-established programs that place teenagers in homes around the globe are AFS International, YFU (Youth for Understanding), and Rotary Youth Exchange. Spending a semester or year abroad is a major undertaking for teenager, and is only appropriate for kids who are independent-natured and have a love of adventure.

Generally, the academic expectations for high school exchange students are not high, as their hosts are well aware of the difficulties of learning a new language. Thus, your teen will probably not have to worry about academic performance in the foreign high school; generally he will not be placed in difficult courses or have his work graded. On the other hand, your child may miss important coursework at home, leading him to fall further behind his peers. It can also be very difficult to coordinate time to study abroad with fulfilling high school graduation requirements. Many students choose to spend their year abroad after finishing high school at home, as part of a "gap" year between high school and college.

Language Learning Software

There are a number of computer programs designed to assist students in learning foreign languages. One of the most widely respected is the Rosetta Stone system, which is used in many schools and is also available for home use. This system is available for about twenty-five different languages and is highly interactive; the student listens to a set of foreign words and phrases while looking at pictures depicting their meaning. Then, when the student feels ready, there is a computer quiz, during which the student must choose the picture that matches the word from a set of four illustrations. As the student's proficiency increases, the level of difficulty rises. The student can opt to look at written words as well as to listen to the language, and the software also affords speaking practice using a microphone and voice recognition software. The computer game-like setting allows the student to control the pace; in most cases, the student rapidly gains a strong vocabulary.

CHAPTER 20

Planning for College and Career

A BIG PART OF HIGH SCHOOL is planning for your teen's life after he graduates. Many students with dyslexia go on to college, often attending prestigious national universities. Some choose to attend their state colleges, or to begin by attending community college or a private two-year junior college. Other students will defer college entrance by a year or more, perhaps exploring volunteer or travel opportunities. Some may join the military, and others may choose to attend a trade school or look for employment immediately. Your child's choices should be governed primarily by his interests and level of motivation. Even if his academic performance in high school has been poor or uneven, a college education is not impossible; but if your child prefers to avoid school, he may do better with options that will lead directly to development of work experience and a career.

College Entrance Exams

If your child is considering college, he will usually need to take and pass college entrance exams. Most colleges will accept either the ACT Assessment or the College Board SAT. Some colleges also require that students take several subject-specific exams, called the SAT II.

The ACT Assessment is a three-hour test containing 215 questions covering topics in English, math, reading, and science. Effective in February 2005, there will also be an optional 30-minute writing exam, which may be required by many colleges. Many students with dyslexia prefer the ACT because questions are more closely tied to the school curriculum. The ACT is scored by counting all right answers, without deducting points for wrong answers; thus there is no penalty for guessing. Also, ACT reports only test results from a specific test administration; the student designates which test score will be sent to the college. Thus, a student can take the test on several occasions and choose to only report her highest score.

Beginning in March 2005, the SAT will be a three-hour, twenty-minute-long test that includes three separate sections on writing, critical reading, and math. The writing section includes multiple-choice questions on grammar and usage, and a student-written essay. The critical reading section includes sentence completions and questions concerning the content of both short and long reading passages. The math section includes concepts taught in college preparatory mathematics up through the third-year level; this generally includes geometry and advanced algebra.

ACT Testing Accommodations

If your child would like accommodations such as extra time to complete the ACT, a written request must be submitted by or before the registration deadline for the exam. A student seeking accommodations such as the use of a large-print test booklet, but who does not need extended time, should submit a written request describing the nature of the disability and the accommodations being requested, and written documentation from his school describing in detail the accommodations he normally receives. A student seeking extended time must complete a special application which includes documentation of a diagnosis and evaluation completed within three years of the testing dates. A student may receive accommodations that have not previously been given by the school, but the evaluation submitted with the application must explain why such modifications are needed if they were not afforded in the past.

SAT Testing Accommodations

If your child qualifies for special accommodations under an IEP or 504 plan, he may qualify for similar modifications for the SAT or SAT II. These accommodations are also available for the Advanced Placement exams and the PSAT. In order to qualify for such accommodations, your child must meet these criteria:

- Must have a disability that necessitates testing accommodations.
- Must have documentation on file at school that supports the need for the requested accommodations and meets College Board guidelines for documentation.
- Must receive the requested accommodations, due to the disability, for school-based tests.

Your child must submit a request for accommodation well before the date of the exam. In general, the deadlines for requests are about six weeks prior to scheduled test dates, but it is recommended that the student submit the SSD Student Eligibility Form as soon as possible. The accommodations that may be available are as follows:

Extended time. Students who read very slowly may be granted up to 50 percent more time to complete the test; if the student needs an audiocassette version of the test, the student may be granted up to twice the usual amount of time to complete the tests.

Large-format test booklets and/or answer sheets. Students with visual tracking problems may benefit from using an enlarged format answer sheet, rather than the standard Scantron (the familiar fill-in-the-bubble format).

Audiocassette/reader. Students who are not able to read on their own because of very poor decoding skills may qualify for an oral test using audiocassettes; the student is expected to bring his own equipment and to be familiar with using it.

Computer. Students who cannot write the essay section due a documented disability such as dysgraphia may be granted the use of a computer for that portion of the exam only. The grade on the written essay will not be reduced for poor handwriting, so a computer will not be afforded if the student is able to write or print legibly, even if writing is messy.

Extra/extended breaks. Students with attention, concentration, or distractibility problems or who need medication may be granted additional short five- to ten-minute breaks between test sections.

Keep in mind that the College Board requires specific documentation of any learning disability, including recent evaluations by qualified professionals. Students will only be granted accommodations that are similar to modifications that have also been afforded at school; your child will probably not be able to qualify for modifications that are different than he has been routinely afforded in the past.

Not All Colleges Require Exams

Many excellent colleges do not require students to submit standardized test scores. Colleges are becoming increasingly aware that standardized test scores are of dubious value in predicting success rates, especially because they often reflect the level of student preparation through coaching or studying for the test, rather than school achievement. Many students with dyslexia simply do not ever test well, whether or not they receive accommodations.

The National Center for Fair and Open Testing has compiled a list of more than 700 colleges and universities nationwide that admit a substantial number of students without regard to test scores. Their list, available at the Web site *www.fairtest.org*, includes a wide variety of institutions, from small, private liberal arts colleges to large, public university systems. Colleges that de-emphasize or do not require test scores base their admission decisions on a variety of other factors, including high school academic record, letters of recommendation, application essays, specific talent or accomplishments of the student, or a student portfolio.

 **FACT**

> The late Senator Paul Wellstone, who was a professor at one of the nation's top liberal arts colleges for many years before entering politics, had dyslexia and was initially denied entrance to graduate school because of his poor scores on the Graduate Record Exam (GRE); fortunately, he was able to gain admittance by appealing to a sympathetic dean.

Choosing a College

Your child's choice of college will be governed by many factors. Even the most prestigious and highly selective colleges will provide accommodations for students with learning disabilities, so his dyslexia should not be a barrier. However, in choosing a college, it is important for your teenager to consider his own learning style and preferences. He may find that he prefers a college with flexible graduation requirements, or he may want a college where class sizes are small to allow close interaction between students and instructors. Encourage your child to obtain the course catalogues for colleges he is interested in, as these provide information about school policies and course sequences that are not covered in the glossy brochures. By comparing catalogs from different schools, your teen will see that requirements for majors can differ considerably; this can be important if there are specific courses that your child would like to avoid.

Keep in mind that there are literally hundreds of excellent colleges your child can choose from. Many have very lenient admission standards, and will accept your child even he has received mostly Bs and Cs in high school. Attending a smaller, less well-known college can be a distinct advantage for a student who sometimes struggles with learning, as the school environment may be less competitive and the instructors more willing to provide support and guidance.

College Support for Students with Dyslexia

Because of provisions of the Americans with Disabilities Act and Section 504, almost every college will make some provisions for students with learning disabilities; the only colleges exempt from the federal legal requirements are some small religious colleges that do not accept any federal funding or benefits for their students. However, the law requires only that colleges make "reasonable accommodations" for students; it neither dictates what is "reasonable" or mandates extra support services. Thus, the level and type of support can be very different from one institution to the next.

In addition to the usual questions your child may have about college, such as admissions requirements, academic programs, and dorm life, your teenager needs to make additional inquiries, either through correspondence, review of brochures or Web site material, or while visiting the campus. Find out what special programs and support services are in place at each college your child is considering, and how long the support program has existed. You and your child should specifically ask about types of assistance he is most likely to need, such as arrangements for students who need help taking notes or writing papers, or availability of recorded books.

 FACT

Jonathan Mooney, author of *Learning Outside the Lines*, has severe dyslexia and didn't learn to read until age twelve. He graduated from an Ivy League college, Brown University, with a degree in English literature after gaining admittance as a transfer student. He attributes his success in part to choosing a college with an "academic culture" that "values self-directed learning, independent study, and diversity."

Ask what the procedures are for negotiating accommodations and modifications with instructors. Are students on their own, or will the college help with advocacy? What is the procedure for resolving disputes with professors?

Find out whether support services like tutoring or a writing lab are included in the tuition, or whether your child will be assessed additional fees. Ask whether tutoring and academic counseling are handled through the learning disabilities support center or through academic departments and general counseling offices. It is often important that advisors and tutors have experience with students who have learning disabilities. Ask whether there are courses available in basic writing and study skills, and whether such courses earn academic credit.

Ask how many students receive support each year, and what percentage of students receiving extra services graduate. Low numbers may indicate a weak level of support.

Ask what sort of documentation is needed to obtain support services. Some colleges may accept the high school IEP, but others may require a recent evaluation by a qualified professional.

College Classes and Graduation Requirements

Your child's success in college may depend on many factors unrelated to services specifically afforded to students with dyslexia. In choosing a college, encourage your child to ask these questions:

What is the average class size in her areas of academic interest? Do classes consist mostly of lectures, discussion, or laboratory sessions? Do professors usually give multiple-choice tests, or essay-based exams; or do they rely largely on student papers or projects for grading? Ask about the college grading system, and whether it is possible to take some courses on a pass/fail basis.

Does the college, or your child's likely major, have a mathematics or foreign language requirement? If these subjects are likely to present a problem, may other courses such as computer courses, an international studies course, or American Sign Language be substituted to satisfy such requirements? If not, does the college ever waive these requirements for students with documented disabilities?

Ask what the minimum number of credits are required each semester or quarter in order to be considered a full-time student, and how many credits are typically earned for a single class. Find out if the college has core requirements that must be fulfilled in the first year, and what those are. Your child may do better if he is able to limit course load. You should also find out whether there is a maximum number of courses allowed, and whether there are extra fees for taking courses beyond a certain amount of credit; it is possible that your child may at some point have to repeat a course to make up for a failing or incomplete grade. Find out what the college polices are for students who take more than four years to complete their degrees, especially with regard to financial aid.

Find out what is sort of work-learn programs and internships are available. If your teenager learns best from hands-on experience, consider choosing a college that encourages and offers academic credit for work experience in his field of interest.

Financing College

Many families wonder whether there are special scholarships available for students with dyslexia. While there are a few sources of funding, the vast majority of college grants and scholarships are either awarded to students solely on the basis of financial need, or else based on merit or an outstanding accomplishment, or talent in arts or sports. Colleges generally use scholarship money to entice particularly strong candidates to attend, rather than to subsidize students who need extra help; thus your search for college funding should begin with a focus on your child's strengths. Your child may also be eligible for scholarships available through your employer, via local service groups, or special scholarships geared to students from a particular ethnic or religious group. Financial assistance for college is also available to students who provide a year of public service through Americorps, or to students who enroll in the military reserves or college ROTC programs.

Funding for Students with Disabilities

There are a growing number of resources earmarked specifically for students with disabilities. Two scholarships specifically geared to students with learning disabilities are:

Marion Huber Learning through Listening Awards, offered by Recording for the Blind and Dyslexic to high school seniors who have been RFB&D members for at least one year. Awards are for $6,000 or $2,000; there are six awards given annually.

Anne Ford Scholarship, offered by the National Center for Learning Disabilities to a high school senior; the annual award is $10,000.

Financing to attend a trade school or a college program geared to qualifying for specific employment may also be available through the vocational rehabilitation system. Every state has a job training program for high school graduates who have difficulty obtaining or keeping employment because of a disability, including dyslexia. This can pay up to 100 percent of college costs, including tuition, books, living expenses, and transportation.

Need-Based Aid

Because of the high cost of college tuition and housing, students are often eligible for a significant amount of assistance based on financial need, even when their parents earn well over median income levels. To determine eligibility for federally subsidized financial aid, students must annually submit a form provided by the U.S. Department of Education called the Free Application for Federal Student Aid (FAFSA). Based on information provided about family income and assets with this form, an expected family contribution (EFC) is calculated. If the total amount of expected college costs exceed the EFC, your child will be eligible to receive federally subsidized loans and to participate in work-study to earn money on campus. Low-income families may qualify for additional loans and for a federally subsidized Pell Grant.

If the subsidized aid that your child receives is not enough to cover all costs, parents with a good credit history can qualify for a federally guaranteed PLUS loan, which will allow you to borrow amounts needed up to the total costs of college at preferred rates. Interest on both student and parent loans may also be tax-deductible;

there are a number of other tax deductions and credits that are available to parents financing their child's higher education as well.

Barriers to High School Graduation

Many states now require students to pass an exit exam in order to obtain their high school diploma. While motivated by genuine concern about the educational system, these tests often discriminate unfairly against students with dyslexia. Your child may have very limited areas of difficulty, such as a disability with math, which makes it impossible for him to pass the test, even though he has studied hard and earned good grades in high school. In some cases, your child's problem may simply be with test-taking—you may observe that he is functioning quite well working at home or in the classroom, but for some reason he consistently performs poorly on tests.

Unfortunately, many states have also failed to provide adequate accommodations to students with learning disabilities when taking the exit exam. Thus you may find that your child is able to obtain high scores on SAT math exams, where students are urged to bring calculators, but cannot pass the state exit exam, where calculators are not allowed. Lawsuits have been brought in many states to compel authorities to provide appropriate accommodations on these tests, or to provide for alternate forms of assessment to enable students to obtain high school diplomas. Some states offer more than one form of diploma, certificate, or exit credential, some of which do not require the exit exam; but parents are rightly concerned that their child may be left with a second-class diploma which may be viewed negatively by prospective employers or by colleges.

If your child's dyslexia makes it hard for him to pass the exit exam, or if he cannot meet high school graduation requirements for other reasons, he can work toward obtaining a GED (General Education Diploma), which is widely accepted by community colleges and employers as the "equivalent" of a high school diploma. Many four-year colleges also will accept students with GEDs, as well as welcoming transfer students who have completed two-year degrees at community colleges.

Career Planning

A young person with dyslexia can be successful with just about any career he chooses. In many cases, even compensation strategies used to cope with continuing reading difficulties turn out to be an asset. David Boies, a trial lawyer known for his exceptional courtroom skills, attributes his prodigious memory in part to reading difficulties—he learned to rely on memory of testimony he heard or of law books he read, so as to avoid the need to read or re-read written material. Many actors with dyslexia report similar experiences with memorizing their lines: they simply don't want to have to read the script a second time, so they get it right on the first try.

 FACT

> A survey of 300 self-made millionaires found that 40 percent had been diagnosed with dyslexia. A larger survey of 5,000 millionaires found that more than half reported early struggles in school. Some highly successful business leaders with dyslexia are Richard Branson, founder of Virgin Enterprises; investment banker Charles Schwab; Cisco CEO John Chambers; Craig McCaw, who pioneered the cellular industry; and Paul Orfalea, founder of Kinko's.

Of course, there are some careers that present greater barriers than others for a young person with dyslexia. One reason that so many individuals with dyslexia end up leading their own businesses may be that they didn't do so well working for someone else; it helps to be in a managerial position where a secretary or administrative assistant can take care of typing, proofreading, and filing. But it's hard to get to be the boss without working one's way up; that is one reason that a college degree is particularly useful to your child.

Generally, young people with dyslexia tend to do better with jobs that allow them to express creativity through their work, such as working as a graphic artist. This includes writing, such as television writer Steven Cannell; of course professional writers have editors available to proofread their work, if they haven't yet mastered the nuances of spelling and punctuation. Many youngsters do well with jobs involving sales, relying on their interpersonal skills.

The key to success is to mesh interests with natural abilities. Many teens are quite proficient with computers and will do well in computer-related fields; but it would be difficult for a person who did not have a natural aptitude for computer work. If your teen plans to defer college, it may be helpful for him to work with a vocational or career counselor for ideas about where to start looking for work or training when he finishes high school. Many youngsters will find their own way, led by their own interests, with long-term employment evolving from a high school job or volunteer position.

 **FACT**

> General George C. Patton apparently had dyslexia and did not learn to read until age twelve. He went on to lead a distinguished military career, becoming one of the most effective Army field commanders during World War II.

Keep in mind that making the transition from childhood to adult employment is difficult for many youngsters, and your child may explore many options before he finds his niche. Your child's imaginative approach and divergent learning style may lead him to take an unorthodox path, but as he moves into adulthood what he needs most from you is your faith, encouragement, and support. Recognize that success in many endeavors depends far more on social skills and personal qualities such as persistence and resilience than on the academic skills so important to school success, and your now-grown child will do best in areas that excite his passions. Encourage your child to follow his dreams—in the end, you may find yourself pleasantly surprised, or perhaps astounded, by how much your once-struggling child is able to accomplish in his adult life.

Famous People with Dyslexia

Historical Figures

The following individuals had characteristics of thinking and learning that are commonly associated with dyslexia. Although we cannot know for certain if they had dyslexia, many had significant difficulties learning to read or other academic problems during childhood; yet they grew to be successful and influential adults. Here is what they said about their learning problems:

Leonardo da Vinci

Wrote his notes in reverse, mirror image; manuscripts contain many spelling errors characteristic of dyslexia.

Quote: "You should prefer a good scientist without literary abilities than a literate one without scientific skills."

Andrew Jackson

Had difficulty writing; disliked reading. His spelling was so notoriously bad that it became an issue during his 1828 campaign for president.

Quote: "It's a damn poor mind that can only think of one way to spell a word."

Thomas Edison

Poor school performance, difficulty with mathematics, unable to focus, difficulty with words and speech.

Quote: "My teachers say I'm addled . . . my father thought I was stupid, and I almost decided I must be a dunce."

William Butler Yeats

Extreme difficulty learning to read as a child; never learned to spell.
Quote: "My father was an angry and impatient teacher and flung the reading book at my head."

Winston Churchill

Did poorly in school; had a childhood stutter.
Quote: "I was, on the whole, considerably discouraged by my school days. It was not pleasant to feel oneself so completely outclassed and left behind at the beginning of the race."

Albert Einstein

Considered to be a slow learner as a child; denied admission to Swiss Federal Institute of Technology after failing entrance exams.
Quote: "One had to cram all this stuff into one's mind for the examinations, whether one liked it or not. This coercion had such a deterring effect on me that, after I had passed the final examination, I found the consideration of any scientific problems distasteful to me for an entire year."

Pablo Picasso

Difficulty recognizing letters and numbers in childhood; unable to read until teenage years.
Quote: "Painting is just another way of keeping a diary."

Contemporary Figures

Here is what some contemporary figures have said about their dyslexia and learning problems.

George Burns, actor

Quote: "For me the toughest thing about dyslexia was learning to spell it."

Steven J. Cannell, screenwriter and producer

Quote: "Since I was the stupidest kid in my class, it never occurred to me to try and be perfect, so I've always been happy as a writer just to entertain myself."

Cher, singer and actress

Quote: "I never read in school. I got really bad grades—D's and F's and C's in some classes, and A's and B's in other classes. In the second week of the eleventh grade, I just quit."

Agatha Christie, writer

Quote: "I, myself, was always recognized . . . as the 'slow one' in the family. It was quite true, and I knew it and accepted it. Writing and spelling were always terribly difficult for me. . . . I was . . . an extraordinarily bad speller and have remained so until this day."

Tom Cruise, actor

Quote: "I had to train myself to focus my attention. I became very visual and learned how to create mental images in order to comprehend what I read."

Magic Johnson, athlete

Quote: "The looks, the stares, the giggles . . . I wanted to show everybody that I could do better and also that I could read."

Keira Knightley, actress

Quote: "When I was very little, kids called me stupid because I couldn't read. . . . . the dyslexia didn't help, but it's amazing what a child calling you stupid would do to make you read pretty quickly."

Danny Glover, actor

Quote: "Kids made fun of me because I was dark-skinned, had a wide nose, and was dyslexic. Even as an actor, it took me a long time to realize why words and letters got jumbled in my mind and came out differently."

Dr. John R. Horner, paleontologist

Quote: "I barely made it through school. I read real slow. But I like to find things that nobody else has found, like a dinosaur egg that has an embryo inside. Well, there are 36 of them in the world, and I found 35."

Bruce Jenner, Olympic gold medalist

Quote: "I just barely got through school. The problem was a learning disability, at a time when there was nowhere to get help."

Keanu Reeves, actor

Quote: "Growing up, I had a lot of trouble reading , and so I wasn't a good student at all. Eventually I got fed up and I didn't bother to finish high school. I thought it was a waste of time—at least for me it was."

Nolan Ryan, athlete

Quote: "When I had dyslexia, they didn't diagnose it as that. It was frustrating and embarrassing. I could tell you a lot of horror stories about what you feel like on the inside."

Nelson Rockefeller, former governor of New York and U.S. vice president

Quote: "I was one of the 'puzzle children' myself—a dyslexic . . . And I still have a hard time reading today."

Charles Schwab, investment banker

Quote: "I couldn't read. I just scraped by. My solution back then was to read classic comic books because I could figure them out from the context of the pictures. Now I listen to books on tape."

Jackie Stewart, international racecar driver

Quote: "For a dyslexic who does not yet know they are dyslexic, life is like a big high wall you never think you will be able to climb or get over. The moment you understand there is something called dyslexia, and there are ways of getting around the problem, the whole world opens up."

Victor Villasenor, author

Quote: "Once the fog lifts, dyslexics are prone to genius. Because theirs is such a unique way of looking at reality."

Roger Wilkins, Pulitzer Prize–winner

Quote: "My problem was reading very slowly. My parents said, 'Take as long as you need. As long as you're going to read, just keep at it.' We didn't know about learning disabilities back then."

Henry Winkler, actor

Quote: "As a child, I was called stupid and lazy. . . . The great thing about a learning problem, is it forces you to become a problem solver."

Loretta Young, actress

Quote: "I hated school. . . . One of the reasons was a learning disability, dyslexia, which no one understood at the time. I still can't spell."

Internet Resources for Dyslexia and Learning

Comprehensive Information about Dyslexia, Literacy, and Learning

All Kinds of Minds
A non-profit institute for the understanding of differences in learning
✐ www.allkindsofminds.org

BrainConnection
The brain and learning
✐ www.brainconnection.com

Dyslexia Online
Online magazine offering new perspectives on dyslexia
✐ www.audiblox2000.com/dyslexia_dyslexic/dyslexia.htm

Dyslexia Parents Resources
Resources for parents of children with dyslexia
✐ www.dyslexia-parent.com

Dyslexia, the Gift
Information and resources for dyslexia
✐ www.dyslexia.com

DyslexiaTalk
Dyslexia discussion board
✐ www.dyslexiatalk.com

Dyslexia.tv
Free thinkers off the page
✍ *www.dyslexia.tv*

International Dyslexia Association
Promoting literacy through research, education, and advocacy
✍ *www.interdys.org*

International Reading Association
Promoting literacy by improving the quality of instruction
✍ *www.reading.org*

LDOnline
Learning disabilities information for parents, teachers, and professionals
✍ *www.ldonline.org*

LD Resources
Resources for the learning disabilities community
✍ *www.ldresources.com*

Learning Disabilities Association of America
✍ *www.ldanatl.org*

Learning Disabilities Resource Community
✍ *www.ldrc.ca*

Reading Rockets
Launching young readers
✍ *www.readingrockets.org*

Resource Room
Free-spirited structured multisensory learning
✍ *www.resourceroom.net*

SchwabLearning.org

A parent's guide to helping kids with learning difficulties

✍*www.schwablearning.org*

Schools for Children with Dyslexia

This is just a sampling of a few of the more well-known schools for dyslexia. There are dozens of schools and programs that could not be included here.

ASSETS School

School for Gifted and/or Dyslexic Children
Honolulu, Hawaii
Day School, Grades K–12
✍*www.assets-school.net*

Charles Armstrong School

Belmont, California
Day School, Grades 1–8
✍*www.charlesarmstrong.org*

The Gow School

South Wales, New York
Boarding for Boys, Grades 7–12
✍*www.gow.org*

The Greenwood School

Putney, Vermont
Boarding for Boys, ages 9–15
✍*www.thegreenwoodschool.org*

Horizon Academy

Roeland Park, Kansas
Day School, Grades 1–10
✍*www.horizon-academy.com*

The Lab School of Washington

Arts-based program for students with learning disabilities
Washington, D.C.
Day School, Grades K–12
Baltimore, Maryland
Day School, Grades 1–8
✒*www.labschool.org*

Landmark College

Putney, Vermont
College for students with dyslexia and ADHD
Two-year program leading to liberal arts degree
✒*www.landmarkcollege.org*

Landmark School

Prides Crossing, Massachusetts
Day and Boarding, ages 7–20
✒*www.landmarkschool.org*

Shedd Academy

Mayfield, Kentucky
Day and Boarding, Grades 1–12
✒*www.sheddacademy.org*

Westmark School

Encino, California
Day School, Grades 2–12
✒*www.westmark.pvt.k12.ca.us*

Programs and Therapies

Audiblox

Cognitive exercises to build foundational skills
✒*www.audiblox2000.com*

Balametrics
Products for balance and sensory integration
✐*www.balametrics.com*

BrainSkills
Brain-training program for enhancing mental skills
✐*www.brainskills.com*

College of Optometrists in Vision Development
Vision therapy resources and referral list
✐*www.covd.org*

Davis Dyslexia Correction
Information and provider directory
✐*www.dyslexiahelp.com*

Davis Math Mastery
Math program for dyslexia
✐*www.davismath.com*

Dore Achievement Centers
Individualized exercise program to enhance cerebellar development
✐*www.dorecenters.com*

Earobics
Software to build phonemic awareness skills
✐*www.earobics.com*

Fast ForWord Learning Products
Software to build reading and phonemic awareness skills
✐*www.scilearn.com*

Great Leaps Reading
Building fluency, phonics, and motivation
✐*www.greatleaps.com*

Interactive Mathematics
www.cut-the-knot.org

Interactive Metronome
Advanced training for the brain
www.interactivemetronome.com

Internet Special Education Resources
Referral information for assessment, treatment, and advocacy
www.iser.com

Irlen Institute
Treatment for scotopic sensitivity syndrome
www.irlen.com

The Kurtz Center
Successful treatment for learning disabilities
www.learningdisabilities.com

Levinson Medical Center
Medical center for learning disabilities
www.levinsonmedical.com

Lexia Reading Software
Information on Lexia's reading software and professional development programs
www.lexialearning.com

Lindamood Bell Learning Systems
Process-based education: phonemic awareness, concept imagery, symbol imagery, math computation, and reasoning
www.lindamoodbell.com

P.A.V.E.—Parents Active for Vision Education
National, nonprofit organization that raises awareness of the relationship between vision and achievement
www.pave-eye.com

Read America!
Phono-Graphix reading program
✑*www.readamerica.net*

Reading and Language Arts Centers
Offers Phonics First based on the Orton-Gillingham approach.
✑*www.rlac.com*

Sensational Strategies for Teaching Beginning Readers
Program based on Orton-Gillingham method
✑*www.ortongillingham.com*

Spalding Education International
Resource for Spalding "Writing Road to Reading" materials
✑*www.spalding.org*

Legal Resources and Information

Home School Legal Defense Association
✑*www.hslda.org*

IDEA Practices (U.S. Department of Education)
✑*www.ideapractices.org*

National Association of Protection and Advocacy Systems
✑*www.napas.org*

Technical Assistance Alliance for Parent Centers
✑*www.taalliance.org*

Wrightslaw—Special Education Law & Advocacy
✑*www.wrightslaw.com*

Curriculum Materials and Support

AVKO Spelling Materials
www.spelling.org
Onion Mountain Technology
Low tech tools for learning assistance
www.onionmountaintech.com

Recording for the Blind and Dyslexic
Learning through listening
www.rfbd.org

Math-U-See
Manipulative materials for understanding math concepts
www.mathusee.com

RightStart Mathematics
Hands-on and visual system for learning math
www.alabacus.com

Rosetta Stone Language Learning Software
Foreign language instruction
www.rosettastone.com

Sparknotes
Study guides and literature
www.sparknotes.com

Strive Books
Inspiring different minds
www.strivebooks.com

Total Physical Response
Foreign language instruction
www.tpr-world.com

Assistive Technology

AlphaSmart
www.alphasmart.com
Dyslexic.com
www.dyslexic.com

Scansoft (Dragon Naturally Speaking)
www.scansoft.com/naturallyspeaking

TextHelp
www.texthelp.com

College and Career Resources

Colleges of Distinction
Profiles many lesser-known colleges with excellent programs
www.collegesofdistinction.com

FAFSA—Free Application for Federal Student Aid
www.fafsa.ed.gov

FinAid! The SmartStudent Guide to Financial Aid
www.finaid.org

Grants and Scholarships for Dyslexic Students
www.dyslexia.com/scholarships.htm

Scholarship Information for people with disabilities
www.hsu.edu/dept/dis/schloarship.htm

Student Aid on the Web
www.studentaid.ed.gov

Vocational Rehabilitation State Offices
www.jan.wvu.edu/sbses/VOCREHAB.HTM

Recommended Reading

Negotiating the Special Education Maze: A Guide for Parents & Teachers
By Winifred Anderson, Stephen Chitwood, and Deidre Hayden. Woodbine House; 3rd edition (June 1997)

Strong-Willed Child or Dreamer? Understanding the Crucial Differences Between a Strong-Willed Child and a Creative-Sensitive Child
By Ron Braund, Dana Spears. Thomas Nelson, February 1996

Homework Without Tears: A Parent's Guide for Motivating Children to do Homework and to Succeed in School
By Lee Canter and Lee Hausner, Ph.D. HarperResource, January 2005

Learning How to Learn: Getting into and Surviving College When You Have a Learning Disability
By Joyanne Cobb. Child Welfare League of America, Incorporated (NBN), Revised edition, February 2003

Learning Outside the Lines: Two Ivy League Students with Learning Disabilities and ADHD Give You the Tools for Academic Success and Educational Revolution
By David Cole and Jonathan Mooney. Fireside, September 2000

The Gift of Dyslexia: Why Some of the Smartest People Can't Read and How They Can Learn
By Ronald D. Davis, Eldon M. Braun. Perigee, April 1997

The Gift of Learning: Proven New Methods for Correcting ADD, Math & Handwriting Problems
By Ronald D. Davis, Eldon M. Braun. Perigee, August 2003

The Secret Life of the Dyslexic Child: How She Thinks. How He Feels. How They Can Succeed.
By Robert Frank, Kathryn E. Livingston. Rodale Press, June 2004

Right-Brained Children in a Left-Brained World: Unlocking the Potential of Your ADD Child.
By Jeffrey Freed and Laurie Parsons. Fireside, 1998.

Smart Moves: Why Learning Is Not All in Your Head
By Carla Hannaford. Great Ocean Publishers, 1995.

Your Child's Growing Mind: Brain Development and Learning from Birth to Adolescence
By Jane Healy. Broadway, 3rd edition, May 2004

Reading by the Colors: Overcoming Dyslexia and Other Reading Disabilities Through the Irlen Method
By Helen Irlen. Perigee Books, January 2001

Uniquely Gifted: Identifying and Meeting the Needs of the Twice Exceptional Student
By Kiesa Kay (editor). Avocus Publishing, July 2000

The Out-of-Sync Child: Recognizing and Coping with Sensory Integration Dysfunction
By Carol Stock Kranowitz and Larry B. Silver. Perigee Books, 1998.

The Human Side of Dyslexia: 142 Interviews with Real People Telling Real Stories About Their Coping Strategies with Dyslexia— Kindergarten through College
By Shirley Kurnoff. London Universal Publishing, November 2001

A Mind at a Time
By Mel Levine. Simon & Schuster, January 2003

The Myth of Laziness
By Mel Levine. Simon & Schuster, January 2003

Reading Reflex: The Foolproof Phono-Graphix Method for Teaching Your Child to Read
By Carmen and Geoffrey McGuinness. Fireside, August 1999

The LCP Solution: The Remarkable Nutritional Treatment for ADHD, Dyslexia, and Dyspraxia
By Malcolm J. Nicholl and Jacqueline Stordy, Ballantine Books, 2000

The Dyslexic Scholar: Helping Your Child Succeed in the School System
By Kathleen Nosek. Taylor Trade Publishing, April 1995

Dreamers, Discoverers and Dynamos: How to Help the Child Who Is Bright, Bored and Having Problems in School
By Lucy Jo Palladino. Ballantine Books, January 1999

Peterson's Colleges for Students With Learning Disabilities or ADD
By Petersons. Petersons Guides, seventh edition, October 2003

Colleges That Change Lives: 40 Schools You Should Know About Even If You're Not a Straight-A Student
By Loren Pope. Penguin USA, Revised edition, August 2000

The Complete IEP Guide: How to Advocate for Your Special Ed Child
By Lawrence M. Siegel and Marcia Stewart. Nolo Press, March 1999

Overcoming Dyslexia: A New and Complete Science-Based Program for Reading Problems at Any Level
By Sally Shaywitz, M.D. Knopf, April 2003

Upside-Down Brilliance: The Visual Spatial Learner
By Linda Kreger Silverman. DeLeon Publishing, Inc., November 2002

The Writing Road to Reading: The Spalding Method for Teaching Speech, Spelling, Writing, and Reading
By Romalda Bishop Spalding and Mary Elizabeth North. HarperResource, 5th Revised edition, February 2003

The LD Child and ADHD Child: Ways Parents and Professionals Can Help
By Suzanne H. Stevens. John F Blair Pub, Revised edition, February 1996

How to Reach and Teach Children and Teens with Dyslexia: A Parent and Teacher Guide to Helping Students of All Ages Academically, Socially, and Emotionally
By Cynthia M. Stowe. Jossey-Bass, June 2002

Dyslexia: Practical and Easy-to-Follow Advice
By Robin Temple. HarperCollins-UK, January 1999

Unicorns Are Real: A Right-Brained Approach to Learning
By Barbara Meister Vitale. Jalmar Press, 1982

In the Mind's Eye: Visual Thinkers, Gifted People with Dyslexia and Other Learning Difficulties, Computer Images and the Ironies of Creativity

By Thomas G. West. Prometheus Books, Updated edition, September 1997

Teaching Kids with Learning Difficulties in the Regular Classroom: Strategies and Techniques Every Teacher Can Use to Challenge and Motivate Struggling Students

By Susan Winebrenner and Pamela Espeland. Free Spirit Publishing, May 1996

Children's Books

My Name Is Brain Brian

By Jeanne Betancourt. Scholastic, Reissue edition, November 1996

Story about a sixth-grade boy with dyslexia—appropriate for kids ages 9–14.

Charlie's Challenge

By Linda Gladden with Ann Root. July 1995

Follows a young boy with dyslexia from diagnosis through receiving special education in school; very positive account geared to young kids grades K–5.

All Kinds of Minds: A Young Student's Book about Learning Abilities and Learning Disorders

By Melvin D. Levine. Educators Pub Service, June 1992

Geared specifically toward children; a collection of short stories involving characters with different learning abilities.

Thank You, Mr. Falker

By Patricia Polacco. Philomel Books, May 1998

Author's account of how her fifth-grade teacher helped her overcome her dyslexia; picture book suitable for children ages 5–10.

INDEX

THE EVERYTHING®
PARENT'S GUIDES SERIES
Expert Advice for Parents in Need of Answers

THE
EVERYTHING
PARENT'S GUIDE TO
RAISING A
SUCCESSFUL
CHILD

All you need to encourage your
child to excel at home and school

Denise D. Witmer

ISBN: 1-59337-043-1

How do I make sure my child is successful? What defines a successful child? Is my child already "successful"?

As parents struggle with these questions on a daily basis, *The Everything® Parent's Guide to Raising a Successful Child* helps put their fears to rest, providing them with professional, reassuring advice on how to raise a "successful" child according to their own standards.

This title walks parents through all emotional, intellectual, and physical aspects of development, including: building character, choosing—and limiting—extracurricular activities, disciplining effectively, ensuring a quality education, and instilling morals and values.

For parents of children with autism, daily activities such as grocery shopping or getting dressed can become extremely challenging. *The Everything® Parent's Guide to Children with Autism* offers practical advice, gentle reassurance, and real-life scenarios to help your family get through each day. Written by Adelle Jameson Tilton, the About.com Guide to Autism, this sensitive work helps you:

- Communicate effectively with your child
- Deal with meltdowns—public or private
- Keep your family together as one unit
- Find a school that suits your child's needs—integration vs. special education
- Learn about assistive devices, such as computers and picture boards
- Find intervention and support groups

THE
EVERYTHING
PARENT'S GUIDE TO
CHILDREN
WITH
AUTISM

A reassuring guide to know what
to expect, find the help you need,
and get through the day

Adelle Jameson Tilton

ISBN: 1-59337-041-5

All titles are trade paperback, 6"x 9", $14.95 (CAN $22.95)

THE

EVERYTHING

PARENT'S GUIDE TO

POSITIVE

DISCIPLINE

Professional advice for
raising a
well-behaved child

Carl E. Pickhardt, Ph.D.

ISBN: 1-58062-978-4

The Everything® Parent's Guide to Positive Discipline gives you all you need to help you cope with behavior issues. Written by noted psychologist Dr. Carl E. Pickhardt, this authoritative, practical book provides you with professional advice on dealing with everything from getting your kids to do their homework to teaching them to respect their elders. This title also shows parents how to:

- Set priorities
- Promote communication
- Establish the connection between choice and consequence
- Enforce punishment
- Change discipline style to reflect the age of the child
- Work with your partner as a team

While children with Asperger's are generally of average or above average intelligence, they xperience challenges with social skills, communicaton, and coordination, among other issues.

The Everything® Parent's Guide to Children with sperger's Syndrome is an informative resource that elps parents recognize areas in which their child eeds support. Filled with helpful hints and practical uidance, this authoritative work is designed to proide parents with the latest information on the best eatments and therapies available, education options, nd ways to make life easier for parent and child on day-to-day basis.

Also including information on resources, and etted for accuracy by Diane Twachtman-Cullen, h.D., this title is a must-read for parents of children ffected by ASD.

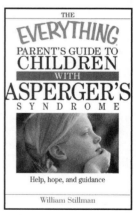

THE

EVERYTHING

PARENT'S GUIDE TO

CHILDREN

WITH

ASPERGER'S

S Y N D R O M E

Help, hope, and guidance

William Stillman

ISBN: 1-59337-153-5

Available wherever books are sold.
Or call 1-800-872-5627 or visit us at *www.everything.com*

OTHER *EVERYTHING*®
PARENTING TITLES:
All titles are $14.95 unless otherwise noted.

Everything® Baby Names, 2nd Ed.
ISBN: 1-59337-578-6

Everything® Baby Shower Book, 2nd Ed.
ISBN: 1-59869-552-5

Everything® Baby's First Year Book
ISBN: 1-58062-581-9

Everything® Birthing Book
ISBN: 1-59337-141-1

Everything® Breastfeeding Book
ISBN: 1-58062-582-7

Everything® Father-To-Be Book
ISBN: 1-58062-974-1

Everything® Get Ready for Baby Book, 2nd Ed.
ISBN: 1-59869-402-2

Everything® Getting Pregnant Book
ISBN: 1-59337-034-2

Everything® Parenting a Teenager Book
ISBN: 1-59337-035-0

Everything® Potty Training Book
ISBN: 1-58062-740-4

Everything® Pregnancy Book, 3rd Ed.
ISBN: 1-59869-286-0

Everything® Pregnancy Fitness Book
ISBN: 1-58062-873-7

Everything® Pregnancy Nutrition Book
ISBN: 1-59337-151-9

Everything® Toddler Book
ISBN: 1-58062-592-4

Everything® Tween Book
ISBN: 1-58062-870-2